Exploring Vulnerability in the Criminal Justice System in England and Wales

Providing a comparative analysis of both vulnerable witnesses and vulnerable suspects, this book discusses the increasingly difficult issue faced by many in modern policing, forensic psychology, criminology, and social justice studies.

Examining recent legislation, guidance, current psychological theory, and contemporary research and literature, the book enhances the currently limited knowledge of vulnerability in the criminal justice system (CJS) through the presentation of theoretical understanding, case law, and real-life case studies. It also explores how vulnerable victims, witnesses, and suspects progress through the system in England and Wales from initially being identified as vulnerable through to the measures used to assist them during interviews and at trial. In doing so, it provides a historical overview of how vulnerability has previously been considered, and how effective those with vulnerabilities were perceived to be in actively participating in the CJS. Further chapters consider how vulnerable individuals are safeguarded, the differences in services available to them, and what this may lead to in terms of effective participation in the system. How vulnerable groups are interviewed, what is considered best practice, and whether such practices are suitable also come under scrutiny.

Exploring Vulnerability in the Criminal Justice System in England and Wales is important reading for students and scholars of policing, forensic psychology, criminology, and social justice studies. It will also be of use for any organisations that conduct internal investigations such as non-government organisations, security and defence organisations, and corporate organisations.

Laura Farrugia is an Assistant Professor and Programme Leader in Psychology with Criminology at Northumbria University. She also works as a Registered Intermediary (accredited by the Ministry of Justice), assisting with vulnerable victims/witnesses at the police interview and trial stage.

Exploring Vulnerability in the Criminal Justice System in England and Wales

Laura Farrugia

Routledge
Taylor & Francis Group
LONDON AND NEW YORK

Designed cover image: Getty Images

First published 2025
by Routledge
4 Park Square, Milton Park, Abingdon, Oxon OX14 4RN

and by Routledge
605 Third Avenue, New York, NY 10158

Routledge is an imprint of the Taylor & Francis Group, an informa business

British Library Cataloguing-in-Publication Data
A catalogue record for this book is available from the British Library

Library of Congress Cataloging-in-Publication Data
Names: Farrugia, Laura, author.
Title: Exploring vulnerability in the criminal justice system in England and Wales / Laura Farrugia.
Description: Abingdon, Oxon ; New York, NY : Routledge, 2024. | Includes bibliographical references and index.
Identifiers: LCCN 2024014956 (print) | LCCN 2024014957 (ebook) | ISBN 9781032479552 (hardback) | ISBN 9781032479590 (paperback) | ISBN 9781003386735 (ebook)
Subjects: LCSH: Criminal justice, Administration of--England. | Criminal justice, Administration of--Wales. | Mentally ill offenders--England. | Mentally ill offenders--Wales. | Mentally ill--Crimes against--England. | Mentally ill--Crimes against--Wales.
Classification: LCC HV9960.G7 F375 2024 (print) | LCC HV9960.G7 (ebook) | DDC 364.942--dc23/eng/20240403
LC record available at https://lccn.loc.gov/2024014956
LC ebook record available at https://lccn.loc.gov/2024014957

ISBN: 978-1-032-47955-2 (hbk)
ISBN: 978-1-032-47959-0 (pbk)
ISBN: 978-1-003-38673-5 (ebk)

DOI: 10.4324/9781003386735

Typeset in Sabon
by KnowledgeWorks Global Ltd.

‘The greater the obstacle, the more glory in overcoming it’ (Moliere).

For those who doubted, and for those who continue to support.

Contents

List of figures and tables *viii*

1 Historical Overview of Vulnerability in the Criminal Justice System 1

2 Defining and Identifying Vulnerability in Witnesses and Suspects 14

3 Safeguarding the Vulnerable in the Criminal Justice System 29

4 Interviewing Vulnerable Witnesses 53

5 Interviewing Vulnerable Suspects 74

6 Vulnerable Witnesses at Trial 97

7 Vulnerable Defendants at Trial 110

8 Future Directions 125

Index *143*

Figures and tables

Figures

4.1 Interview phases from ABE guidance (MOJ, 2022) 56
5.1 The nine-step Reid Interrogation Technique (Inbau et al., 2013) 76
5.2 The PEACE model of interviewing (College of Policing, 2020) 81

Tables

2.1 Gudjonsson's four main types of vulnerability (2006) 15
4.1 Question types 58
5.1 Seven key principles of investigative interviewing 83

1 Historical Overview of Vulnerability in the Criminal Justice System

Introduction

The criminal justice system (CJS) in England and Wales and around the world has developed significantly over many decades, with progress made as to how victims, witnesses, and suspects are treated. However, crime has always been and will continue to be a political, social, and contentious issue with the media regularly casting spotlight onto what can be perceived as shocking crimes. Between the 1950s and the early 1990s, crime had risen fairly steadily and was seen as being out of control (Rock, 2004). For example, rates of crime in England and Wales were relatively large in comparison to Europe, with high numbers of assaults, sexual offences, and burglaries (Council of Europe, 1999). Crime surveys reported that those living in England had the highest risk of encountering theft and burglary crimes compared to 11 other industrialised countries in and around Europe (Mayhew & van Dijk, 1997), with offending behaviour becoming part of 'normal' life (Young, 1999). Thus, whilst England and Wales had previously prided themselves on suppressing crime and disorder (Durston, 2001; Gurr et al., 1977), the rates of crime were one of the highest. It was not until the early 1990s that the rates of officially reported crime began to fall. British Crime Surveys conducted around the time revealed that the number of recorded offences between 1995 and 1997 fell by 15% (Home Office, 1998). Similar reductions in crime were also reported by many other countries, including those in Europe (Barclay & Tavares, 2002).

Whilst there continues to exist a strong focus on maintaining low crime rates, there have also been many interventions developed in recent decades that focus on ensuring that those who are required to enter the CJS (victims, witnesses, and suspects) are treated fairly and can effectively participate in criminal proceedings. This is particularly so should an individual be vulnerable – however, this was not always the case. To understand the concept of vulnerability and explore its contemporary trends in the justice system, it is important to first consider the historical response to vulnerability in England and Wales, and further afield internationally. This is where the chapter now turns.

Vulnerability, Asylums, and Deinstitutionalisation

Historically, committing a crime relied on proving intentional action and culpability and thus an individual's capability to discern good from evil (Walker, 1968). From the 10th to the 16th century in England and Wales, juries were required to convict an individual regardless of his or her mental condition and whether the act was intentional or not. The Court would then grant a 'charter of pardon' to any 'insane' individual found guilty of an offence (Moran, 1985). From the first recorded case of an acquittal based on mental disorder in

DOI: 10.4324/9781003386735-1

1505, until custodial legislation was introduced at the start of the 19th century, individuals acquitted on the grounds of having vulnerabilities (largely mental health difficulties) were entitled to their full release (Walker, 1985). That said, it did not mean that those with mental health conditions did not find their way into a prison. By the 16th and 17th centuries, bridewells or houses of correction were confining 'more dangerous or troublesome lunatics' (Seddon, 2007, p. 2) with scholars and reformers highlighting how by the late 18th century, prisoner cells were largely occupied by 'lunatics' who were not privy to appropriate treatment and care (Howard, 1780/1784). This was particularly so in prisons in Ireland who were noted for their poor implementation of legislation to protect the health of their prisoners (Howard, 1780/1784). Others raised concerns about the violent and often dangerous nature of 'lunatics' held in prisons in England, with reference made to the threat they posed to prison order and prisoner officers' lives. The suggestion that such individuals be moved to a place of seclusion went unheeded leading to vulnerable individuals in prisoners often committing suicide (DeLacy, 1986).

It was not until the 18th century that institutions for controlling 'deviant' individuals began to be implemented in England and Wales (Symonds, 1995) with the development of hospitals and workhouses for those who were 'poor, decrepit and dependent' (Symonds, 1995, p. 96). The implementation of the Lunacy Act (1845) in England and Wales meant that the building of asylums for 'pauper insane people' (Symonds, 1995, p. 96) became a reality. What this meant was that those individuals who had mental health difficulties were distinguished from other vulnerable individuals and tended to be isolated. Until the 20th century, admission to an asylum or similar institution arose either from a petition from the individual's family or from somebody in the position of power such as a Magistrate, that the individual was mentally unwell (Houston, 2019). Perhaps the most famous institution in England was Bethlem Hospital in London. Individuals could be admitted, discharged, and re-admitted depending on their mental health needs and whilst asylums were seen as caring and controlled environments based on whether they could prevent suicide in their patients, institutions such as Bethlem Hospital in 1815 tended to show off its patients to the public for a price. Overall, the hospital earned an annual revenue of almost £400 (the equivalent to over £35,000 today; Dvoksin et al., 2020). Asylums and similar institutions were implemented around the world, albeit at different times. For example, in France, the first Hospital-General opened in Paris in 1656 and was designed for the 'insane' as well as those who posed a threat to 'normality' (Dvoksin et al., 2020). Institutionalisation in Wales did not begin until the early 20th century but in Ireland half of the committals to asylums were ordered by the Magistrates under the Lunacy (Ireland) Act due to the perceived dangerousness of the individual in question, a concept the chapter turns to later on. Regardless of the timing of the enactment of asylums, they were often criticised for being 'overcrowded, inhumane, and ineffective regimes of confinement' housing 'inactive, apathetic, and isolated patients' (Lomax, 1921, p. 10). Others suggested that they were also overcrowded and resulted in the mistreatment of patients (Scull, 1979).

However, significant changes in psychiatry launched in the decades after World War II whereby an international consensus arose regarding the need for change in mental health care. The main declared goal of the reforms was to transform the old asylum-based system of care and establish new community-based approaches (Freeman et al., 1985). This led to a move away from the traditional mental health hospital and led to a considerable discharge of patients; thus, the term' deinstitutionalisation' was coined (Novella, 2010). In this post-War period, asylums were closed thus shifting the care and support for those in psychiatric custodial institutions to community-based settings (Fakhoury & Priebe, 2002).

The assumption was that individuals with mental health difficulties should not be confined and isolated in mental health hospitals but should be actively treated and supported in the community (Ballerini, 2002; Schmiedebach et al., 2002). This process occurred at varying paces across the world. Early in the 19th century, for example, the concept of 'moral treatment' developed in America. The assumption was that those struggling with mental illness would recover if treated kindly and thus advocated for specially constructed hospitals that provided quiet and peaceful country settings and opportunities for meaningful work (D'Antonio, n.d.). In the United Kingdom, the number of in-patient psychiatric hospital beds was reduced dramatically, and community mental health teams have since been established throughout the country. In Germany, deinstitutionalisation initially led to patients staying in renamed sections of hospitals or in homes for the disabled (Von Cranach, 2000) due to an initial lack of community mental health teams and psychiatric nurses (Richter & Nollau, 2000). However, this has recently changed to large numbers of vulnerable individuals living in the community, albeit in supported accommodation (Bauer et al., 2001; Kaiser et al., 2001; Salize et al., 2007). The success of deinstitutionalisation in New Zealand was originally reported to be under par with other Western countries and they faced significant difficulties in caring for those with mental health difficulties in the community and also reported similar issues to that of Germany in terms of under-developed community services (Wilson, 2000). In several South American countries, deinstitutionalisation has only started to progress since the 1990s. In other countries, such as Hong Kong and Japan, mental health care remains largely institutionalised (Kuno & Asukai, 2000; Yip, 2000). Recent reports around the world still refer to deinstitutionalisation and mental health reforms as 'ongoing processes' (Becker & Barquero, 2001).

Despite the process of deinstitutionalisation occurring at various stages around the world, there have been many that have voiced concerns. For example, some have indicated that less severely ill patients are prioritised rather than those with more persistent and serious difficulties – this criticism is reported not only in the United Kingdom but also in the United States and the Netherlands (Pijl et al., 2000). In addition, McCulloch et al. (2000) indicated that the conservative and safety-oriented practices now adopted in community-based settings would lead to further alienation and stigmatisation of vulnerable individuals, particularly those with mental health difficulties. Many deinstitutionalised individuals face hostility and opposition from other community members (Fakhoury & Priebe, 2002) which can lead to vulnerable individuals having to compete for access to employment and housing opportunities; this can lead to further stigmatisation. Furthermore, those with mental health difficulties are at a heightened risk of entering the CJS; research has documented the increase in numbers of those vulnerable individuals entering prison or other forensic institutions and this has been reported around the world (Blaauw et al., 2000). For example, in Australia, individuals with cognitive disability are over-represented in the justice system (Baldry et al., 2013) as well as those with multiple combinations of mental health difficulties and/or alcohol and substance abuse disorders (Hayes et al., 2007). Furthermore, high rates of intellectual disability have been found in prisons in Australia, America, and the United Kingdom, including Ireland (Indig et al., 2011) although prevalence rates for comparison can be difficult to make (Holland & Persson, 2011). This is not limited to vulnerable adults. The rate of mental health difficulties and other vulnerabilities is of significant concern amongst juvenile offenders due to prevalence rates being three times higher than in the general population (Indig et al., 2011). Once inside the justice system, mental health difficulties tend to worsen. The Guardian newspaper recently reported a number of homicide cases involving prison inmates struggling with mental health difficulties with the article highlighting that the English prison system has recreated Bedlam due to the poorly equipped prison service (Cox & Marland, 2018). Similar media articles have been reported in Ireland where prison conditions have been blamed for exacerbating psychological problems that later cause self-harm or violent behaviour and in 2005, the United Nation's special rapporteur highlighted the impact of overcrowding, enforced isolation, and violence on mental health difficulties (Humphreys, 2013). This has led to vulnerable individuals, particularly those with mental health conditions, being stigmatised and labelled as more dangerous than those without such difficulties; this is an important concept to consider when one considers vulnerability in the CJS.

Vulnerability and the Concept of Dangerousness

Given the impact of institutionalising vulnerable individuals, namely those with mental health conditions, to asylums and other secure psychiatric facilities, it is not surprising that such vulnerable individuals are often seen as more dangerous than the average member of the public. In accordance with popular beliefs, asylums were designed after all to remove those with mental health difficulties from society to a confined space in order to treat their 'disordered minds' (Link et al., 1999). The history of how such individuals have been treated has dramatic consequences for how they may now be stereotyped. Following deinstitutionalisation, scholars reported that community members did not necessarily want to be living in the same area as a recently released patient. The 'not in my back yard' responses during this process of deinstitutionalisation have helped shape the nature of perceptions relating to those with mental health difficulties (Arens, 1993). For example, early research in America identified a strong stereotype of dangerousness and a desire for social distance from such individuals (Link et al., 1999), thus reflecting a similar theme in other research findings at the time (Link et al., 1989; Pescosolido et al., 1999; Rosenfield, 1997). Unfortunately, more recent research continues to suggest that individuals with mental health difficulties are still perceived by many as dangerous and unpredictable (Daff & Thomas, 2014), and are considered to be responsible for a disproportionate level of serious and violent crime (Jorm et al., 2012; Yap et al., 2014). This perception is reported to have increased recently in other countries such as Australia (Reavley & Jorm, 2012).

Beliefs concerning dangerousness in people with mental health difficulties are due to a number of complex and varied factors and can relate to the characteristics of both the individual who holds the belief and the vulnerable individual, exposure to mental health conditions and exposure to violence by individuals with mental health conditions, as well as the media reporting of crimes committed by vulnerable individuals (Jorm et al., 2012). For example, research has documented that the more contact an individual has with somebody who has mental health difficulties, than the lower the belief they have in associated dangerousness (Jorm et al., 2012; Reavley et al., 2016). In addition, a greater belief in dangerousness has been found in those who have reported negative experiences such as threats of violence or physical harm from those who have mental health conditions (Phelan & Link, 2004). The way that the media reports crimes committed by vulnerable individuals has also been shown to have an impact on beliefs in dangerousness particularly as newspapers, for example, are more likely to describe those with mental health conditions within the context of dangerousness and/or violence rather than treatment or recovery (Corrigan et al., 2005). This has been particularly prevalent at times in America in relation to gun violence (Jorm & Reavley, 2014; McGinty et al., 2013).

Other research has suggested that dangerousness can be dependent upon the type of mental health condition the individual has. A study conducted in Australia sought to assess the associations between beliefs in dangerousness of people with mental health conditions and exposure to media reports of violence and/or personal experiences of fear or threat and harm. Participants were provided with a vignette of an individual with depression or with early schizophrenia and were asked if they believed him to be dangerous. Whilst participants reported that media reports and having felt afraid of someone were associated with beliefs about dangerousness, these were not as strongly associated with the depression vignette compared to the early schizophrenia vignette (Reavley et al., 2016) – earlier research has reported similar findings (Reavley & Jorm, 2011). The reality is that the majority of individuals with mental health difficulties are not violent and are more likely to be victims of violence rather than perpetrators (Pulay et al., 2008; Rodway et al., 2014). In addition, where relationships have been found between severe mental health conditions and violence, substance abuse has been found to play a pivotal role (Douglas et al., 2009; Fazel et al., 2010). Still, it is concerning that decades after deinstitutionalisation, the prevalent view still remains the same; that those with mental health conditions are 'ticking time bombs' perceived to be dangerous and responsible for a disproportionate level of serious and violent crime (Appelbaum, 2004, p. 1105). Thus, the primitive association between mental health illness and a violation of morals, values, and the law are yet to be completely resolved. This has implications for their treatment within the CJS in England and Wales, and around the world.

The Vulnerable Victim and Witness

For many years, victims and witnesses were the forgotten actors in the CJS (Sanders, 2002). The history of victims' rights has been markedly different from that of suspect or defendant rights (Holder et al., 2021). Their views were not given much interest by the police nor prosecution, except in relation to the sort of evidence they would provide in Court. It meant that information relevant in deciding whether to accept guilty pleas or lesser charges, or information pertaining to the impact of the crime upon the victim or witness and thus important for sentencing, was infrequently collected. Victims and witnesses were often left in the dark in terms of progress of their case given the limited communication from the Court, and they were generally viewed as citizens who may or may not be used as witnesses – a decision usually left to the prosecution (Sanders, 2002).

Consideration of the victim, as opposed to the offender, therefore, is a relatively new development in terms of psychological and legal studies. It was not until the 1950s in America that attention was first drawn to the experiences of victims and the under-reporting of crime (Edwards, 2014). In the Netherlands, victim awareness grew from 1970s onwards largely due to the rise in crime (Leferink, 2012). Changes to compensation orders in the 1990s now mean that there is no longer a fixed maximum for a claim, and from 2005, victims were given the right to speak at criminal justice proceedings (Elbers et al., 2022) which, from 2016, has since become unlimited and thus allows the victim or witness to inform the Court of their views about the impact of the crime, the culpability of the offender and what they believe would be an appropriate sentence. In addition, victims and witnesses now have the right to be informed about the progression of the case, to be treated respectfully, the right to access the case file should they wish to and the right to be legally represented (see Title IIIA, Article 51 of the Dutch Code of Criminal Procedure for more information). On an international level, the first steps taken towards victims' rights were in 1985 when the United Nations Declaration of Basic Principles of Justice for Victims of Crime and Abuse of Power were incorporated. Within the Declaration it was stated that victims should get access to justice, fair treatment, restitution, compensation, and assistance (Elbers et al., 2022). In 2001, the European Union (EU) Council adopted a legally binding Framework Decision on the standing of victims in criminal proceedings which prescribed that victims' rights should include receiving information, protection, and respect. This was replaced in 2012 by the EU Directive 2012/29/EU of the European Parliament and Council of Europe which laid out the minimum standards for the rights, support, and protection of victims. Many countries in the EU implemented the EU Directive accordingly and so victim rights have since gained traction where there is regional jurisdiction (Holder et al., 2021).

In England and Wales, victims and witnesses started to receive attention from the 1960s and their needs started to become the subject of greater recognition; this was further developed with the implementation of bodies such as the Criminal Injuries Compensation Board which was established in 1964. However, until the mid-1990s, the position of victims in the CJS was ill-defined and often contested in England and Wales (Rock, 2004). There was much debate about who was eligible as a victim and what their entitlements should be. There were concerns that whilst victims and witnesses were expected to meet the demands of the CJS by supporting the prosecution and giving evidence, they would become 'over-mighty' and upset the integrity of the justice system by pushing for increased punishments and longer sentences (Rock, 2004). In addition, whilst publications were raising the awareness of victim rights, these remained limited. For example, under the first published Victims Charter in 1990, the formal position of victims in England and Wales remained unchanged; that is, they were not party to any proceedings and had no enforceable rights (Sanders, 2002). Whilst many professionals working in the justice system may have believed that victims and witnesses deserved better treatment, they also believed that they should not have any rights, nor be party to any proceedings nor be heard in Court unless testifying under oath (Rock, 2004). However, at the same time, the small number of cases moving through the justice system was a particular concern. For example, less than half of offences known to victims were reported, only half of those were recorded and only 3% of those offences resulted in a caution or conviction (Home Office, 1999). Thus, there developed a focus on increasing the number of convictions of perpetrators involved in committing these crimes by coaxing victims and witnesses to report crime and go to trial (Rock, 2004).

Victims and witnesses' right in the United Kingdom have since progressed due to the growing recognition of the interests of witnesses fuelled in part by the activism of victim groups and organisations and the growing attention from politicians. In addition, victims and witnesses can now make victim impact statements, now known as victim personal statements, for the Court and the Parole Board. This allows the victim or witness to inform the Court of the impact the crime has had on their lives and should be considered when sentencing the defendant although early evaluations of the scheme, indicated that many victims felt that their statements had been ignored (Hoyle et al., 1998), something reflected in other studies around the world (Sebba, 1996). Furthermore, in England and Wales, the development of the Witness Service at Court supports victims and witnesses to give their evidence by ensuring they are regularly kept up to date with the progression of the trial and supported whilst attending Court. Thus, many countries now make commitments to victims and witnesses, exemplified in legislation and guidance which sets out what can be expected from the agencies involved in the justice system (Kilcommins et al., 2010).

Appearing as a victim or witness in a criminal trial is often described as a stressful and terrifying ordeal with high rates of revictimisation (Almeida et al., 2021). If this is the case for victims and witnesses without any vulnerabilities, it must be even more so for those who are vulnerable (Ellison, 1999). Vulnerable victims and witnesses are often targets because of their vulnerabilities, and, for the same reason, may be denied access to justice (Plotnikoff & Woolfson, 2015). As recently as the 1990s, a 16-year-old victim's evidence in a rape trial was deemed unacceptable because her 'mental age' was stated to be less than eight, and it was thought that children under the age of eight years old could not give evidence under oath (McCormack, 1991). There was no consideration that the victim's actual age and a subjective view of her mental age were not synonymous.

The Case of Laura Kelly

In February 2006, Laura Kelly attended her brother's 21st birthday party hosted at her sister's home in Navan. During the birthday party, it was alleged that shortly after Laura (who has Down's syndrome) was put to bed, Laura's sister entered the bedroom and saw a man in bed with her. Most of Laura's clothes had been removed and the man was found naked from the waist down. The sexual assault was reported to gardai the next day and Laura was taken to the sexual assault unit of the Rotunda Hospital. The case progressed to trial in 2007 and despite Laura having the mental age of a four-year-old, she was treated under the law as an adult in Court. Laura's mother reports that Laura was brought into Court and asked questions about numbers, and colours, and days of the week which bore no relevance in Laura's mind, especially as Laura knew she had to go into Court to tell them what had happened to her. Laura was deemed incompetent to testify at Court after the Judge ruled that Laura had failed a competency test; her case was dismissed, and the defendant was acquitted.

It was not until 2010, in a recent Court of Appeal case in England and Wales, that it was highlighted that, 'until recently, there was no possibility of the Court even considering the evidence of complainants with serious communication difficulties' (R v Watts [2010] EWCA 1824, para 56). This has been echoed around the world and is not wholly surprising. For example, victims and witnesses with intellectual disabilities may have broad deficits in memory encoding, storage, and retrieval (Ternes & Yuille, 2008), and other limitations in cognitive functioning, including being susceptible to a range of psychological vulnerabilities. This can result in significant difficulties when providing an account of the crime (Farrugia, 2022; Perlman et al., 1994) and can also significantly impair their capacity to give evidence during trial – for example, such individuals may become highly suggestible or acquiescent and are more likely to engage in nay-saying than those in the general population (Gudjonsson, 2018). Victims and witnesses with vulnerabilities may also have difficulties in understanding the legal process including understanding legal terminology (Ericson & Perlman, 2001). Such vulnerabilities can be exacerbated by the environment in which they are providing their evidence (Gudjonsson, 2018). That said, whilst the impact of an individual's vulnerability can affect their ability to effectively engage with the CJS, it does not mean that they should not be allowed to, or their evidence be discredited. Many scholars have indicated that vulnerable individuals can give reliable evidence if their difficulties are accounted for (Gudjonsson, 2003, 2018).

The recognition of vulnerable victims and witnesses participating in the CJS is a milestone (Stanko, 1999). That said, it was not until 1998, that the Labour Government in England

and Wales published its consultation document that underpinned the proposed legislation to assist vulnerable victims and witnesses. 'Speaking Up for Justice' was the result of an interdepartmental working group on the treatment of vulnerable and/or intimidated victims and witnesses in the justice system and was published to propose 'a coherent and integrated scheme to provide appropriate support and assistance' for this vulnerable group (Home Office, 2001, p. 1). Described as a 'radical departure in the treatment of some victims by the criminal justice system' (Stanko, 1999, p. 101), there is an explicit acknowledgement of the difficulties that vulnerable victims and witnesses face when engaging in the justice system. As such, recommendations stipulated in the consultation document included improvements in identifying vulnerability and/or intimidation in victims and witnesses, greater communication, and implementation of a range of special measures for use at trial, the banning of defendants cross-examining victims of rape and sexual assault and the implementation of pilot projects for other special measures. These measures have been designed to protect and safeguard vulnerable victims and witnesses in the justice system and ensure that they can effectively participate.

It was around the same time that similar measures were implemented in European countries. Under the European Framework Decision on the Standing of Victims in Criminal Proceedings (2001), member States (including Ireland, Portugal, Finland, and Romania) now have a duty to recognise the difficulties that vulnerable victims and witnesses may face and to ensure that this does not affect their evidence. For example, member States are required to take necessary measures to protect the vulnerable victim or witness from being questioned any more than is necessary for the purpose of the criminal proceedings (Article 3), minimise communication difficulties affecting understanding and/or involvement in criminal proceedings (Article 5), and ensure protection against secondary victimisation (Article 15). The recognition of comprehension difficulties and the impact on and treatment of the vulnerable victim and witness participating in the CJS has come a long way.

Summary

Crime continues to be a political, social, and contentious issue with little crime being reported until the mid-1990s. The reporting of crime results in thousands and thousands of individuals entering the CJS in England and Wales and further afield internationally as victims, witnesses, and suspects, many of whom are vulnerable. But, for a long time, mental illness and other vulnerabilities were viewed not as a disease or medical condition, but as a manifestation of evil spirits (Høyersten, 1996). Institutions, commonly known as asylums, were implemented internationally at various stages between the 16th and 18th century for controlling 'deviant' individuals. However, significant changes in psychiatry in the decades after World War II led to a move away from the traditional mental health hospital and to community-based care; a term coined as deinstitutionalisation. Although this meant many vulnerable individuals now received care in the community, it also placed them at a heightened risk of entering the CJS; thus, vulnerable individuals continue to be stigmatised and termed dangerous in comparison to other members of the community.

Other key players in the justice system, victims, and witnesses, were forgotten about until much more recently. The history of their rights has been markedly different from that of the suspect, and they were often left in the dark regarding the progression of their case through the justice system. It was not until the 1950s onwards that attention was given to victims and witnesses and their role in the CJS. What this led to was their role becoming more defined and their rights becoming established. This now means that victims and witnesses are informed about the case, are able to provide evidence at trial, and are treated respectfully and as integral to the progression of a case. However, vulnerable victims and witnesses who are often targeted because of their difficulties may still be denied access to justice. It was not until a Court of Appeal case in 2010 in England and Wales that the evidence of victims and witnesses with communication difficulties would have been considered. This has been echoed around the world. However, although such vulnerable individuals may have impairments that make communication difficult, it does not mean that they cannot effectively participate in the CJS. This is starting to be recognised at varying paces around the world. Whilst progress has been made in the way that vulnerable individuals are treated within the CJS, such provisions can only be put in place if the individual is identified as vulnerable. Being able to define and thus identify a vulnerable individual is paramount to ensuring their effective participation in the justice system – this is where the next chapter turns.

Key Learning Points

- The way that vulnerable individuals have been treated as part of the CJS stems back to the 10th century.
- By the late 18th century, many prison cells were occupied by those who were mentally unwell.
- In 1845, the implementation of the Lunacy Act in England and Wales meant that those who were mentally ill were isolated in asylums or other secure psychiatric services. The most famous asylum in England and Wales was Bethlem Hospital. Institutionalisation occurred at varying rates around the world.
- Following significant changes in psychiatry after World War II, deinstitutionalisation occurred and those who were mentally unwell were moved to the community for treatment. Those with mental illness continue to be stigmatised and viewed as more dangerous.
- Victims and witnesses were the forgotten actors in the CJS and consideration of them are a new development in psychological and legal studies.
- The position of victims and witnesses was ill-defined and often contested in England and Wales.
- Victim and witness rights have since developed in the United Kingdom and around the world.
- However, it was not until recently, that the Court would consider the evidence of vulnerable victims and witnesses; their participation in the CJS is seen as a milestone.

References

Almeida, I., Fernandes, A., Frade, C., Nobre, C., & Osorio, L. (2021). Vulnerable victims in court: From childhood to senescence. *Annals of Medicine*, *53*, S133–S134.

Appelbaum, P. (2004). Law & psychiatry: One madman keeping loaded guns: Misconceptions of mental illness and their legal consequences. *Psychiatric Services*, *55*(10), 1105–1106.

Arens, A. (1993). What do the neighbours think now? Community residences on Long Island, New York. *Community Mental Health Journal*, *29*(3), 235–245.

Baldry, E., Clarence, M., Dowse, L., & Trollor, J. (2013). Reducing vulnerability to harm in adults with cognitive disabilities in the Australian criminal justice system. *Journal of Policy and Practice in Intellectual Disabilities*, *10*(3), 222–229.

Ballerini, A. (2002). The Italian paradox: Expansion of community psychiatry and marginalisation of psychopathology. *Archives of Psychiatry*, *65*, 13–26.

Barclay, G., & Tavares, C. (2002). *International comparisons of criminal justice statistics 2000.* Home Office.

Bauer, M., Kunze, H., Von Cranach, M., & Fritze, J. (2001). Psychiatric reform in Germany. *Acta Psychiatrica Scandinavica Supplementum*, *104*(410), 27–34.

Becker, I., & Barquero, J. (2001). The European perspective of psychiatric reform. *Acta Psychiatrica Scandinavica*, *410*, 8–14.

Blaauw, E., Roesch, R., & Kerkhof, A. (2000). Mental disorders in European prison systems: Arrangements for mentally disordered prisoners in the prison systems of 13 European countries. *International Journal of Law and Psychiatry*, *23*, 649–663.

Corrigan, P., Watson, A., Gracia, G., Slopen, N., Rasinski, K., & Hall, L. (2005). Newspaper stories as measures of structural stigma. *Psychiatric Services*, *56*(5), 551–556.

Council of Europe. (1999). *European sourcebook of crime and criminal justice*. European Committee on Crime Problems.

Cox, C., & Marland, H. (2018). 'We are recreating Bedlam': A history of mental illness and prison systems in England and Ireland. In A. Mills & K. Kendall (Eds.), *Mental health in prisons* (pp. 25–47). Palgrave.

D'Antonio, P. (n.d.). *History of psychiatric hospitals. Nursing, history and healthcare.* Retrieved June 1, 2023, from https://www.nursing.upenn.edu/nhhc/nurses-institutions-caring/historyof-psychiatric-hospitals/

Daff, E., & Thomas, S. (2014). Bipolar disorder and criminal offending: A data linkage study. *Social Psychiatry and Psychiatric Epidemiology*, *49*, 1985–1991.

DeLacy, M. (1986). *Prison reform in Lancashire, 1700–1850: A study in local administration*. Stanford University Press.

Douglas, K., Guy, L., & Hart, S. (2009). Psychosis as a risk factor for violence to others: A meta-analysis. *Psychological Bulletin*, *135*(5), 679–706.

Durston, G. (2001). *Criminal and constable: The impact of policing reform and crime in nineteenth century London* [PhD thesis]. London School of Economics and Political Science.

Dvoksin, J., Knoll, L., & Silva, M. (2020). A brief history of the criminalisation of mental illness. *CNS Spectrums*, *25*, 638–650.

Edwards, C. (2014). Pathologising the victim: Law and the construction of people with disabilities as victims of crime in Ireland. *Disability and Society*, *29*(5), 685–698.

Elbers, N., Meijer, S., Becx, I., Schijns, A., & Akkermans, A. (2022). The role of victims' lawyers in criminal proceedings in the Netherlands. *European Journal of Criminology*, *19*(4), 830–848.

Ellison, L. (1999). The protection of vulnerable witnesses in court: An Anglo-Dutch comparison. *International Journal of Evidence and Proof*, *3*, 29–43.

Ericson, K., & Perlman, N. (2001). Knowledge of legal terminology and court proceedings in adults with developmental disabilities. *Law and Human Behaviour*, *25*(5), 529–545.

European Union. (2001). *European framework decision on the standing of victims in criminal proceedings.* https://www.eumonitor.eu/9353000/1/j9vvik7m1c3gyxp/vitgbgi8vbys#:~:text=The%20rules%20and%20practices%20as,protected%20at%20the%20various%20stages

Fakhoury, W., & Priebe, S. (2002). The process of deinstitutionalisation: An international overview. *Current Opinion in Psychiatry*, *15*, 187–192.

Farrugia, L. (2022). *Interviewing of suspects with mental health conditions and disorders in England and Wales. A paradigm shift.* Routledge.

Fazel, S., Lichtenstein, P., Grann, M., Goodwin, G. M., & Langstrom, N. (2010). Bipolar disorder and violent crime: New evidence from population-based longitudinal studies and systematic review. *Archives of General Psychiatry*, *67*(9), 931–938.

Freeman, H., Fryers, T., & Henderson, J. (1985). *Mental health services in Europe: 10 years on*. WHO Regional Office for Europe.

Gudjonsson, G. H. (2003). *The psychology of interrogations and confessions: A handbook*. John Wiley & Sons.

Gudjonsson, G. H. (2018). *The psychology of false confessions: Forty years of science and practice*. John Wiley & Sons Ltd.

Gurr, T., Grabosky, P., & Hula, R. (1977). *The politics of crime and conflict: A comparative history of four cities*. Sage Publications.

Hayes, S., Shackell, P., Mottram, P., & Lancaster, R. (2007). The prevalence of intellectual disability in a major UK prison. *British Journal of Learning Disabilities*, *35*, 162–167.

Holder, R., Kirchengast, T., & Cassell, P. (2021). Transforming crime victims' rights: From myth to reality. *International Journal of Comparative and Applied Criminal Justice*, *45*(1), 1–13.

Holland, S., & Persson, P. (2011). Intellectual disability in the Victorian prison system: Characteristics of prisoners with an intellectual dis- ability released from prison in 2003–2006. *Psychology, Crime & Law*, *17*, 25–41.

Home Office (1998). *British crime survey, 1998, England and Wales*. Home Office.

Home Office (1999). *Information on the criminal justice system in England and Wales: Digest 4*. Home Office.

Home Office (2001). *Speaking up for justice*. Home Office.

Houston, R. (2019). Asylums: The historical perspective before, during, and after. *The Lancet Psychiatry*, 7(4), 354–362.

Howard, J. (1780/1784). *The state of the prisons in England and Wales*. William Eyres.

Høyersten, J. (1996). Possessed! Some historical, psychiatric and current moments of demonic possession. *Tidsskr Nor Laegeforen*, *116*(30), 3602–3606.

Hoyle, C., Cape, E., Morgan, R., & Sanders, A. (1998). *Evaluation of the 'one stop shop' and victim statement pilot projects*. Home Office.

Humphreys, J. (2013). The prison trap: mental strains of solitary confinement. *Irish Times*. Retrieved June 1, 2023, from https://www.irishtimes.com/news/crime-andlaw/the-prison-trapmental-strains-of-solitary-confinement-1.1528684

Indig, D., Vecchiato, C., Haysom, L., Beilby, R., Carter, J., Champion, U., Gaskin, C., Heller, E., Kumar, S., Mamone, N., Muir, P., van den Dolder, P., & Whitton, G. (2011). *2009 NSW young people in custody health survey: Full report*. Justice Health and Juvenile Justice.

Jorm, A., & Reavley, N. (2014). Public belief that mentally ill people are violent: Is the USA exporting stigma to the rest of the world? *Australian and New Zealand Journal of Psychiatry*, *48*, 213–215.

Jorm, A., Reavley, N., & Ross, A. (2012). Belief in the dangerousness of people with mental disorders: A review. *Australian and New Zealand Journal of Psychiatry*, *46*(11), 1029–1045.

Kaiser, W., Hoffmann, K., Isermann, M., & Priebe, S. (2001). Long-term patients in supported housing after deinstitutionalisation: Part VB of the Berlin deinstitutionalisation. *Psychiatrische Praxis*, *28*(5), 235–243.

Kilcommins, S., Leane, M., Donson, F., Fennell, C., & Kingston, A. (2010). *The needs and concerns of victims of crime in Ireland, Dublin*. Commission for the Support of Victims of Crime.

Kuno, E., & Asukai, N. (2000). Efforts toward building a community-based mental health system in Japan. *International Journal of Law and Psychiatry*, *23*(3–4), 361–373.

Leferink, S. (2012). *Victims' rights. Do they justice to victims?* Slachtofferhulp Nederland.

Link, B., Cullen, F., Struening, E., Shrout, P., & Dohrenwend, B. (1989). A modified labelling theory approach to mental disorders: An empirical assessment. *American Sociological Review*, *54*(3), 400–423.

Link, B., Phelan, J., Bresnahan, M., Stueve, A., & Pescosolido, B. (1999). Public conceptions of mental illness: Labels, causes, dangerousness, and social distance. *American Journal of Public Health*, *89*(9), 1328–1333.

Lomax, M. (1921). *The experiences of an asylum doctor: With suggestions for asylum and lunacy law reform*. Allen & Unwin.

Mayhew, P., & van Dijk, J. (1997). *Criminal victimisation in eleven industrialised countries*. Ministry of Justice.

McCormack, B. (1991). Sexual abuse and learning disabilities. *British Medical Journal*, *303*, 143–144.

McCulloch, A., Muijen, M., & Harper, H. (2000). New developments in mental health policy in the United Kingdom. *International Journal of Law and Psychiatry*, *23*(3–4), 261–276.

McGinty, E., Webster, D., & Barry, C. (2013). Effects of news media messages about mass shootings on attitudes toward persons with serious mental illness and public support for gun control policies. *American Journal of Psychiatry*, *170*(5), 494–501.

Moran, R. (1985). The origin of insanity as a special verdict: The trial for treason of James Hadfield 1800. *Law and Society Review*, *19*(3), 487–519.

Novella, E. (2010). Mental health care in the aftermath of deinstitutionalisation: A retrospective and prospective view. *Health Care Analysis*, *18*, 222–238.

Perlman, N. B., Ericson, K. I., Esses, V. M., & Isaacs, B. J. (1994). The developmentally handicapped witness: Competency as a function of question format. *Law and Human Behaviour*, *18*(2), 171–187.

Pescosolido, B., Monahan, J., Link, B., Stueve, A., & Kikuzawa, S. (1999). The public's view of the competence, dangerousness, and need for legal coercion among persons with mental health problems. *American Journal of Public Health*, *89*, 1339–1345.

Phelan, J., & Link, B. (2004). Fear of people with mental illnesses: The role of personal and impersonal contact and exposure to threat or harm. *Journal of Health and Social Behaviour*, *45*(1), 68–80.

Pijl, Y., Kluiter, H., & Wiersma, D. (2000). Change in Dutch mental health care: An evaluation. *Social Psychiatry and Psychiatric Epidemiology*, *35*(9), 402–407.

Plotnikoff, J., & Woolfson, R. (2015). *Intermediaries in the criminal justice system. Improving communication for vulnerable witnesses and defendants*. Policy Press.

Pulay, A., Dawson, D., Hasin, D., Goldstein, R., Ruan, W., Pickering, R., Huang, B., Chou, P., & Grant, B. (2008). Violent behaviour and DSM-IV psychiatric disorders: Results from the National Epidemiologic Survey on Alcohol and Related Condition. *Journal of Clinical Psychiatry*, *69*(1), 12–22.

R v Watts [2010] EWCA 1824. Retrieved July 1, 2023, from https://www.casemine.com/judgement/uk/5b46f1fb2c94e0775e7ef591

Reavley, N., & Jorm, A. (2011). Stigmatising attitudes towards people with mental disorders: Findings from an Australian National Survey of Mental Health Literacy and Stigma. *Australian and New Zealand Journal of Psychiatry*, *48*(12), 1086–1093.

Reavley, N., & Jorm, A. (2012). Stigmatising attitudes towards people with mental disorders: Changes to Australia over 8 years. *Psychiatry Research*, *197*(3), 302–306.

Reavley, N., Jorm, A., & Morgan, A. (2016). Beliefs about dangerousness of people with mental health problems: The role of media reports and personal exposure to threat or harm. *Social Psychiatry and Psychiatric Epidemiology*, *51*, 1257–1264.

Richter, R., & Nollau, M. (2000). Perspectives of psychiatric care in Leipzig: Deinstitutionalisation from the viewpoint of neurologist/psychiatrist in private practice and the work of consortium of community psychiatric services. *Psychiatrische Praxis*, *27*, 95–99.

Rock, P. (2004). *Constructing victims' rights: The home office, new labour and victims*. Oxford University Press.

Rodway, C., Flynn, S., While, D., Rahman, M., Kapur, N., Appleby, L., & Shaw, J. (2014). Patients with mental illness as victims of homicide: A national consecutive case series. *Lancet Psychiatry*, *1*(2), 129–134.

Rosenfield, S. (1997). Labelling mental illness: The effects of services versus stigma. *American Sociological Review*, *62*, 660–672.

Salize, H., Rossler, W., & Becker, T. (2007). Mental health care in Germany. Current state and trends. *European Archives of Psychiatry and Clinical Neuroscience*, *257*, 92–103.

Sanders, A. (2002). Victim participation in criminal justice. *The Centre for Crime and Justice Studies*, *49*, 30–31.

Schmiedebach, H., Beddies, T., Schulz, J., & Priebe, S. (2002). Housing and work as criteria of the 'social integration' of the mentally ill – developments in Germany from 1900 to 2000. *Psychiatrische Praxis*, *29*, 285–294.
Scull, A. (1979). *Museums of madness. The social organisation of insanity in nineteenth century England.* Pengrum.
Sebba, L. (1996). *Third parties: Victims and the criminal justice system.* Ohio State University Press.
Seddon, T. (2007). *Punishment and madness: Governing prisoners with mental health problems.* Routledge.
Stanko, E. (1999). Identities and criminal violence: Observations on law's recognition of vulnerable victims in England and Wales. *Studies in Law, Politics, and Society*, *19*, 99–120.
Symonds, B. (1995). The origins of insane asylums in England during the 19th century: A brief sociological review. *Journal of Advanced Nursing*, 22, 94–100.
Ternes, M., & Yuille, J. (2008). Eyewitness memory and eyewitness identification performance in adults with intellectual disabilities. *Journal of Applied Research in Intellectual Disabilities*, *21*(6), 519–531.
Von Cranach, M. (2000). Housing for psychiatric patients inside and outside of hospitals. *Psychiatrische Praxis*, *27*, 59–63.
Walker, N. (1968). *Crime and insanity in England (volume 1).* Edinburgh University Press.
Walker, N. (1985). The insanity defence between 1800. *The Annals of the American Academy of Political and Social Science*, *477*, 25–30.
Wilson, J. (2000). Mental health services in New Zealand. *International Journal of Law and Psychiatry*, *23*, 215–228.
Yap, M., Mackinnon, A., Reavley, N., & Jorm, A. (2014). The measurement properties of stigmatising attitudes towards mental disorders: Results from two community surveys. *International Journal of Methods in Psychiatric Research*, *23*(1), 49–61.
Yip, K. (2000). Have psychiatric services in Hong Kong been impacted by the deinstitutionalisation and community care movements? *Admin and Policy Mental Health*, *27*, 443–449.
Young, J. (1999). *The exclusive society.* Sage.

2 Defining and Identifying Vulnerability in Witnesses and Suspects

Introduction

Vulnerability is a key concern within policing and across public and private health partners (Murray et al., 2018). This is not surprising given the process of deinstitutionalisation resulting in a large number of vulnerable individuals now being treated in the community; it is a disproportionate number of these individuals that come into contact with the justice system (Sirdifield & Brooker, 2012). In England, Wales, and Scotland, increasing prioritisation is now given to identifying, assessing, and managing vulnerable victims, witnesses (here on referred to as witnesses) and suspects (College of Policing 2018; Police Scotland, 2017). For example, there is an expanding focus on the experiences of vulnerable witnesses in particular to disability hate crime and the legal responses to such incidents (Hoong Sin et al., 2009) with the continuing association between disability and vulnerability regularly scrutinised (Roulstone et al., 2011). Similarly, attention is given to vulnerable suspects – for example, how they may fare within particular stages of the criminal justice system (CJS) and whether current safeguards are adequate (see Farrugia & Gabbert, 2019a, 2019b, 2020). However, the very concept of vulnerability is difficult to define leading to implications for the vulnerable individual entering the justice system. Should they not be identified as such, their access to justice and a fair trial can be impeded upon. Defining and identifying vulnerability is where the focus of this chapter lies.

Theoretical Concepts of Vulnerability

The use of the term 'vulnerability' is increasing in public, political and academic discourse (Misztal, 2011) and generally refers to the neediest of those facing difficulty, risk or exposure. Indeed, being vulnerable is said to refer to the possibility of being physically or emotionally attacked or harmed. Similarly, vulnerability has also been described as a state or condition whereby an individual is in danger, under threat, experiencing health challenges, at risk, and/or requiring support or protection (Larkin, 2009). However, defining vulnerability is complex and problematic when one considers the concept within the justice system. As a narrative in criminal justice, it has widespread implications (Bartkowiak-Theron & Asquith, 2012). For example, a conventional and popular view of vulnerability would be one that ties it to individuals who have been victims of crime (Dehaghani & Newman, 2017). This is reflected in a recent scoping review where international definitions of vulnerability in law enforcement and public health were assessed. Enang and colleagues (2019) reported fragmented definitions of vulnerability and indicated that explicit definitions were present in only four out of 34 articles reviewed. Definitions reported in these four articles

DOI: 10.4324/9781003386735-2

related largely to victimology – for example, being at risk of abuse, experience of abuse, being unable to take care of oneself or protect oneself against exploitation (Whitelock, 2009), and being vulnerable in social and physical risk environments (McNeil & Small, 2014). Thus, their scoping review highlighted the difficulties in defining vulnerability and tended to approach it from a victim perspective.

Scholars have long attempted to define the concept of vulnerability, and this is reflected in the vast amount of conflicting literature. What this has led to is an ill-defined concept where 'the exact meaning and parameters remain somewhat elusive' (Munro & Scoular, 2012, p. 189). Even the definitions isolated to specific disciplines such as psychology and law allude to many constructs within vulnerability (McLean & Ryan, 2018). These include characteristics which are innate such as youth or old age, physical and mental health, and low socioeconomic status, and levels of risk based on the circumstances the individual finds themselves in (Brown, 2015). There may also be different levels of vulnerability (Smith & O'Mahony, 2018). Consequently, many academics argue that there is no internationally agreed definition of vulnerability in relation to witnesses and suspects, and that the concept of vulnerability is therefore dependent upon the lens and context (e.g., witness or suspect) in which it is being encountered within. Similarly, some highlight that vulnerability is constructed based upon the need to serve political and economic interests (Green, 2007). Within the justice system, vulnerability is often developed with reference to interviewing and the risk that vulnerability poses to obtaining evidence and evidence integrity (Smith & O'Mahony, 2018). One major body of psychological knowledge concerning vulnerability reflects this.

Gudjonsson's Concept of Vulnerability

Gudjonsson (2006) defines vulnerability within the CJS as, 'psychological characteristics or mental state which renders an [individual] prone, in certain circumstances, to providing information which is inaccurate, unreliable or misleading' (p. 68). In doing so, Gudjonsson identifies four main types of vulnerability (see Table 2.1).

Gudjonsson's psychological concept of vulnerability focuses largely on the degree of risk and characteristics that may impede on the forensic interview. Using this definition amongst vulnerable witnesses and suspects can be problematic as it suggests that such individuals are susceptible to providing unreliable or misleading evidence. Inferring risk can also lead to problematic conceptual divides leading to governmental and policing bodies failing to address central issues around vulnerability such as ensuring appropriate identification and safeguards (Bartkowiak-Theron & Asquith, 2012). Thus, whilst it contributes to definitions on vulnerability, it cannot be used in isolation in defining vulnerability in witnesses and suspects. Other attempts to define vulnerability include that of Fineman's work.

Table 2.1 Gudjonsson's four main types of vulnerability (2006)

Type of vulnerability	*Definition*
Mental disorder	Includes mental illness such as mood disorders, schizophrenia, personality disorder, and learning disability.
Abnormal mental state	States include anxiety, intoxication, or withdrawal from alcohol/drugs.
Intellectual functioning	Refers to level of IQ.
Personality	Includes psychological constructs such as suggestibility, compliance, and acquiescence.

Fineman's Vulnerability Theory

Rather than identifying specific characteristics that identify an individual as vulnerable (Turner, 2006), Fineman's work highlights vulnerability as a conceptual tool with the aim of compelling the state to respond (Fineman, 2013). Fineman defines vulnerability as 'universal and constant...' that must be '...understood as particular, varied, and unique on the individual level' (Fineman, 2013, p. 21). In Fineman's work, two forms of vulnerability are identified. The first is physical which includes mental and intellectual states. The second relates to a socially constructed state due to the various overlapping and complex relationships individuals are situated in (Fineman, 2013). Thus, the central notion to Fineman's theory of vulnerability is that all individuals are vulnerable and prone to dependency, and that the state, therefore, has an obligation to deal with the individual's vulnerability (this is explored further in Chapter 3).

Whilst Fineman's work seeks to encapsulate vulnerability as a concept that covers all individuals, others suggest that the wider use of vulnerability definitions or terminologies creates a problem of over-inclusiveness, subsequently resulting in those most vulnerable becoming less visible (Smith & O'Mahony, 2018). In contrast, when a clustering approach is taken to vulnerability, whereby vulnerable groups are viewed together as possessing similar characteristics of vulnerability, scholars indicate that this may operate too inclusively or discriminatory in some cases (Aihio et al., 2017). For example, the use of terms like 'most' vulnerable and 'least' vulnerable in recent Australian research (see McLean & Ryan, 2018) fail to describe wider nuances when discussing vulnerability (Gudjonsson, 2010). Others suggest that vulnerability could be ranged along a spectrum rather than definitive categories, and that the individuals' needs not be assumed (Burton et al., 2006).

In practice, it can be very difficult to define who is, and who may not be vulnerable. Defining vulnerability appropriately is important because not only are all individuals entitled to justice, 'those who are vulnerable must not be excluded or marginalised' (Cooper et al., 2018, p. 18). That said, should a person be labelled as vulnerable, it may mean that they are deemed not credible or reliable depending on the interpretation of existing definitions of vulnerability – thus, affecting the overall progression in the justice system. The way that vulnerability is constructed in the CJS, therefore, is important, particularly in legislative guidance.

Legislative Concepts of Vulnerability

Vulnerability in the justice system must be properly considered in order to ensure there is access to justice for all. Using psychological theories may not adequately capture vulnerability and so it is important to consider legislative guidance too. In doing so, the College of Policing in England and Wales have adopted the following definition: 'a person is vulnerable if, as a result of their situation or circumstances, they are unable to take care of or protect themselves or others from harm or exploitation' (College of Policing, 2020, p. 4). However, whilst some police forces adopt this definition, others follow different explanations. For example, the definition within the Code of Practice for Victims of Crime is followed by Durham and Cumbria Police Services. Here, vulnerability is defined as follows: 'a natural person who has suffered harm, including physical, mental or emotional harm, or economic loss which was directly caused by a criminal offence or a close relative of a person whose death was directly caused by a criminal offence' (Ministry of Justice [MoJ], 2015, p. 53). In addition, it is recognised that 'the language of policing vulnerabilities is not universal with some countries using other vernacular to describe the same individuals' (Bartkowiak-Theron & Asquith, 2012, p. 45). Thus, even in legislative guidance there is a lack of consistency around how vulnerability is operationalised (Cooper et al., 2018; HMIC, 2015). This is particularly so when one considers the vulnerable witness versus the vulnerable suspect (something we will visit later).

In England and Wales, perhaps the two most important pieces of legislation that define vulnerable witnesses and vulnerable suspects is the Youth Justice and Criminal Evidence Act (YJCEA, 1999) and the Police and Criminal Evidence Act (PACE, 1984; Home Office, 2018), and the accompanying Codes of Practice respectively.

Vulnerable Witnesses: The Youth Justice and Criminal Evidence Act (1999)

Generally, there is a legal presumption that all witnesses are competent to give evidence unless information is provided to suggest otherwise (Roberts & Zuckerman, 2010). The YJCEA was designed to deal with vulnerable witnesses through two main methods: s.16 and s.17. The original YJCEA defined vulnerability in terms of age; witnesses under the age of 17 years, as well as being vulnerable whereby the evidential quality of an individual is diminished as a result of significant impairments in intelligence, functioning and physical disability (Roberts & Zuckerman, 2010). More recently, vulnerable witnesses are defined as being under the age of 18 years (section 16 [1], or those witnesses as per section 16(2):

- i who have a mental disorder as defined by the Mental Health Act 1983 (as amended by the Mental Health Act, 2007).
- ii who are significantly impaired in relation to intelligence and social functioning.
- iii who have a physical disability.

Section 17 defines 'intimidated' witnesses as those whose quality of evidence is likely to be diminished by reason of fear or distress in relation to giving evidence in the case. For example, those who are involved in sexual offences (although not limited to these types of offences) would automatically fall into this category, unless they wished to opt out.

Where an individual is identified as vulnerable (section 16) or intimidated (section 17), they are entitled to Special Measures. Designed to improve the quality of the evidence 'in terms of completeness, coherence and accuracy' (s.16[5]), they include allowing a vulnerable witness to give evidence in court from behind a screen (s.23), the use of live link for cross examination (s.24), the removal of court dress such as wigs and gowns (s.26), pre-recorded cross examination (s.28), and the use of a Registered Intermediary (s.29). These will be discussed in more detail in the next chapter.

Although the implementation of the YJCEA has resulted in large numbers of vulnerable witnesses being assisted through the justice system, it is not without its criticisms. For example, guidance or legislation that focuses specifically on vulnerability has been critiqued for using over-inclusive terminology and a preoccupation with definitions (Bartkowiak-Theron & Asquith, 2012; Gibbs, 2018). This can lead to the labelling of some vulnerable witnesses and thus lead to negative impacts on individuals (Walklate, 2011). Consider witnesses under the age of 18 years; they are automatically eligible for Special Measures which implies that they are vulnerable. Whilst it is not being suggested that this should be changed, such labelling may be seen as over-inclusive and not truly representative of that individuals' needs or their levels of resilience (Brown, 2011). Furthermore, not every individual who has a mental health condition may be vulnerable in their dealings with the justice system. This may also be the case for individuals who have experienced or been involved in specific crime types (Gibbs, 2018; Sherman et al., 2017). For example, adult witnesses involved in sexual offences or modern-day slavery are identified as intimidated under s.17 of the YJCEA. This means that adult witnesses involved in these crime types would receive Special Measures to assist in ensuring the quality of their evidence. However, their evidence may be complete, coherent, and accurate anyway, thus indicating the potential for over-categorisation of vulnerability in relation to specific crime types. Whilst there is no doubt that such individuals may fear crime, this is not a conclusive measure of vulnerability and does not make them inherently vulnerable (Green, 2007). Thus, some advocate for the move away from policies and laws which provide a descriptive list of vulnerability themes (Bartkowiak-Theron & Asquith, 2012), as any attempt to define or reduce vulnerability to specific terms, groups or crime types can result in negative labelling and stereotyping, and limit the overall assessment of who is vulnerable.

However, in contrast, some say that certain social and neurological factors are ignored in the YJCEA. These relate to adults with no specific impairment but those that may have a reduced hearing or visual ability for example, or those with neurodiverse needs. By including language such as 'significant impairments' or 'obvious physical disability', those with less visible conditions may not be considered as vulnerable and thus not receive the appropriate Special Measures to assist in ensuring the quality of their evidence. In addition, the onus is on the police officer and other professionals working in the justice system to identify an individual as vulnerable and perform the necessary assessments to ensure Special Measures are put in place. This may lead to a decrease in the number of options available to vulnerable witnesses depending on access to resources and subsequent cost implications (Doak et al., 2012). Research has indicated that a large number of vulnerable witnesses may not receive the Special Measures they are entitled to, with many advocating that 'vulnerability is ranged along a spectrum and needs and wishes need to be ascertained, not assumed' (Burton et al., 2006, p. 14). This is particularly important given that defining vulnerability and thus using appropriate evidence gathering techniques has an impact on later trial processes (Surgenor, 2012). This is also significant when considering vulnerable suspects.

Vulnerable Suspect: The Police and Criminal Evidence Act (1984)

The impact of an individual's vulnerability on the criminal investigation is well documented. There has been a substantial amount of research that has consistently identified a relationship between heightened suggestibility and compliance and the increased likelihood to provide a false confession (Gudjonsson, 2010, 2018; Otgaar et al., 2020). Indeed, there is an over-representation of vulnerable individuals in proven false confession cases (Kassin et al., 2010). Thus, the way that vulnerable suspects are treated within the justice system is paramount to their likely outcomes.

In England and Wales, it is the PACE (1984) and the associated Codes of Practice that govern how individuals entering custody should be treated. In particular, Code C (2018) provides requirements for the detention, treatment and questioning of suspects, including those that are vulnerable. Before updates to Code C were implemented in 2018, a suspect was considered vulnerable if they were a juvenile (although exceptions could be made for 17-year-olds), or if an officer held any suspicion or had been told in good faith that the individual was mentally disordered or otherwise mentally vulnerable, and if there was no clear evidence to suggest otherwise (para 1.4, Code C, 2017). Thus, officers were only required to have a suspicion of any vulnerability, resulting in the suspect having access to the safeguards in which they were entitled without proof of vulnerability. Scholars labelled this the 'benefit of the doubt' test (Dehaghani & Bath, 2019). However, significant revisions were made to Code C following a public consultation by the Home Office (2017). What resulted was significant revisions made to how vulnerability was constructed.

The recently revised Code C (2018) includes updated definitions as to who may be vulnerable. There are no longer exceptions made for 17-year-old individuals in custody meaning that all individuals under the age of 18 are to be treated as juveniles. Furthermore, instead of using terms such as 'mentally disordered' and 'mentally vulnerable', the overall term, 'vulnerable person' is now used. As such, a 'vulnerable person' is anyone, who, because of a mental health condition or mental disorder:

i may have difficulty in understanding or communicating effectively regarding the full implications for them of any procedures and processes connected with:

- their arrest and detention; or (as the case may be)
- their voluntary attendance at a police station or their presence elsewhere for the purpose of a voluntary interview; and
- the exercise of their rights and entitlements.

ii does not appear to understand the significance of what they are told, of questions they are asked or of their replies; and

iii appears to be particularly prone to:

- becoming confused and unclear about their position
- providing unreliable, misleading or incriminating information without knowing or wishing to do so
- accepting or acting on suggestions from others without consciously knowing or wishing to do so, or
- readily agreeing to suggestions or proposals without any protest or questions (para 1.13d).

In addition, Note 1G highlights that although a suspect may be vulnerable due to existing mental health conditions or disorders, the absence of any such condition does not exclude them from being vulnerable; that is, an individual does not have to have a diagnosed mental health condition to be considered and thus treated as a vulnerable individual, and that consideration should be given to the factors listed in paragraph 1.13(d) in case they should apply to the individual. Subsequently, the new definitions of vulnerability take into account definitions provided in the psychological literature (e.g., Gudjonsson, 2006) as well as the situational factors that may impact upon the individual entering custody – these include, the particular circumstances of the individual and the nature of the investigation. Academics working in this area have welcomed such considerations (Dehaghani & Bath, 2019).

Although the revised Code C (2018) has updated the definition of vulnerability for those entering custody, there remains both positive and negative responses. For example, police officers are required to make reasonable enquiries relating to available information about an individual's potential vulnerability, document what specific factors apply and make such record available to the appropriate safeguards, such as the Appropriate Adult (see Chapter 3). Psychological constructs such as suggestibility and compliance, known to place a vulnerable individual at a heightened risk of falsely confessing, are alluded to when considering if an individual is vulnerable and there has been a move away from the subjective test of identifying vulnerability, e.g., officers having a suspicion of vulnerability, to a more objective test e.g., a reason to suspect vulnerability (National Appropriate Adult Network [NAAN], 2018). However, many indicate that there still remains work to be done. For example, whilst the move away from a subjective test to a more objective test may be considered positive, it now requires an increased threshold for someone to be considered vulnerable. That is, it may lead to individuals not being considered vulnerable and thus not receiving the appropriate safeguards to assist them if a specific factor cannot be identified (NAAN, 2018). In addition, the definition of vulnerability appears more complex and police officers are under an expectation to be able to understand how different mental health conditions or disorders may impact upon an individual and map across the factors listed in paragraph 1.13(d). Indeed, whilst police officers can 'screen' for vulnerability, they are not trained as clinical experts (Dehaghani & Bath, 2019) and concerns have already been raised in how vulnerability is interpreted upon an individual entering custody (Farrugia, 2021). The implementation of new definitions of 'vulnerability' in legislative guidance is yet to be thoroughly examined.

Who Is More Vulnerable? The Vulnerable Witness vs. the Vulnerable Suspect

Clearly, vulnerable suspects cannot be categorised as victims per se, but that does not mean that they find the CJS any less intimidating or are any less vulnerable. Indeed, in addition to the vulnerabilities that having a mental health condition or disorder may lead to, the vulnerable suspect can be vulnerable in other ways with regards to their positions as defendants. Some identify that such individuals are placed in a weak position in comparison to the state. For example, the state prosecuting has unlimited access to the necessary expertise to navigate the legal system (Ashworth, 1996) whereas those accused of a crime are not in a fair position to defend themselves without a lawyer (Dehaghani & Newman, 2017). In addition, the physical arrangements of custody, the interview room, and the courtroom, as well as the behaviour of professionals working in the justice system, all work to alienate the suspect (Dehaghani & Newman, 2017). Consequently, unless vulnerable suspects are afforded the same safeguards within legislative guidance as vulnerable witnesses, they are at an increased risk as they progress through the justice system. Some have identified that populist policies have seen a systemic focus on attempts to support victims whilst ignoring the rights of those suspected or accused of crimes (Cape, 2004). For example, when considering the legal terminology used within criminal proceedings, the position of 'victim', 'witness' and 'suspect' directs attention to Special Measures. Research has found that a defendant's needs for intermediaries are often overlooked because of their role as a defendant in the process, despite the positive impact an intermediary can have (Henderson, 2015). Scholars have continuously indicated that defendants should be included for consideration in Special Measures (Oxburgh et al., 2016; Plotnikoff & Woolfson, 2007). Whilst some Special Measures may be implemented for vulnerable defendants at the discretion of the trial judge, this does not equate to the same statutory support available to vulnerable witnesses (Jacobson & Talbot, 2009). This is explored in much further detail in Chapter 7 but see the case of *R v Sevenoaks Youth Court* [2009] EWHC 3088.

Differences in legislative guidance when dealing with vulnerable witnesses compared to vulnerable suspects can also lead to heightened vulnerability for the latter individual. For example, legislative guidance for vulnerable witnesses considers the impact of race, gender, culture, and ethnic backgrounds, as well as other life experiences that may impact upon the quality of evidence provided (see MoJ, 2022, para 2.111, for example). This is in stark contrast to the guidance provided in Code C (2018) for vulnerable suspects. Whilst some progress has been made in updating the definition of vulnerability in Code C (2018), attention must still be paid to the way that vulnerable suspects are perceived by those working in the justice system. There are high numbers of vulnerable individuals that have difficulties that impact upon their ability to effectively engage in and cope with the CJS (Loucks, 2007). Consequently, many have argued that all vulnerable individuals involved in the justice system should be considered worthy of equal attention (Dehaghani & Newman, 2017). Seeing vulnerable suspects as equally vulnerable to witnesses encourages arguments for a properly functioning justice system that upholds everyone's rights (Dehaghani & Newman, 2017) thus reducing the risk of creating unequal services to witnesses and suspects, disparity, and inequality. One key element in ensuring that vulnerable individuals are treated as such is being able to identify vulnerability in the first instance.

Identifying Vulnerability

Vulnerable individuals coming into contact with the CJS as a witness or a suspect is not a new phenomenon (Farrugia, 2021). Whilst the main duties of a police officer focus on the detection and investigating of a crime, they are increasingly becoming the first point of contact for many vulnerable individuals. Defining vulnerability is problematic because of the multiplicity of meanings and definitions and the way that vulnerability has been legally and socially constructed (Brown, 2017). As such, being able to identify vulnerability is fraught with difficulties and not an easy task, particularly when psychological and legal research has typically operated in isolation (Smith & O'Mahony, 2018). This has not served vulnerable individuals well. How vulnerability is identified in vulnerable witnesses and vulnerable suspects will subsequently be explored.

Identifying Vulnerable Witnesses

When a vulnerable witness encounters the justice system in England and Wales, the onus is on the investigating officer to identify if a vulnerability exists based on the legislative guidance provided in the YJCEA (1999) and the Achieving Best Evidence in Criminal Proceedings guidance (ABE; MoJ, 2022). That may include an initial contact with the witness not only to take an initial account, but also to collate relevant information about the witness. This usually occurs via a witness assessment carried out by the interviewing officer to ascertain if the witness is vulnerable, and if so, what the nature of those vulnerabilities may be. The assessment may also explore factors relating to age, gender, culture, religion, language and communication, social and cognitive functioning, welfare and social care issues, the relationship to the suspect, the need for any safeguarding and whether there are any physical disabilities. Should vulnerability be identified, then the vulnerable witness is likely to receive some Special Measures (see Chapter 3). The ABE guidance acknowledges the difficulties in identifying vulnerability, particularly in adults (Chown, 2010) and this is exacerbated if individuals are reluctant to disclose any vulnerability (Crane et al., 2016). Currently, there is no accepted or consistent approach to the assessment of a vulnerable witness and their competence to engage in the justice process in England and Wales (Farrugia & Maras, 2023). Indeed, training manuals around vulnerability are often organisationally and situationally based (Majeed-Ariss et al., 2019) which may lead to some investigators considering vulnerability in a narrow lens, as well as sporadic approaches to conducting assessments. Often, reports and Special Measure applications are submitted based on the organisation or policy requirements, or if requested by the prosecutor (Charles, 2012; HMIC, 2015), and it has been acknowledged that many assessments and thus identification of vulnerable witnesses rely initially on perception and judgements (Majeed-Ariss et al., 2019).

There has been a consistent failure to identify vulnerable witnesses with some research indicating that up to half of all witnesses who would benefit from some form of Special Measures as per the YJCEA (1999) are not identified (Ewin, 2010). This may be due to a lack of assessment (or a fragmented assessment), a lack of clarity regarding defining vulnerability, or simply not recognising relevant factors during evidence gathering (Burton et al., 2006). For example, in most research work there is an emphasis on vulnerability being identified or measured using statistical frameworks and concerning witness populations who automatically become vulnerable due to the crime type, age or gender (Gibbs, 2018). This could result in inadequate measures of those witnesses who have some learning or developmental needs but where assessment does not take place as the individual has not been a victim of a certain offence. Research has documented that those involved in minor offences may receive less investigative attention relating to vulnerability and the use of Special Measures (HMIC, 2015). This is potentially dangerous given that any crime type can involve a vulnerable or intimidated witness (HMIC, 2015), and can lead to a bias within the early identification of vulnerability in witnesses. It can also lead to the number of applications for Special Measures being limited. Thus, this is important to consider given how subtle vulnerability is subjected to variables and bias; that is an individual can and is often considered more vulnerable due to the type of crime (HMIC, 2015). Indeed, this has been reiterated by recent research that suggests that police responses to crimes, usually associated with vulnerability such as sexual offences, and those implicated, are often based on myths and over-stated facts (Gibbs, 2018; Sherman et al., 2017). This can detract from other crimes and lead to vulnerable individuals not receiving the same attention when needed and being left without support (Asquith, 2012).

Identifying Vulnerable Suspects

Research has frequently highlighted that mental health disorders are over-represented in individuals entering custody (McKinnon & Grubin, 2010); an issue that has been documented worldwide (Chariot et al., 2014; Dorn et al., 2014; Fazel & Seewald, 2012; Heide et al., 2012; Ogloff et al., 2011). There are typically higher levels of mental ill health and other vulnerabilities in individuals in custody than compared to the general population (Ceelen et al., 2012; Dorn et al., 2014). In England and Wales, that figure is estimated to be between 33% and 63% (McKinnon & Grubin, 2014). Whilst international responses in police custody vary considerably, it is the PACE (1984) and Code C (2018) that provide the legal framework in England and Wales under which custody services operate. When an individual is brought into custody, they undergo a 'booking in' procedure that involves being asked a number of questions by a custody officer as part of a risk assessment. Such questions include those relating to the individuals' physical and mental health, including use of substances or withdrawal from substances, risk of self-harm and any medication requirements. The purpose of the risk assessment is to confirm the level of risk the suspect may pose to themselves or to others, and whether a healthcare professional or an Appropriate Adult is required (Brooker et al., 2018; NAAN, 2020). The responsibility of the individual's care falls to the custody officer, who quite frequently works under significant pressure in busy and complex custody suites (Carter & Mayhew, 2010; McKinnon & Grubin, 2012; Payne-James et al., 2010).

However, much like vulnerable witnesses, there are significant difficulties and failures in being able to effectively identify vulnerability in suspects. Research reports there is ambiguity in the understanding of what vulnerability means in custody officers despite current legislative guidance, and whilst each police force in England and Wales considers vulnerability as a priority, there remains a lack of consistency in terms of how vulnerability is defined (Farrugia, 2021). In Australia, scholars have identified a lack of a standardised approach in identifying and assessing intellectual and adaptive functioning for individual with intellectual disability and they highlight the difficulties that such vulnerable individuals may face as they may not be appropriately identified as being vulnerable (Baldry et al., 2013). In addition, those who are responsible for identifying vulnerability in the first instance often receive very little to no formal training in mental health (Bather et al., 2008; Vigurs & Quy, 2017). The difficulties in identifying vulnerable suspects does not mirror the vast amounts of research work conducted around the world.

International contemporary work has focused largely on the suspects' health needs or prevalence rates of individuals in custody (Chariot et al., 2014; Dorn et al., 2014; Heide et al., 2018; McKinnon & Grubin, 2010), or on developing and comparing new and existing screening measures (McKinnon & Finch, 2018; McKinnon & Grubin, 2012; Noga et al., 2015; Sondi & Williams, 2018; Young et al., 2013). However, such screening tools have been deemed not 'fit for purpose' in England and Wales as they are known to miss many cases of mental ill health, as well as failing to identify the need for appropriate safeguards in almost half of cases that required one (McKinnon & Grubin, 2012). Thus, the difficulties in effectively identifying vulnerable suspects continues.

Summary

Vulnerability is not a new phenomenon especially given the process of deinstitutionalisation. Unfortunately, a disproportionate number of vulnerable individuals now being treated in the community regularly come into contact with the justice system and so there is an increased need and prioritisation to be able to identify, assess and manage such individuals. However, this is not an easy task. Theoretical explanations of vulnerability define it generally as those in need or at risk and within the context of the CJS, it is often described in relation to an individual's age, physical and mental health, socioeconomical status and situational factors. Whilst there is no internationally agreed definition of vulnerability in the psychological literature, Gudjonsson's work is often drawn upon in understanding how a vulnerable individual may be at a heightened risk during the justice process, particularly the police interview. Legislative guidance regarding vulnerability includes the YJCEA (1999) and the PACE (1984) and Code C (2018). Here definitions of vulnerability focus on the individual's evidential quality being diminished due to mental disorder, significant impairments in intelligence and social functioning, and physical disability. However, they are not without their criticisms and scholars indicate that there remains much work to be done in reducing the ambiguity and complex nature of defining vulnerability, particularly when considering the vulnerable witness v the vulnerable suspect.

If there are difficulties in defining and explaining what vulnerability is, then it seems obvious that there are problems in identifying vulnerability in both witnesses and suspects. Whilst guidance advocates for the use of an assessment in identifying vulnerable witnesses, there is no consistent approach to doing so – coupled with witnesses involved only in certain crimes that automatically makes them eligible for Special Measures, it is not surprising that up to half of all vulnerable witnesses are not identified. This is mirrored somewhat in identifying vulnerable suspects. Despite a risk assessment being conducted when a suspect first enters custody in England and Wales, there remains difficulties in being able to effectively identify a vulnerable suspect. Scholars have highlighted this is down to lack of consistency in how vulnerability is defined and is an issue that is reflected worldwide, despite the large amount of contemporary work conducted on screening tools and prevalence rates of vulnerable suspects in custody. Thus, there remains a lot of work to be completed in defining and identifying vulnerability in both witnesses and suspects. If a vulnerable individual enters the justice system, and is not recognised as such, they may not receive the appropriate support to assist them. Such safeguards are vital for ensuring equal justice for both vulnerable witnesses and vulnerable suspects – the various safeguards available to vulnerable individuals in the justice system is where the next chapter shall turn.

Key Learning Points

- Since the process of deinstitutionalisation, increasing numbers of vulnerable individuals come into contact with the justice system.
- Defining vulnerability is difficult; there is no internationally agreed definition of vulnerability in relation to witnesses and suspects.
- Gudjonsson's work identifies four main types of vulnerability, including mental disorder, abnormal mental state, intellectual functioning, and personality.
- Legislative concepts of vulnerability are captured in the YJCEA (1999) and the PACE (1999) and accompanying Codes of Practice, in particular Code C (2018).
- Identifying vulnerability in witnesses and suspects has proven problematic with vast numbers of both going unrecognised.
- There is no accepted or consistent approach to the assessment of a vulnerable witness.
- It is the custody officer who completes a risk assessment with a vulnerable suspect when they enter custody.
- There remain significant issues in defining vulnerability and subsequently being able to appropriately identify vulnerable witnesses and vulnerable suspects.

References

Aihio, N., Frings, D., Wilcock, R., & Burrell, P. (2017). Crime victims' demographics inconsistently relate to self-reported vulnerability. *Psychiatry, Psychology and Law*, *24*(3), 379–391.

Ashworth, A. (1996). Legal aid, human rights and criminal justice. In R. Young & D. Wall (Eds.), *Access to criminal justice* (pp. 55–77). Blackstone.

Asquith, N. (2012). Vulnerability and the art of complaint making. In I. Bartkowiak-Théron & N. L. Asquith (Eds.), *Policing vulnerability* (pp. 147–161).

Baldry, E., Clarence, M., Dowse, L., & Trollor, J. (2013). Reducing vulnerability to harm in adults with cognitive disabilities in the Australian criminal justice system. *Journal of Policy and Practice in Intellectual Disabilities*, *10*(3), 222–229.

Bartkowiak-Theron, I., & Asquith, N. L. (2012). The extraordinary intricacies of policing vulnerability. Australasian policing. *A Journal of Professional Practice and Research*, *4*(2), 43–49.

Bather, P., Fitzpatrick, R., & Rutherford, M. (2008). *Briefing 36: Police and mental health*.

Brooker, C., Tocque, K., Mitchell, D., & Pearce, M. (2018). Findings from a health needs assessment in Durham and Darlington. *Journal of Forensic and Legal Medicine*, *57*, 91–95.

Brown, K. (2011). 'Vulnerability': Handle with care. *Ethics & Social Welfare*, *5*(3), 313–321.
Brown, K. (2015). *Vulnerability and young people: Care and social control in policy and practice.* Policy Press.
Brown, K. (2017). Introduction: Vulnerability and social justice. *Social Policy and Society*, *16*(3), 423–427.
Burton, M., Evans, R., & Sanders, A. (2006). *An evaluation of the use of special measures for vulnerable and intimidated witnesses.* Home Office, Research, Development, and Statistics Directorate.
Cape, E. (2004). Overview: Is reconciliation possible? In E. Cape (Ed.), *Reconcilable rights? Analysing the tension between victims and defendants* (pp. 1–18). Legal Action Group.
Carter, J., & Mayhew, J. (2010). Audit of hospital transfers January to March 2006 from Sussex police custody. *Journal of Forensic Legal Medicine*, *17*, 38–40.
Ceelen, M., Dorn, T., Buster, M., Stirbu, I., Donker, G., & Das, K. (2012). Healthcare issues and healthcare use among detainees in police custody. *Journal of Forensic Legal Medicine*, *19*, 324–331.
Chariot, P., Lepresle, A., Lefevre, T., Boraud, C., Barthes, A., & Tedlaouti, M. (2014). Alcohol and substance screening and brief intervention for detainees kept in police custody. A feasibility study. *Drug and Alcohol Dependence*, *134*, 235–241.
Charles, C. (2012). *Special measures for vulnerable and intimidated witnesses: Research exploring the decisions and actions taken by prosecutors in a sample of CPS case files.* Crown Prosecution Service.
Chown, N. (2010). 'Do you have any difficulties that I may not be aware of?' A study of autism awareness and understanding in the UK police service. *International Journal of Police Science and Management*, *12*(2), 256–273.
College of Policing. (2018). *Mental health: Mental health vulnerability and illness.* https://www.college.police.uk/app/mental-health/mental-vulnerability-and-illness
College of Policing (2020). *National vulnerability action plan (NVAP) revised 2020-2022.* National Police Chiefs' Council.
Cooper, P., Dando, C., Ormerod, T., Mattison, M., Marchant, R., Milne, R., & Bull, R. (2018). One step forward and two steps back? The '20 Principles' for questioning vulnerable witnesses and the lack of an evidence-based approach. *The International Journal of Evidence and Proof*,
Crane, L., Maras, K. L., Hawken, T., Mulcahy, S., & Memon, A. (2016). Experiences of autism spectrum disorder and policing in England and Wales: Surveying police and the autism community. *Journal of Autism and Developmental Disorders*, *46*(6), 1–14.
Dehaghani, R., & Bath, C. (2019). Vulnerability and the appropriate adult safeguard: Examining the definitional and threshold changes within PACE code C. *Criminal Law Review*, *3*, 213–232.
Dehaghani, R., & Newman, D. (2017). 'We're vulnerable too': An (alternative) Analysis of vulnerability within English criminal legal aid and police custody. *Onati Socio-Legal Series*, *7*(6), 1199–1228.
Doak, J., McGourlay, C., & Doak, J. (2012). *Evidence in context* (3rd ed.). Routledge.
Dorn, T., Ceelan, M., Buster, M., Stirbu, I., Donker, G., & Das, K. (2014). Mental health and healthcare use of detainees in police custody. *Journal of Forensic and Legal Medicine*, *26*, 24–28.
Enang, I., Murray, J., Dougall, N., Wooff, A., Heyman, I., & Aston, E. (2019). Defining and assessing vulnerability within law enforcement and public health organisations: A scoping review. *Health and Justice*, *7*, 1–13.
Ewin, R. (2010). The vulnerable and intimidated witness: A study of the special measure practitioner. *Journal of Applied Psychology and Social Science*, *2*(1), 12–40.
Farrugia, L. (2021). Identifying vulnerability in police custody: Making sense of information provided to custody officers. *Journal of Forensic and Legal Medicine*, *80*.
Farrugia, L., & Gabbert, F. (2019a). The appropriate adult: What they do and what they should do in police interviews with mentally disordered suspects. *Criminal Behaviour and Mental Health*, *29*(3), 134–141.
Farrugia, L., & Gabbert, F. (2019b). Vulnerable suspects in police interviews: Exploring current practice in England and Wales. *Journal of Investigative Psychology and Offender Profiling*, *17*(1), 17–30.
Farrugia, L., & Gabbert, F. (2020). Forensic interviewing of mentally disordered suspects: The impact of interview style on investigation outcomes. *Current Psychology*, *41*(5), 3216–3224.

Farrugia, L., & Maras, K. (2023). Achieving best evidence from victims and witnesses. In G. Oxburgh, T. Myklebust, M. Fallon, & M. Hartwig (Eds). *Interviewing and interrogation: A review of research and practice since* World War II. Torkel Opsahl Academic EPublisher.

Fazel, S., & Seewald, K. (2012). Severe mental illness in 33,588 prisoners worldwide: Systematic review and meta-regression analysis. *The British Journal of Psychiatry, 200*, 364–373.

Fineman, M. (2013). Equality, autonomy, and the vulnerable subject in law and politics. In M. Fineman & A. Grear (Eds.), *Gender in law, culture, and society: Vulnerability: Reflections on a new ethical foundation for law and politics* (pp. 12–28). Ashgate.

Gibbs, P. (2018). *Love, fear and control – Does the criminal justice system reduce domestic abuse?* Transform Justice.

Green, S. (2007). Crime, victimisation and vulnerability. In S. Walklate (Ed.) *Handbook of victims and victimology* (pp. 91–118). https://www.taylorfrancis.com/chapters/edit/10.4324/9780203118207-10/crime-victimisation-vulnerability-simon-green

Gudjonsson, G. (2018). *The psychology of false confessions: Forty years of science and practice.* John Wiley & Sons Ltd.

Gudjonsson, G. H. (2006). Disputed confessions and miscarriages of justice in Britain: Expert psychological and psychiatric evidence in Court of Appeal. *Manitoba Law Journal, 31*, 489–521.

Gudjonsson, G. H. (2010). Psychological vulnerabilities during police interviews. Why are they important? *Legal and Criminological Psychology, 15*(2), 161–175.

Heide, S., Chariot, P., Green, P., Fabian, J., & Payne-James, J. (2018). Healthcare and forensic medical aspects of police detainees, suspects and complainants in Europe. *Journal of Forensic and Legal Medicine, 57*, 58–65.

Heide, S., Stiller, D., Lessig, R., Lautenschlager, C., Birkholz, M., & Fruchtnicht, W. (2012). Medical examination for fitness of police custody in two large German towns. *International Journal of Legal Medicine, 126*, 27–35.

Henderson, E. (2015). Bigger fish to fry: Should the reform of cross-examination be expanded beyond vulnerable witnesses? *The International Journal of Evidence & Proof, 19*(2), 83–99.

HMIC (2015). *Police effectiveness 2015 (vulnerability)—A national overview.* HMIC.

Home Office. (2017). *Revised code of practice for the detention, treatment and questioning of persons by police officers.* Police and Criminal Evidence Act (PACE) 1984, Code C.

Home Office. (2018). *Police and Criminal Evidence Act (1984) and codes of practice.*

Hoong Sin, C., Hedges, A., Cook, C., Mguni, N., & Comber, N. (2009). *Disabled people's experiences of targeted violence and hostility.* Equality and Human Rights Commission.

Jacobson, J., & Talbot, J. (2009). *Vulnerable defendants in the criminal courts: A review of provision for adults and children.* Project Report. Prison Reform Trust.

Kassin, S., Drizin, S., Grisso, T., Gudjonsson, G., Leo, R., & Redlich, A. (2010). Police induced confessions: Risk factors and recommendations. *Law and Human Behaviour, 34*, 3–38.

Larkin, M. (2009). *Vulnerable groups in health and social care.* Sage Publications.

Loucks, N. (2007). *Prisoners with learning difficulties and learning disabilities – Review of prevalence and associated needs.* Prison Reform Trust.

Majeed-Ariss, R., Brockway, A., Cook, K., & White, C. (2019). 'Could do better': Report on the use of special measures in sexual offences cases. *Criminology & Criminal Justice*, https://doi.org/10.1177/1748895819840396

McKinnon, I., & Finch, T. (2018). Contextualising health screening risk assessments in police custody suites – Qualitative evaluation from the HELP-PC study in London, UK. *BMC Public Health, 18*, 393–406.

McKinnon, I., & Grubin, D. (2010). Health screening in police custody. *Journal of Forensic and Legal Medicine, 17*, 209–212.

McKinnon, I., & Grubin, D. (2012). Health screening of people in police custody – Evaluation of current police screening procedures in London, UK. *European Journal of Public Health, 23*, 399–405.

McKinnon, I., & Grubin, D. (2014). Evidence-based risk assessment screening in police custody: The HELP-PC study in London, UK. *Policing, 8*, 174–182.

McLean, F., & Ryan, S. (2018). *Vulnerability: A review of reviews*. College of Policing. Available at: https://assets.production.copweb.aws.college.police.uk/s3fs-public/2021-11/Recognising-responding-vulnerability-related-risks-scope-of-practice.pdf

McNeil, R., & Small, W. (2014). Safer environment interventions: A qualitative synthesis of the experiences and perceptions of people who inject drugs. *Social Science and Medicine*, *106*, 151.

Ministry of Justice (MoJ). (2015). *Code of practice for victims of crime*. HMSO.

Ministry of Justice (MoJ). (2022). *Achieving best evidence in criminal proceedings: Guidance on interviewing victims and witnesses and using special measures*. HMSO.

Misztal, B. (2011). *The challenges of vulnerability: In search of strategies for a less vulnerable social life*. Palgrave Macmillan.

Munro, V. E., & Scoular, J. (2012). Abusing vulnerability? Contemporary law and policy responses to sex work in the UK. *Feminist Legal Studies*, *20*(3), 189–206.

Murray, J., Heyman, I., Wooff, A., Dougall, N., Aston, L., & Enang, I. (2018). *Law enforcement and public health: Setting the agenda for Scotland*. Scottish Institute for Policing Research Annual Review.

National Appropriate Adult Network (NAAN). (2018). *PACE Update: Changes to Code C, E, F, and H*.

National Appropriate Adult Network (NAAN). (2020). *There to help: Ensuring provision of appropriate adults for mentally vulnerable adults detained or interviewed by police*. Available at: https://www.appropriateadult.org.uk/policy/research/there-to-help-research-series

Noga, H., Walsh, E., Shaw, J., & Senior, J. (2015). The development of a mental health screening tool and referral pathway for police custody. *European Journal of Public Health*, *25*, 237–242.

Ogloff, J., Warren, L., Tye, C., Blaher, F., & Thomas, S. (2011). Psychiatric symptoms and histories among people detained in police cells. *Social Psychiatry and Psychiatric Epidemiology*, *46*, 871–880.

Otgaar, H., Schell-Leugers, J., Howe, M., Villar, A., Houben, S., & Merckelbach, H. (2020). The link between suggestibility, compliance and false confessions: A review using experimental and field studies. *Applied Cognitive Psychology*, *35*, 445–455.

Oxburgh, L., Gabbert, F., Milne, R., & Cherryman, J. (2016). Police officers' perceptions and experiences with mentally disordered suspects. *International Journal of Law and Psychiatry*, *49*, 138–146.

Payne-James, J., Green, P., McLachlan, G., & Moore, T. (2010). Healthcare issues of detainees in police custody in London, UK. *Journal of Forensic and Legal Medicine*, *17*, 11–17.

Plotnikoff, J., & Woolfson, R. (2007). *The 'Go-between': Evaluation of intermediary pathfinder projects. Research summary*. https://www.researchgate.net/publication/344219930_The_%27Go-Between%27_evaluation_of_intermediary_pathfinder_projects

Police Scotland. (2017). *Policing 2026: Our 10-year strategy for policing in Scotland*. https://www.scotland.police.uk/spa-media/jjkpn4et/policing-2026-strategy.pdf?view=Standard

Roberts, P., & Zuckerman, A. A. S. (2010). *Criminal evidence*. Oxford University Press.

Roulstone, A., Thomas, P., & Bladerston, S. (2011). Between hate crime and vulnerability: Unpacking the British criminal justice system's construction of disablist hate crime. *Disability and Society*, *26*(3), 351–364.

Sherman, L., Strang, H., & O'Connor, D. (2017). Introduction - key facts about domestic abuse: Lessons from eight studies. *Cambridge Journal of Evidence Based Policing*, *1*, 59–63.

Sirdifield, C., & Brooker, C. (2012). Detainees in police custody: Results of a health needs assessment in Northumbria, England. *International Journal of Prisoner Health*, *8*, 60–67.

Smith, K., & O'Mahony, B. (2018). Vulnerability and criminal investigations. In A. Griffiths & R. Milne (Eds.), *The psychology of criminal investigation; From theory to practice* (pp. 91–112). Routledge.

Sondi, A., & Williams, E. (2018). Health needs and co-morbidity among detainees in contact with healthcare professionals within police custody across the London Metropolitan Police Service area. *Journal of Forensic and Legal Medicine*, *57*, 96–100.

Surgenor, S. (2012). Better representing the vulnerable. *Criminal Law and Justice Weekly (Formerly Justice of the Peace)*, *12*, 176–454.

Turner, B. (2006). *Vulnerability and human rights*. Pennsylvania State University.

Vigurs, C., & Quy, K. (2017). *What works: Crime reduction systematic review series. No. 6: Police responses to people with mental health needs: A systematic map of the literature*. University College London.

Walklate, S. (2011). *Handbook of victims and victimology*. Routledge.

Whitelock, A. (2009). Safeguarding in mental health: Towards a rights-based approach. *The Journal of Adult Protection*, *11*(4), 30–42.

Young, S., Goodwin, E., Sedgwick, O., & Gudjonsson, G. (2013). The effectiveness of police custody assessments in identifying suspects with intellectual disabilities and attention deficit hyperactivity disorder. *BMC Medicine*, *11*, 248–259.

Youth Justice and Criminal Evidence Act (YJCEA). (1999). London: HMSO.

3 Safeguarding the Vulnerable in the Criminal Justice System

Introduction

The criminal justice system (CJS) is becoming well versed in vulnerability, particularly given the prevalence rates. It has been reported that mental ill-health, for example will affect one in four of us at some point in our lives (World Health Organisation, 2001). It is a complex area within policing and one that can be very time-consuming. For example, it is estimated that anywhere between 20% and 75% of police time is spent assisting vulnerable individuals, particularly those with mental health concerns (HMICFRS, 2018). Whilst mental health care needs to be seen as a part of the core business of policing, the steep rise in funding cuts has led to many community services being reduced, resulting in a lot of unmet need, and a demand for services and support that the police are unable to meet. Recent reports have documented that the police in England and Wales may be working beyond their duty when responding to mental health needs although they are good at recognising when individuals are in crisis and thus at risk. However, the importance of collaboration and working with the appropriate services in assisting vulnerable individuals was also identified (HMICFRS, 2018). Some of these services come in the form of safeguards enshrined in legislation to assist a vulnerable witness or suspect when they come into contact with the CJS.

Although there exists many issues and difficulties in identifying vulnerability as previous chapters have alluded to, when vulnerable individuals are recognised as such, they should be afforded safeguards including the Registered Intermediary and the Appropriate Adult – two main safeguards for vulnerable victims and witnesses (hereon referred to as witnesses) and suspects, respectively in England and Wales and other parts of the world. The development of these roles and their efficacy will be the main focus of this chapter, with reference made to other practices around the world. In addition, how vulnerable witnesses are safeguarded compared to vulnerable suspects will be considered throughout.

The Vulnerable Witness

The central principle within the majority of adversarial justice systems is that of orality; whereby a witness is expected and relied upon to be able to provide an oral account of the events they have experienced or witnessed. Usually, this account is initially provided to the police where it is recorded as a written statement or a video interview, and then to the Court during any subsequent trial. Indeed, evidence testified in Court by witnesses is most commonly tested by cross-examination; this process is designed to establish the truth, observe witness demeanour, and clarify any inconsistences (Henderson, 2014; Roberts & Zuckerman, 2010). However, whilst many legal professionals including barristers and

DOI: 10.4324/9781003386735-3

Judges believe that a witness being physically present in Court to give their evidence is best (O'Mahony et al., 2011), not all witnesses may be capable of engaging with the usual process of orality, particularly those that are vulnerable or intimidated (Brunel & Py, 2013). The CJS has acknowledged this and with the implementation of the Youth Justice and Criminal Evidence Act (YJCEA, 1999) came considerations to the way that vulnerable and intimidated witnesses provide their evidence.

Many suggest that the YJCEA has changed the approach to traditional methods of vulnerable witnesses providing their evidence both at the investigation stage and the trial stage (Ewin, 2015). Designed to help such witnesses in the 'orality task', the YJCEA provides Special Measures to help enable vulnerable and intimidated witnesses to provide their evidence given the impact of their vulnerability and/or the impact of the type of crime committed. It does not remove the need to provide oral evidence but does change the way in which it is recorded, and the approach taken to obtain it (Ewin, 2015). For example, the use of screens to shield the witness from the defendant (s.23) is often used to ease the distress and anxieties the vulnerable or intimidated witness may feel at the prospect of coming 'face-to-face' with the defendant. They may also provide their evidence via a live video link (s.24) to remove the need for their physical presence in the Court; an environment that many have not encountered before and may find distressing. Other Special Measures include their initial account to the police being video recorded via an Achieving Best Evidence interview and then submitted to the Court as their evidence-in-chief (s.27). This reduces the amount of time the vulnerable or intimidated witness is required to spend at Court and means that their account can be played to the Court (via the video interview) rather than them having to explain in detail at trial what has allegedly happened to them. The use of pre-recorded cross-examination (s.28) builds on this concept – a relatively new Special Measure, this allows for a vulnerable or intimidated witness to go to Court before the trial commences and be recorded giving their evidence through cross-examination. Subsequently, the witness does not have to then attend Court during the trial and endure lengthy delays before they are called to give their evidence.

One type of Special Measure for vulnerable and intimidated witnesses is that of the Registered Intermediary (s.29), whose role primarily is to communicate

a to the witness, questions put to the witness, and
b to any person asking such questions, the answers given by the witness in reply to them, and to explain such questions or answers so far as necessary to enable them to be understood by the witness or person in question (s.29(2)).

The Development of the Registered Intermediary Scheme in England and Wales

Described as 'new players in the criminal justice system' (Plotnikoff & Woolfson, 2015, p. 3), the Registered Intermediary scheme was only rolled out nationally in England and Wales in 2008. However, the very concept of the intermediary role dates back to the 1950s and is not limited to that of England and Wales, although was initially used to assist children only. For example, in 1955, Israel introduced the 'youth examiner' which was in effect a social worker responsible for questioning children (Libai, 1969). Similarly, legislation was passed in South Africa in 1977 to allow an intermediary to relay questions to children from lawyers (Henderson, 2012). It was not until the late 1980s that England and Wales followed the Israeli model and proposed the use of a 'child examiner' to relay lawyers' questions to children whilst their evidence was videotaped before trial (Williams, 1987a,

1987b). An advisory group, led by Judge Thomas Pigot QC endorsed this idea and recommended that all children's evidence, including cross examination, should be captured before trial and that the lawyers' questions should 'be relayed through a person approved by the court who enjoys the child's confidence' (Home Office, 1989, para 2.32). What followed was the Criminal Justice Act in 1991 which built upon some of Pigot's recommendations; for example, children's police videotaped interviews were now admissible as their evidence-in-chief but proposals for a child examiner and the pre-trial filming of cross-examination were disregarded (Plotnikoff & Woolfson, 2015). It was not for another seven years that recommendations were made for courts to be given statutory powers to order intermediary assistance in England and Wales where it would assist vulnerable witnesses to give their best evidence (Home Office, 1998; Sanders et al., 1997).

The intermediary role was created under Section 29 of the YJCEA (, 1999) and a number of intermediaries with relevant professional skills were recruited by the Home Office in 2003. Registration and thus performing the role as a Registered Intermediary was subject to passing a training course and a Disclosure Barring Service (DBS). Intermediaries were provided with a Code of Practice, a Code of Ethics, and a Procedural Guidance Manual (Ministry of Justice, 2023). The Home Office initially managed the register and those requiring a Registered Intermediary were encouraged to regard the register as 'the first port of call' (Plotnikoff & Woolfson, 2015, p. 11). Registered Intermediaries were matched to vulnerable witnesses based on the intermediary skillset and the needs of the witness. The Home Office ran a pilot scheme regarding the use of Registered Intermediaries between 2004 and 2005 in six police force areas in England and Wales. Shortly after, research highlighted little recognition of communication difficulties in the CJS, little awareness of Special Measures and thus a failure to recognise who might be eligible for a Registered Intermediary (Cooper & Roberts, 2006). Given that the initial Home Office guidance indicated that eligibility for this type of Special Measure was restricted only to witnesses with profound or significant communication difficulties, it is not surprising that those from the police force areas involved in the pilot rarely used a Registered Intermediary, believing that they were available only for those who could not communicate verbally. Further confusion was caused by the interpretation of the guidance with many police force areas indicating that intermediaries were only for the youngest of witnesses or applying the adult criteria such as a physical or mental disability to those eligible by virtue of age. Thus, children with no diagnosed disability but whose communication difficulties were derived from their developmental stage or trauma were often overlooked (Plotnikoff & Woolfson, 2015).

Having received the feedback regarding how the guidance was interpreted, the Home Office relaunched the scheme in 2005 with new guidance explaining the eligibility criteria. Whilst this did not immediately solve the problem, requests for Registered Intermediaries increased albeit unevenly depending on police force area, and the evaluation report recommended national rollout of the intermediary scheme. This was immediately accepted in 2006 by the Home Office, and the implementation of this was completed in 2008 to all 43 police force areas in England and Wales. Control of the Registered Intermediary register passed to the Ministry of Justice in 2008 who outsourced it to the Witness Intermediary Scheme matching service in 2009; they currently still manage the register now hosted by the National Crime Agency. Requests for Registered Intermediaries are made by the police or the Crown Prosecution Service (CPS) depending on the stage of the case via a Request for Service form which collects information about the needs of the vulnerable witness. This is used to find an appropriate match to a Registered Intermediary with the necessary skills. In the year ending 2020/21, the Witness Intermediary Scheme in England and Wales had received a total of 7,312 requests for the assistance of a Registered Intermediary; a new record for the highest number of requests received in any 12-month period. That figure constitutes a 518% increase in the number of requests since 2010, with approximately 97.8% of all requests being matched (Ministry of Justice, 2021). These requests are dealt with by only a small number of Registered Intermediaries – to date, there are approximately 200 Registered Intermediaries on the national register, with around 150 active at any one time (Ministry of Justice, 2021). Thus, the development of the Registered Intermediary in England and Wales continues to grow.

The Role of the Registered Intermediary in England and Wales

Accredited by the Ministry of Justice in England and Wales, Registered Intermediaries come from a wide variety of professional backgrounds. Perhaps the most common is speech and language therapy, although there are increasing numbers from psychology and social work (Cooper & Wurtzel, 2014). From the outset, Registered Intermediaries in England and Wales are trained to facilitate communication between the legal professional (e.g., interviewing police officer, lawyer, Judge) and the vulnerable witness so as to obtain the best quality evidence from the vulnerable witness (Plotnikoff & Woolfson, 2015; Taggart, 2021). They are also trained to be independent and impartial, with their duty being to the Court irrespective of either counsel (O'Mahony et al., 2011). Upon being matched to the vulnerable witness and receiving the Request for Service form, the Registered Intermediary will complete an assessment of the vulnerable witness' communication needs. Usually conducted prior to the witness being interviewed by the police (or if the case is at trial, prior to the vulnerable witness providing their evidence at Court), the assessment forms the basis of recommendations the Registered Intermediary will make to ensure effective communication. These can include how the vulnerable witness should be communicated with prior to and during questioning, how to monitor any impact of anxiety or other associated mental health symptoms upon their ability to effectively communicate and how best to use communication aids if required. Following the assessment of a vulnerable witness, the Registered Intermediary will produce a report that includes such recommendations and advises how those involved in the communication and/or questioning of the vulnerable witness should adapt their communication. The Registered Intermediary will then be present in the police interview and/or at trial to assist where necessary. This includes attending a Ground Rules Hearing to discuss with the Court, the adjustments to questioning needed, and how they will intervene during cross-examination if they believe a communication issue has arisen (Cooper et al., 2015).

In reality, most of what a Registered Intermediary does in a case is not found in legislation but has evolved through the development of good practice (Taggart, 2021). Described as 'little short of revolutionary' (Henderson, 2015, p. 155), some suggest that what intermediaries have achieved as a body may have done more than anyone to affect a culture change in the way that the courts and legal system now deal with vulnerable witness (Wurtzel & Marchant, 2017). Encouraged to 'think outside of the box' (Plotnikoff & Woolfson, 2015), Registered Intermediaries often have to use a number of innovative methods to assist in obtaining effective communication. These can range from the simple use of pen and paper to encourage the use of sketching, to the use of body maps and dolls to 'show' what happened rather than 'tell' what happened, to more complex tools that can assist in determining a timeline of events particularly if there is more than one alleged offence and to tools that aid in managing the witness' mental health or anxiety and the impact on their communication. For example, the use of a traffic light system where the witness can indicate how stressed they are feeling. How each of these communication aids are developed to assist the vulnerable witness is determined largely by the Registered Intermediary and their assessment, and their need for use must be evidenced as the following case depicts.

'Thinking Outside of the Box'

I received the Request for Service form and knew it was going to be a tricky one. The case was as follows: M was an 18-year-old female with significant impairments to her communication; in effect whilst she had the physical capacity to talk, she was mute and was not able to verbally express herself. Upon speaking with the officer on the case, I was informed that M had been subjected to a number of sexual assaults. Unfortunately, whilst living at home, her mother would 'sell' her daughter to different men for sex. It was only when a neighbour raised the alarm due to the amount of men coming and going from the house, that the police became involved. M was taken out of her family home to be safeguarded and the police wanted to obtain an account from her.

I met with M a number of times – usually the assessment is conducted in one meeting, two maximum, but this was going to take a lot of time. Given M's difficulties, I wanted to take the pressure off verbal communication from the start – something that resulted in a few raised eyebrows from the officer. Instead, I introduced an app called 'text to speech' that I had installed on my iPad. I started to use the app to engage with M and slowly but surely, she started to do the same. During our second meeting, M then started to whisper her responses rather than use the app all of the time. We moved onto other elements of the assessment that I knew would be important for the police interview – for example, the words that she would use for different body parts, sexual acts, positions. In addition to the 'text to speech' app, M was introduced to body maps which we labelled up together, and dolls.

Following my assessment meetings with M, the officer and I started planning the interview. Again, given her needs, we knew it was not going to be straightforward. We used portable recording equipment that we took to where M was currently residing and set aside two full days to capture her evidence in short interview blocks. M was able to give a full account of what she had experienced in a total of around six hours with lots of breaks in between. We assisted her by encouraging M to use the tools we had spent so much time using in the assessment – whilst she was only minimally verbal, she was able to sketch, show and use the 'text to speech' app in her responses. Unfortunately, the case did not progress to trial – we as intermediaries do not always get to know the reasons why. However, what I was able to find out was that she had been permanently moved away from her mother and she was now being protected and safeguarded. Sometimes, that's all you can hope for.

Aide Memoir from the author; a Registered Intermediary

International Developments of the Intermediary Scheme

By the time that Registered Intermediaries were piloted and introduced in England and Wales, similar roles were operating in other countries around the world. As mentioned previously, intermediaries were allowed to assist children in South Africa (Jonker & Swanzen, 2007), and Israel used a system of child examiners who collected evidence from children for use in Court. Similarly, in Norway and Sweden, schemes using an examining Magistrate to take evidence from children in advance of trial were also underway (Cooper & Mattison, 2017; Hanna et al., 2013). More recently, two witness intermediary schemes using the English model have been introduced in Northern Ireland and in New South Wales (NSW) in Australia.

In Northern Ireland, the Criminal Evidence (Northern Ireland) Order 1999 allows for the same range of Special Measures found in the YJCEA (, 1999) in England and Wales. However, it was not until 2013 that the Department of Justice, Northern Ireland launched its intermediary pilot schemes – one for vulnerable witnesses and one for vulnerable defendants, respectively. Article 17 of the Criminal Evidence (Northern Ireland) Order 1999 describes the function of the witness intermediary to communicate:

1 to the witness, questions put to the witness,
2 to any person asking such questions, the answers given by the witness in reply to them, and
3 to explain such questions or answers so far as necessary to enable them to be understood by the witness or person in question (s.2).

Following these pilots in the Crown Court, the Registered Intermediary scheme under the 1999 Order was rolled out to all Crown, Magistrates', and Youth Courts in Northern Ireland from April 2017 (Hoff et al., 2022). Similar to the scheme in England and Wales, Registered Intermediaries are classed as communication specialists and are provided to ensure that the vulnerable witness can effectively participate in the justice system. As with all Special Measures, their need is subject to the approval of the Court where it is considered if 'their use is likely to improve the quality (completeness, coherence, and accuracy) of the evidence given by the witness' (Article 17 of the Criminal Evidence (Northern Ireland) Order 1999).

The intermediary model used in England and Wales was recommended to NSW, Australia by the NSW Office of the Director of Public Prosecutions – they had conducted research into the use of intermediaries for children in countries such as England and Wales, Ireland, Austria, and Norway (Watts, 2013). Following the publishing of the report, 'Every Sentence Tells a Story: Report on Sentencing of Child Sexual Assault Offenders' (Parliament of New South Wales, 2014) recommendations were made including the setting up of a 'Child Sexual Assault Offences Taskforce' who were responsible for exploring a preferred model for a specialist court that would deal with child sexual assault offences in NSW (Cooper & Mattison, 2017). What they recommended a year later was a pilot scheme for the use of intermediaries and the use of pre-recorded cross-examination of child witnesses involved in sexual assault cases; such necessary provisions were enacted in 2015 in the Criminal Procedure Amendment (Child Sexual Offence Evidence Pilot) Act 2015. This legislation sets out the role of the intermediary who is also described as a children's champion. Their role is to communicate:

1 to the witness, questions put to the witness,
2 to any person asking such a question, the answers given by the witness in replying to them, and
3 to explain such questions or answers so far as necessary to enable them to be understood by the witness or person in question.

Other intermediary models varying in form and scope now exist in all Australian jurisdictions apart from the Northern territory (Mackay & Giuffrida, 2020).

Although the description of the intermediary's role is similar (if not identical) in England and Wales, Northern Ireland and NSW, Australia, there remains some significant differences. For example, witnesses in England and Wales under the YJCEA (1999) are eligible for Special Measures including the Registered Intermediary on grounds of age, for example, being a child, or incapacity. However, in NSW, Australia, an intermediary is only likely to be appointed for a witness under the age of 16 years, or, if the witness is older than only if the witness has difficulties communicating and is involved in a sexual offence case (s.89(3) Criminal Procedure Amendment (Child Sexual Offence Evidence Pilot) Act 2015). Furthermore, s.89(4) indicates that an intermediary should not be appointed for a child where 'it is not otherwise in the interests of justice to appoint a children's champion'. However, in Northern Ireland, the eligibility criteria are perhaps the most all-encompassing as it covers not only children and vulnerable adults but also includes vulnerable suspects/defendants (a topic the chapter will turn to later) and is not restricted on offence type. Thus, the practice of an intermediary is highly dependent upon the country in which the scheme operates and how well received it is (see Hepner et al., 2015 and Powell et al., 2014 for full discussions).

Do They Work? The Effectiveness of the Registered Intermediary

There have been a number of Special Measures introduced in England and Wales and around the world in the last 20 years (Collins et al., 2017). Their purpose is to assist the accounts of the most vulnerable and enable them to provide their 'best evidence'. Indeed, research has frequently highlighted how child witnesses become very stressed when providing their evidence which can impact upon their overall accuracy and consistency during cross-examination at trial (Righarts et al., 2015). When these measures were first introduced, there were a handful of studies that examined the effects of Special Measures predominately on children's communication and behaviour. For example, research examining the impact of giving evidence via a live video link (s.24, YJCEA, 1999) on children's testimony has found that child witnesses become more capable of providing their evidence and report being less nervous (Landstrom & Granhag, 2010). Research has reported that child witnesses are less likely to produce errors to misleading questions when communicating via a live video link compared to face to face (Doherty-Sneddon & McAuley, 2000). Other work has conducted an extensive review on Special Measures and found that they can reduce children's feelings of anxiety and improve their overall experience of giving evidence (Hamlyn et al., 2004). More recently, scholars have indicated that with the appropriate preparation and questioning, quality evidence can be gathered from very young children (Marchant, 2016). However, when considering jury decision-making, the vast amount of research indicates that jurors view testimony more positively and are better convinced when they observe children in court rather than across a live video link (Landstrom & Granhag, 2010). That is, research has indicated that jurors perceive children as less credible, accurate and believable when they give their evidence via a live video link (Eaton et al., 2001) and some highlight that this may affect conviction rates with a bias in favour of the defence (Goodman et al., 1998). But, findings have been mixed with other work reporting no differences in jury perceptions of children's evidence when comparing a live video link against court testimony (Orcutt et al., 2001). Thus, despite the use of the live video link increasing children's recall and behaviour when giving their evidence, there is mixed findings in terms of jurors' perceptions relating to credibility and believability.

Other Special Measures, namely that of the Registered Intermediary, has not been subject to such extensive research. Whilst early work found that Registered Intermediaries were found to be helpful in terms of aiding communication and helping vulnerable witnesses cope with the stress of giving evidence (Plotnikoff & Woolfson, 2007), scholarly work around the effectiveness of the Registered Intermediary and the fairness on criminal proceedings is limited (Collins et al., 2017). One area that has received some interest is the perceptions of the jury and the impact on their decision-making where an intermediary is used to assist a vulnerable witness. Experimental work investigating the impact of Registered Intermediary involvement on mock juror perceptions of children and their communication whilst being cross-examined in Court was conducted by Collins and her colleagues in 2017. In their work, mock jurors were required to watch a video clip of children of different age groups being questioned with or without an intermediary and were required to rate the children on a number of factors. The results indicated that ratings for children's communication and the quality of cross examination were greater when a Registered Intermediary was present compared to when they were not present, thus supporting earlier work (Ridley et al., 2015). However, there remains little to no work that has explored this with vulnerable adult witnesses with different vulnerabilities; that is, the majority of the work appears to focus only on child witnesses.

Other work exploring the effectiveness of the Registered Intermediary has focused on the views of legal professionals that are required to work alongside the intermediary. Whilst the intermediary role has been described as a radical scheme, it has also been met with positive responses overall from Judges and other legal professionals in England and Wales (Henderson, 2015) and the role of the Registered Intermediary has become integral to the justice system (Plotnikoff & Woolfson, 2015). Furthermore, recent reports have found that Registered Intermediaries are invaluable in providing assistance to vulnerable witnesses and giving them a voice in the justice system, with positive feedback obtained from police and others when using the Witness Intermediary Scheme (VC, 2018).

That said, the same review (VC, 2018) also reported that not all vulnerable witnesses who are legally entitled and would benefit from an intermediary are receiving their assistance to give evidence. This is not overly surprising given the vast increase in demand for a Registered Intermediary in recent years. Currently, the average waiting time to be matched with a Registered Intermediary is four weeks – this can lead to many cases proceeding without the assistance of one (VC, 2018). It has also been found that there are not enough Registered Intermediaries to meet the current levels of demand, with particular shortages in intermediaries that are able to assist older children and/or adults with mental health needs (VC, 2018). Given issues also being raised around the overall management and governance of the Witness Intermediary Scheme, the Victims' Commissioner has made several recommendations to enhance the overall provisions, including the need for a centralised national service, a fast-track service for very young children due to the impact of delays on forgetting, and regular inspections of how the CPS and police work with Registered Intermediaries (VC, 2018). However, whilst these issues are important, they relate more to the overall running of and access to the service, rather than the efficacy of the Registered Intermediary themselves. Whilst much more work needs to be conducted regarding the latter, key themes emerging from recent studies have highlighted how Registered Intermediaries are important facilitators and enablers for vulnerable witnesses (Henderson, 2015; Plotnikoff & Woolfson, 2015) as we can see in the cases below.

Two-Year-Old Girl Gives Evidence in UK Abuse Case

A two-year-old girl sexually abused by an adult male is believed to have become the youngest person to give evidence in a UK criminal case. The male was sentenced to more than 10 years in prison for his offences. A Registered Intermediary assisting in the case advised the police about the best way to question the two-year-old child who was initially reluctant to engage with unfamiliar adults and clung to her parents. The girl began talking to the intermediary and the police officers and was able to respond to simple 'who', 'what', and 'where' questions, naming the suspect and describing what had happened with the help of communication aids such as a paper figure. The Registered Intermediary also helped obtain a mouth swab from the child for forensic analysis. Initially hiding from the officer wearing blue medical gloves, the intermediary asked for everyone to be given gloves and swabs and they played for several minutes pretending to brush their teeth. Once the girl was comfortable, she was able to provide a mouth swab. The specialist support of the Registered Intermediary ensured the two-year-old girl was well supported and the police interviewer understood how best to talk to the child ultimately gathering powerful evidence of the most serious offending.

Abstract taken from The Guardian (2017a).

Stephen Hawking Style Eye Tracking Tech Helped Convict Vicar Cyril Rowe of Child Abuse

A former church chorister rendered immobile by motor neurone disease has been helped to give courtroom evidence against his abuser using eye-tracking technology. It is believed to be the first time the Eyegaze equipment has been used for cross-examination in a British Crown Court, a retired Anglican vicar has been convicted of three counts of indecent assault dating back to the 1970s. The witness, who was a young boy when the offences occurred, recorded his evidence and was questioned by lawyers via video link as he lay in a hospice bed. He was helped by a Registered Intermediary who assessed his ability to communicate and read out his answers where needed. The witness died on the same day that the guilty verdict was returned.

Abstract taken from The Guardian (2017b).

The Vulnerable Suspect

It is well acknowledged that vulnerable individuals with mental health conditions and other cognitive difficulties are over-represented in custody in England and Wales (Fazel & Seewald, 2012; McKinnon & Grubin, 2010). Approximately 33–63% of those detained in custody have a mental health condition or disorder (McKinnon & Grubin, 2014) and these prevalence rates are echoed around the world (Chariot et al., 2014; Dorn et al., 2014). For example, scholars in Australia estimate that police officers spend 10–15% of their time dealing with individuals only with mental ill health – this percentage is increased when considering individuals with different cognitive impairments (Punter & Bronitt, 2020), and this over-representation increases with each stage of the justice system (Giuffrida & Mackay, 2021). Prisons have been described as quasi mental health institutes due to the high proportion of the prison population with a mental illness or a learning disability (Naylor, 2014) with some prison officers suggesting that prison and staff working within it are now primary carers for those that are mentally unwell (Cunneen et al., 2013).

Individuals entering custody will undoubtedly find the process daunting and stressful (Chariot et al., 2014; Newburn, 2013). When individuals have vulnerabilities such as poor mental health or a learning disability, the process may become exceptionally confusing and exacerbate their existing vulnerabilities (HM Inspectorate of Constabulary, 2015). As such, they may face a number of difficulties in navigating their way through the justice system. Not only are vulnerable individuals more likely to be arrested (Hartford et al., 2005), but they tend to spend longer periods of time in police custody (Hiday & Wales, 2003). Furthermore, research has documented the lack of understanding reported by vulnerable suspects during their time in custody and in subsequent legal procedures such as the police interview; that is, vulnerable suspects are often unsure what to say or do (Hyun et al., 2014). It has also been consistently reported that those with mental health conditions and disorders, as well as learning disabilities are at a heightened risk of falsely confessing to crimes (see, e.g., Gudjonsson, 2018) and may have limited effective participation in police investigations due to the barriers they face as a result of their vulnerability (Bath & Dehaghani, 2020). At the furthest extreme, and has been unfortunately previously reported, the vulnerability of the individual can pose a risk factor leading to suicide ideation (Forrester et al., 2016).

Internationally, police responses and custody procedures vary when identifying and dealing with vulnerable suspects (McKinnon et al., 2016). In Europe for example, there are a number of procedural safeguards that are implemented (European Parliament, 2016). In America and Canada, the use of Crisis Intervention Teams (CIT) are adopted whereby specialised police officers partner with community and health organisations to assist with vulnerable individuals (particularly those that have poor mental health) that enter custody (Ghelani, 2022). In England and Wales, it is the Police and Criminal Evidence Act (PACE, 1984; Home Office, 2018) and the associated Codes of Practice which legislate and regulate police powers in England and Wales, as well as provide the legal framework under which custody services operate. Upon arrival into custody, the suspect will complete a 'booking in' procedure designed to assess the level of risk they may pose to themselves or to others and whether a healthcare professional or other safeguard is required (Brooker et al., 2018) – this involves being asked a number of questions by a custody officer (McKinnon & Grubin, 2013). The risk assessment contains questions that relate directly to the individuals' physical and mental health and includes items such as, 'Are you experiencing any mental ill health or depression?' and 'Have you ever tried to harm yourself?' (College of Policing, 2017). The custody officer is responsible for documenting and recording the risk assessment for every individual brought into custody in England and Wales as well as responding appropriately to any specific risk identified and continuously reviewing the level of risk should circumstances change (see PACE, Code C, para 3.6-3.10; Home Office 2018). Subsequently, individuals in custody will be placed on one of four pre-defined observation levels whilst they are in custody, ranging from a general observation whereby the individual is checked hourly (level 1) up to close proximity where the individual is physically supervised in close proximity and reviewed by a healthcare professional (level 4) (College of Policing, 2017).

When a vulnerable suspect is identified as such, they are entitled to a number of safeguards to assist them as they progress through the custody and justice processes. In addition to clinical attention and assessments from a Forensic Medical Examiner and/or Custody Nurse, the vulnerable suspect is also entitled to an Appropriate Adult.

The Development of the Appropriate Adult in England and Wales

The role of the Appropriate Adult was introduced in England and Wales as part of the legislative framework of the PACE (1984; Home Office, 2018) and accompanying Codes of Practice designed to regulate police powers and suspects rights. The Appropriate Adult's role is defined by Code C (2018) as a parent, guardian, social worker, or other responsible person aged 18 years and above, who does not have any association with the police (para 1.7). The Appropriate Adult's role is to 'safeguard the rights, entitlements and welfare of juveniles and vulnerable persons' (para. 1.7A, p.7). Their duties include supporting and advising, and assisting the vulnerable individual in custody, whilst observing whether the police are acting properly and fairly and raise any concerns if they are not to a senior officer, and assist with and facilitate communication and ensure that the vulnerable individual understands their legal rights. Consequently, the Appropriate Adult should be present when the vulnerable individual is being cautioned (para 7 and 10.12), during the taking of any samples such as fingerprints or DNA and intimate searches (Annex para 2B), during the interview or the signing of written statements (para 11.15), and when Special warnings in relation to adverse inferences are given (para 10.11, para 10.11A), and if the vulnerable individual is being charged (para 16.1).

Initially, it was not uncommon for the parents of vulnerable individuals to take on the role of the Appropriate Adult, particularly if the individual in custody was a child, and especially because the Appropriate Adult must be independent of the police. What this meant was that family members often enacted this role with little or no training. Whilst vulnerable individuals in custody have reported the importance of knowing their Appropriate Adult and thus being able to trust them, conflict with a family member or known person acting as their Appropriate Adult was also reported (Leggett et al., 2007). In addition, research has found that when parents act within the role of the Appropriate Adult, their contributions are more consistent with control or punishment (Brown, 1997; Bucke & Brown, 1997) and assisting the police in obtaining a confession (Dixon et al., 1990). Other research has indicated that where parents have acted as the Appropriate Adult, they do not make much contribution in assisting the vulnerable suspect; Evans (1993), for example found little or no contribution by parents or guardians in 74.8% of interviews analysed in their dataset. This has been found by other scholars (Pierpoint, 2001). More recently, concerns relating to adults with a Learning Disability have been reported regarding how much practical support a family member or carer could provide when enacting the role of the Appropriate Adult (Howard et al., 2015). Thus, although current legislative guidance indicates that a parent or guardian should be considered in the first instance when requiring an Appropriate Adult (College of Policing, 2020), it must be considered whether they understand the role and can sufficiently perform it.

Consequently, recommendations for the use of professionally trained Appropriate Adults were made by the Home Office nearly 30 years ago and have since been encouraged in more recent years (Pierpoint, 2004). As such, organised groups of trained individuals now carry out this role in England and Wales. Described as a professional Appropriate Adult, such individuals either volunteer or are employed within dedicated Appropriate Adult schemes (NAAN, 2015); some of these are organised and funded locally, although the National Appropriate Adult Network (NAAN) is the national membership body supporting and representing organisations delivering Appropriate Adult support. The NAAN is a registered charity and receives funding from membership fees, Home Office grants and other charitable trusts and foundations. They identify as an independent centre of expertise that provide training to approximately 100 member organisations (NAAN, 2023). As a result, there now exists a number of schemes that operate under the NAAN whereby individuals are trained specifically for this role and thus assist vulnerable suspects in police custody.

However, there remains a disparity in such schemes and the provision available (Farrugia, 2023). Currently, there is no statutory duty for any agency to provide an Appropriate Adult for a vulnerable adult (Jessiman & Cameron, 2017) and research consistently documents how some police force areas have little or no access to an Appropriate Adult scheme (Bath et al., 2015). In one report, 14 out of 43 police forces in England and Wales highlighted that a sub-contracted private or third sector organisation fulfilled the Appropriate Adult role (some trained by the NAAN but others not), 12 areas relied upon social services (either via a dedicated team or through social services staff providing the support as part of their role but not necessarily trained to do so), with many other police force areas indicating that there was no provision for vulnerable suspects (Perks, 2010). Thus, despite an earlier report recommending the need for trained individuals to undertake the role of the Appropriate Adult (Bradley, 2009), it is still 'not possible to provide an overall picture of the need for Appropriate Adult's...or understand the level of familial Appropriate Adult's undertaking the role' (Perks, 2010, p. 5). There remains much more to develop in terms of ensuring all police force areas have access to trained Appropriate Adults.

Implementing the Appropriate Adult in England and Wales

Despite the introduction of the Appropriate Adult role, there remains some problems in the implementation of this safeguard even in areas that have do have access to dedicated schemes (Bradley, 2009; NAAN, 2015). Early research reported that just over half of 'psychologically vulnerable' suspects had been interviewed with the use of an Appropriate Adult (Medford et al., 2003); this continues to be supported by more recent work (Young et al., 2013). A number of reasons have been identified as to why Appropriate Adults are not being utilised despite having a vulnerable suspect in custody and these relate not only to inconsistencies in police force area but also to the perceived suitability/quality of the Appropriate Adult, and the severity of the crime and vulnerability of the individual in custody.

The inconsistency in police force areas regarding the use of Appropriate Adults has been reported recently. For example, Bath and Dehaghani (2020) found significant differences in the recorded rate of Appropriate Adult use in different force areas. Sussex Police reported that 25.2% of their cases involved an Appropriate Adult; this is significantly higher than 2.35% and 0.72% reported by Northumbria Police and the West Midlands, respectively. Other work has found similar results. Farrugia (2021) examined the differences in disposal options between police forces when presented with a vulnerable suspect. She found that police forces in the North of England were the least likely to obtain the assistance of an Appropriate Adult when compared to other police force areas. This suggests that an individual's vulnerability and thus the need for an Appropriate Adult may be detected in one police force area but not necessarily another (Farrugia, 2021). However, it must be noted that not all police force areas have access to a dedicated Appropriate Adult scheme and concerns have been frequently raised relating to the suitability/quality and availability of the Appropriate Adult's that may be available (Bath, 2014; Jessiman & Cameron, 2017; NAAN, 2019; Pierpoint, 2000, 2006).

The severity of the crime and the type of vulnerability have also been found to have an impact on whether or not an Appropriate Adult is implemented. For example, Dehaghani (2019) found that those who had been arrested for less serious offences would not necessarily be provided with an Appropriate Adult despite being vulnerable. The type of vulnerability the vulnerable suspect presented with has also been reported as a barrier to the implementation of an Appropriate Adult. Dehaghani (2019) found that those with Autism would not necessarily be provided with an Appropriate Adult if they were deemed to be intelligent and articulate. Furthermore, those with serious mental health conditions including depression and schizophrenia were not considered vulnerable enough to receive the safeguard that should be afforded to them. Her work identified that only vulnerable suspects who had issues with capacity, knowledge and understanding would be provided with an Appropriate Adult despite the presence of a mental health condition. This was also found in her previous work (Dehaghani, 2016). In addition, even when there were issues with reading and writing identified alongside the presence of a mental health condition, an Appropriate Adult would not always be called (Young et al., 2013). Such findings were replicated in an independent piece of work examining how custody officers understand vulnerability and thus implement the Appropriate Adult safeguard. Farrugia (2021) developed six case scenario vignettes in which individuals with different types of vulnerability were presented. A total of 237 custody officers from 25 police forces in England and Wales participated. Her findings suggested that despite having a mental health disorder, an Appropriate Adult would only be considered if the vulnerable individual also had issues with capacity, knowledge and understanding, despite the presence of a mental disorder being a trigger to implement one. Thus, research has identified that even when vulnerability is identified, custody officers make subjective judgments whether the severity of the vulnerability is serious enough to warrant the Appropriate Adult. Furthermore, custody officers have highlighted that if a suspect was taking medication to help manage a mental health condition or other vulnerability but was functioning 'normally' than an Appropriate Adult would not necessarily be required (McKinnon & Finch, 2018).

Thus, there appears to be a number of reasons why the Appropriate Adult safeguard may not be implemented even when there is access to a dedicated scheme. In addition to those noted above, the current guidance may also play a role. For example, Code C (2018) makes reference to an individual being vulnerable and thus requiring an Appropriate Adult if they do not understand the significance of what is being said to them – this direct reference to an individual's understanding suggests that an Appropriate Adult should be used only where there are issues with comprehension rather than the individual's overall vulnerability. It does not explicitly identify that even where there are no issues with comprehension, an individual may still be at risk of providing misleading or inaccurate information, or falsely implicating themselves. A failure to indicate that vulnerability does not always equate to issues with comprehension and capacity may lead to the misunderstanding of the true nature of an individual's vulnerability and thus the need for an Appropriate Adult. This has implications for the criminal justice process as a whole; after all, a breach in the requirement for an Appropriate Adult to assist a vulnerable suspect can result in the exclusion of evidence at trial (as per PACE, 1984; Home Office, 2018) and thus impact upon the outcome of the case for both the vulnerable suspect and the witness.

The Effectiveness of the Appropriate Adult in England and Wales

When a vulnerable suspect has been identified and the Appropriate Adult implemented, it is vital that the Appropriate Adult perform their role effectively to ensure that the vulnerable individual is safeguarded. Seeking the assistance of an Appropriate Adult suggests that there must be an understanding of their role (Farrugia, 2023). However, this is not always the case. Whilst legislative guidance provides some direction to how the Appropriate Adult should execute their role, in reality this can be very difficult. Scholars have highlighted that the role of the Appropriate Adult is a complex, demanding, and confusing one (Bartlett & Sandland, 2003; Bath, 2014; Cummins, 2011) and that both the Appropriate Adult and professionals working with them can find their role difficult to understand. For example, research has reported that many Appropriate Adults may not fully understand their role (Nemitz & Bean, 2001; HMIC, 2015) whilst others suggest that little is known about how the Appropriate Adult constructs and performs their role (Miller, 2015). Other scholars working in this field suggest that the Appropriate Adult role has been socially constructed and that the perception of the Appropriate Adult role lies with the perception holder, for example, the vulnerable individual, the police and the Appropriate Adult themselves. For example, the Appropriate Adult may view their role as a welfare role, or to ensure due process. Others may view it as a crime prevention role or a combination of a welfare role and one of due process (see Pierpoint, 2006 for a full discussion). The confusion around the role of the Appropriate Adult continues to be documented (Jessiman & Cameron, 2017).

This can have an impact on the effectiveness of the AA role and how they perform their duties. Research has shown that when Appropriate Adults are provided with clear provisions, such as the right to request legal advice on behalf of a juvenile individual in custody, the Appropriate Adult is more likely to perform their role more consistently. However, when the requirements of the role were more ambiguous, for example, ensure the interview is being conducted fairly, then the Appropriate Adult tended to impose their own interpretations and engage in duties that fell outside of their role (Pierpoint, 2006). Given that there is a lack of an underpinning conceptual framework and the fact that the Appropriate Adult role can be interpreted in many ways, the effectiveness of the role is undermined (Dehaghani, 2021). This has been highlighted in research that has frequently documented the passivity of the Appropriate Adult when they engage in their role with the vulnerable suspect. Early research reported that Appropriate Adults were not performing their role well in terms of remaining passive when they should have been more active. For example, Evans (1993) reported that the Appropriate Adults in his sample of police interviews were simply observers and made no contributions whatsoever. This has been found in other work too (Bradley, 2009; Medford et al., 2003; Pierpoint, 2001). More recent work sought to examine if this was still the case given the increase in professionally trained Appropriate Adults and the implementation of specific schemes under the NAAN. Farrugia and Gabbert (2019) examined transcripts of police interviews that had been conducted with vulnerable suspects (largely with a mental health condition or disorder) whereby an Appropriate Adult had been present throughout. Their findings reflected earlier work in that Appropriate Adults were significantly more likely to remain passive than to intervene although when they did intervene, such actions were also significantly more likely to be appropriate (in accordance with the legislative guidance). It must be noted however that this may not be completely surprising. To work effectively as an Appropriate Adult, some may argue that a good working relationship with the police is essential. However, research has highlighted that the Appropriate Adult can be actively discouraged from completing their duties during the vulnerable suspects' interview (Dehaghani, 2021; Jessiman & Cameron, 2017) and the legislative guidance specifies that the Appropriate Adult can be asked to leave if they are deemed to be obstructive (Code C, para 11.17A). In very recent research that explored the experiences of Appropriate Adults trained under the NAAN, Appropriate Adults suggested that they may be less likely to perform their duties if faced with excessive conflict from others working in custody (Farrugia, 2023). Such power dynamics have been discussed and reported in depth elsewhere (see, e.g., Dehaghani, 2021).

The passivity of the Appropriate Adult coupled with the complexities of the vulnerable suspect presents a clear challenge in the justice system. Vulnerable suspects are at an increased risk of providing misleading and inaccurate information whilst not fully understanding their legal rights or the custodial process. Unfortunately, well documented miscarriages of justice have occurred as a result of failures to support vulnerable suspects within an interview context (Gudjonsson, 2018). If the Appropriate Adult is not able to fulfil their role effectively and safeguard the vulnerable suspect, then who can?

The Intermediary Role for Vulnerable Suspects/Defendants?

Clearly vulnerable defendants cannot be categorised as a victim, but that does not mean that they do not find the justice process intimidating (McEwan, 2009). Over half of children and adults who offend have communication difficulties as a result of learning difficulties and/or mental health conditions or disorders (Criminal Justice Joint Inspection, 2014). In England and Wales, the term 'Registered Intermediary' is restricted to those who are recruited and trained by the Ministry of Justice who then assist vulnerable witnesses as per the requirements of the YJCEA (, 1999). Vulnerable suspects and defendants are excluded from this Act (s.17(1)); thus, they are not eligible for the same Special Measures including the access to a Registered Intermediary (Plotnikoff & Woolfson, 2015). That said, an amendment to the Act added by s.104 of the Coroners and Justice Act (2009) considers examination of a defendant through an intermediary and provides the following direction:

> ...for any examination of the accused to be conducted through an interpreter or other person approved by the court for the purposes of this section ('an intermediary').
>
> (s.33BA, para 3)

Unfortunately, this amendment is yet to come into force and so when a Judge exercises their inherent jurisdiction to appoint an intermediary for a defendant, the lack of access to a matching service in the same way that exists for a vulnerable witness and Registered Intermediaries makes it difficult to find a suitable defendant intermediary. That said, in reality those that take on defendant work are likely to be already working as a Registered Intermediary with vulnerable witnesses and are therefore willing to take on defence cases. In England and Wales, there are private sector organisations that recruit and train intermediaries for vulnerable defendants (e.g., Intermediaries for Justice, Plotnikoff & Woolfson, 2015).

In England and Wales, having an intermediary to assist a vulnerable defendant is a contentious issue (McEwan, 2009). They are likely to be appointed only whilst the vulnerable defendant provides their evidence at trial rather than during the earlier police interview and the remainder of the trial. There have been numerous legal cases where this has been heavily criticised and courts have recognised in some instances, that without the appropriate assistance throughout the entirety of the trial, the vulnerable defendant would not be able to have a fair trial given the impact of their difficulties. There exist many cases that evidence this, namely the case of R (AS) v Great Yarmouth Youth Court [, 2011] EWHC 2059 (Admin) and this is discussed in much further depth in later chapters. More recently, however, the Divisional Court directed that it is not essential for an intermediary to be present to assist the defendant for the duration of the trial as other than giving evidence, the needs of the vulnerable defendant can be met by other more general support. Thus, the reality is that the needs of the vulnerable suspect and/or defendant do not appear to have the 'same statutory rights to help and support as vulnerable witnesses' (Jacobson & Talbot, 2009, p. 1) as reported below by a Registered Intermediary.

> I met with H when he was serving a custodial sentence in a prison. The referral for a Registered Intermediary had come through the usual channels via the Witness Intermediary Team. H is a 35-year-old male who prior to being imprisoned had been seriously assaulted by another male. During my assessment with H, we spoke of his experience navigating the justice system. This was not the first time H had received a custodial sentence. H explained that when he was interviewed as a suspect, he did not receive the assistance of an Appropriate Adult despite informing the officer that he had complex mental health difficulties (indeed during the assessment, he spoke of his hallucinations and delusional thoughts). Following the assault he had sustained, and thus now being treated within a vulnerable witness context, he was able to access the various Special Measures that were now available to him; one being me as his Registered Intermediary. During the assessment, it became apparent at the impact of his vulnerability on his ability to understand the judicial process and his ability to effectively engage with the court and provide his best evidence. After the assessment, I walked out of the prison bewildered that only now as vulnerable witness, H was able to access the safeguards and support he needed to be able to engage effectively with the justice system. It appeared that no one thought twice about him when he was a vulnerable suspect/defendant.
>
> *Aide Memoir from the author; a Registered Intermediary*

The contentious issue of the defendant intermediary in England and Wales differs in many other countries. For example, in Northern Ireland, an intermediary is permitted for use both during the police suspect interview and during trial (Taggart, 2018). In Australia, vulnerable defendants are provided with 'access to justice...on an equal basis with others, including through the provision of procedural...accommodations, in order to facilitate their direct role as direct and indirect participants...in all legal proceedings' (Convention on the Rights of Persons with Disabilities, Article 13 (1)). What this means is that vulnerable defendants are entitled to support so that they can meaningfully participate in the trial (Gooding & O'Mahony, 2016). Without such assistance, some vulnerable defendants are unable to effectively participate in their defence effectively – the provision of intermediaries to vulnerable suspects and defendants is crucial to safeguarding the right to a fair trial and may go some way to prevent wrongful convictions (Collins et al., 2017). There is now a growing body of evidence and support to ensure that all reasonable steps are taken to assist vulnerable suspects and defendants to give their best evidence and to be able to understand and participate in the justice system (Taggart, 2021). One other alternative is to try and divert the vulnerable suspect from custody.

Diverting Vulnerable Suspects from Custody

Liaison and diversion services are a relatively new concept in England and Wales and in other countries around the world. They exist to improve the health and criminal justice outcomes for vulnerable individuals. Quite often, those with vulnerabilities such as mental health conditions or disorders, learning disabilities, etc., only access the relevant care services when they have been arrested (Farrugia, 2022). As such, liaison and diversion services seek to identify such vulnerable individuals, where the range of their complex needs are identified as factors in the offending behaviour, and divert them away from the justice system and towards the appropriate health and social care services that they require (College of Policing, 2016; Haines et al., 2012). Following recommendations from the Bradley Report (2009), a number of organisations including the Department of Health, the Ministry of Justice, and the Home Office, engaged in a national programme involving six pilot youth justice liaison and diversion schemes for vulnerable juveniles. Following this, the government committed to developing a delivery plan in 2009 and launched the 'Improving Health, Supporting Justice: The national delivery plan of the Health and Criminal Justice Programme Board'. Commitments to improve mental health support for vulnerable individuals who entered custody and divert them away were made (Petrosino, 2010).

What followed has been a number of initiatives that led to the launch and implementation of the 'Liaison and Diversion Operating Model' in 2014 at 10 trial sites in England and a further 13 sites in 2015. The National Model now provides 24 hours, seven days a week services for all vulnerable individuals (adults and juveniles) who have a range of vulnerabilities including mental and physical health, and learning disabilities (NHS England Liaison and Diversion Programme, 2014). However, it was only a few years ago that liaison and diversion services achieved 100% coverage across England (NHS, 2020).

Although liaison and diversion services appear to be a positive way to divert vulnerable individuals away from the justice system and into the relevant support agencies, there does not yet exist a strong evidence base for their success (Kane et al., 2020). Of the work that has been completed, generally it promotes positive correlations between liaison and diversion interventions and changing offending behaviour, and improvements in at least one critical area of mental health outcomes, thus reducing mental health act sections for such vulnerable individuals (Disley et al., 2021; Kane et al., 2020). Others indicate that whilst liaison and diversion services were generally seen as a positive addition to existing services, the methodologies exploring the actual impact on mental health outcomes and reoffending were only moderately rigorous and did not consist of high-quality research studies (Kane et al., 2018; Scott et al., 2013). What is needed, however, is future research that incorporate high-quality, systematic evaluations of outcomes (Schucan & Shemilt, 2019).

Summary

The young and vulnerable are targeted precisely because of their vulnerability; for the same reason, they may be denied access to justice whether that be as a vulnerable witness or suspect (Plotnikoff & Woolfson, 2015). In England and Wales (and around the world), changes to existing legislation that allows for vulnerable witnesses to be protected when they provide their evidence means that those who would not have previously been thought of as able to provide their evidence, can. One of those measures in England and Wales is that of the Registered Intermediary. Dating back to the 1950s, many countries introduced the concept of a 'youth examiner' or a 'child examiner' to assist children in giving their evidence. It was not until the late 1980s that England and Wales introduced the same concept and following some of Pigot's recommendations, the Registered Intermediary safeguard was piloted and rolled out nationally. The Registered Intermediary's role is to assist vulnerable witnesses (juveniles and adults) to give their best evidence. Following an assessment, the Registered

Intermediary provides guidance and recommendations to the police and to the Court to assist with this. Other countries, including Northern Ireland and Australia, have followed the English model and incorporated the role of the Registered Intermediary to assist with their vulnerable witnesses. Originally described as 'new players in the criminal justice system' (Plotnikoff & Woolfson, 2015, p. 3), it is not unusual now to see a Registered Intermediary assisting a vulnerable witness of any age in England and Wales and many other countries around the world to give their best evidence.

Many say that vulnerable suspects also require the same type of support when entering custody and engaging in the justice process. What exists for this vulnerable group is a far cry from what is available for vulnerable witnesses. The development of the Appropriate Adult safeguard was introduced in England and Wales in 1984 as per the PACE (1984; Home Office, 2018) and accompanying Codes of Practice. Developed to 'safeguard the rights, entitlements and welfare of juveniles and vulnerable persons' (para. 1.7A, p.7), their duties include supporting and advising the vulnerable individual in custody, whilst observing whether the police are acting properly and fairly and raise any concerns if they are not to a senior officer, as well as assist with and facilitate communication and ensure that the vulnerable suspect understands their legal rights. Originally, it would be the parent or guardian that would act as an Appropriate Adult, especially if the vulnerable suspect was a juvenile. However, with the development of specific Appropriate Adult schemes and a national membership body known as the NAAN, there now exists trained individuals to assist all vulnerable suspects in custody. However, there remains issues with the implementation and effectiveness of this safeguard leading to many vulnerable suspects not receiving the support they require. Thus, there is now a shift towards the use of intermediaries for vulnerable suspects and defendants. Whilst this practice has already been adopted in some countries around the world, for example, Northern Ireland and Australia, the use of an intermediary for a vulnerable suspect/defendant in England and Wales remains a contentious issue. Whilst one may be requested for a vulnerable defendant, it is usually only when they are providing their evidence and not for the duration of the trial, nor for any prior police interview. As such, there remains a lot more to be done to safeguard the vulnerable suspect/defendant. One relatively new method is the recent development of liaison and diversion services to divert vulnerable individuals out of the justice system and towards the health and social care services they require. However, it was only a few years ago that liaison and diversion services achieved 100% coverage across England (NHS, 2020) and the efficiency of these services are still be evaluated.

As vulnerable individuals progress through the CJS, albeit as witnesses or suspects, they must be treated with caution to ensure that their best evidence can be captured. One key stage of the justice process is the police interview; this is where the next few chapters shall turn where we explore how vulnerable witnesses and vulnerable suspects are interviewed, respectively.

Key Learning Points

- Policing mental ill health and other vulnerabilities takes up a considerable amount of police time around the world, whether that involves a vulnerable witness or a vulnerable suspect.
- The Youth Justice and Criminal Evidence Act (1999) provides Special Measures for vulnerable witnesses; one of these is the Registered Intermediary.

- Rolled out nationally in England and Wales, the Registered Intermediary's role is to assist with and facilitate communication with vulnerable witnesses.
- Other countries around the world have followed the English model and adopted the Registered Intermediary.
- Vulnerable suspects are provided with an Appropriate Adult safeguard as per the Police and Criminal Evidence Act (1984), and the accompanying Codes of Practice (Code C, 2018, in particular).
- Initially parents and guardians would act as the Appropriate Adult for many vulnerable suspects, particularly juveniles. There now exists dedicated Appropriate Adult schemes in England and Wales, many of whom operate under the National Appropriate Adult Network; a national membership body that supports and represents organisations delivering this safeguard.
- Despite the introduction of the Appropriate Adult role, there remains issues with the implementation and effectiveness of this safeguard for vulnerable suspects. Many countries adopt an intermediary for vulnerable defendants although this remains a contentious issue in England and Wales.
- The recent introduction of liaison and diversion services seek to divert vulnerable individuals away from custody and into health and social care services that are more appropriate to their needs. The efficiency of these services is yet to be fully evaluated.

References

Bartlett, P., & Sandland, R. (2003). *Mental health law policy and practice.* Oxford University Press.

Bath, C. (2014). *NAAN briefing: Liaison and diversion and the provision of appropriate adults for mentally vulnerable adults.* National Appropriate Adult Network.

Bath, C., Bhardwa, B., Jacobson, J., May, T., & Webster, R. (2015). *There to help: Ensuring provision of appropriate adults for mentally vulnerable adults detained or interviewed by police.* National Appropriate Adult Network.

Bath, C., & Dehaghani, R. (2020). *There to Help 3. The identification of vulnerable adult suspects and application of the appropriate adult safeguard in police investigations in 2018/19.* National Appropriate Adult Network.

Bradley, K. (2009). *The Bradley report: Lord Bradley's review of people with mental health problems or learning disabilities in the criminal justice system.* Department of Health.

Brooker, C., Tocque, K., Mitchell, D., & Pearce, M. (2018). Findings from a health needs assessment in Durham and Darlington. *Journal of Forensic and Legal Medicine, 57*, 91–95.

Brown, D. (1997). *PACE ten years on: A review of the research* HORS 155. Home Office.

Brunel, M., & Py, J. (2013). Questioning the acceptability of the cognitive interview to improve its use. *L'Année Psychologique, 113*(3), 427–458.

Bucke, T., & Brown, D. (1997). *In police custody: Police powers and suspects' rights under the revised PACE Codes of Practice.* HORS 174. HMSO.

Chariot, P., Lepresle, A., Lefevre, T., Boraud, C., Barthes, A., & Tedlaouti, M. (2014). Alcohol and substance screening and brief intervention for detainees kept in police custody. A feasibility study. *Drug and Alcohol Dependence, 134*, 235–241.

College of Policing. (2016). *Mental health and the criminal justice system.* https://www.college.police.uk/app/mental-health/mental-health-and-criminal-justice-system

College of Policing. (2017). *Detention and custody. Risk assessment.* https://www.college.police.uk/app/detention-and-custody/detention-and-custody-risk-assessment

College of Policing. (2020). *Detention and custody. Children and young persons*. https://www.college.police.uk/app/detention-and-custody/detainee-care/children-and-young-persons

Collins, K., Harker, N., & Antonopoulos, G. A. (2017). The impact of the registered intermediary on adults' perceptions of child witnesses: Evidence from a mock cross examination. *European Journal on Criminal Policy and Research*, *23*, 211–225.

Cooper, P., Backen, P., & Marchant, R. (2015). Getting to grips with Ground Rules Hearing– a checklist for judges, advocates and intermediaries. *Criminal Law Reports*, *6*, 417–432.

Cooper, P., & Mattison, M. (2017). Intermediaries, vulnerable people and the quality of evidence: An international comparison of three versions of the English intermediary model. *The International Journal of Evidence and Proof*, *21*(4), 351–370.

Cooper, D., & Roberts, P. (2006). *Special measures for vulnerable and intimidated witnesses*. Crown Prosecution Service.

Cooper, P., & Wurtzel, D. (2014). Better the second time around? Department of justice registered intermediaries schemes and lessons from England and Wales. *Northern Ireland Legal Quarterly*, *65*(1), 39–61.

Coroners and Justice Act. (2009). https://www.legislation.gov.uk/ukpga/2009/25

Criminal Evidence (Northern Ireland) Order. (1999). https://www.legislation.gov.uk/nisi/1999/2789/contents

Criminal Justice Joint Inspection. (2014). *Achieving best evidence in child sexual abuse cases: A joint inspection*. HMCPSI Publications.

Criminal Procedure Amendment (Child Sexual Offence Evidence Pilot) Act. (2015). https://legislation.nsw.gov.au/view/pdf/asmade/act-2015-46

Cummins, I. (2011). The other side of silence': The role of the appropriate adult post Bradley. *Ethics and Social Welfare*, *5*(3), 306–312.

Cunneen, C., Baldry, E., Brown, D., Schwartz, M., Steel, A., & Brown, M. (2013). *Penal Culture and hyperincarceration: The revival of the prison*. Routledge.

Dehaghani, R. (2016). He's just not that vulnerable: Exploring the implementation of the appropriate adult safeguard in police custody. *Howard Journal of Crime and Justice*, *55*(4), 396–413.

Dehaghani, R. (2019). *Vulnerability in police custody. Police decision-making and the appropriate adult safeguard*. Routledge.

Dehaghani, R. (2021). Interpreting and reframing the appropriate adult safeguard. *Oxford Journal of Legal Studies*, *42*(1):187–206.

Disley, E., Gkousis, E., Hulme, S., Morley, K., Pollard, J., Saunders, C., Sussex, J., & Sutherland, A. (2021). *Outcome evaluation of the national model for liaison and diversion*. RAND.

Dixon, D., Bottomley, C., Coleman, M., Wall, G., & Wall, D. (1990). Safeguarding the rights of suspects in police custody. *Policing and Society*, *1*, 115–140.

Doherty-Sneddon, G., & McAuley, S. (2000). Influence of video-mediation on adult-child interviews: Implications for the use of the live link with child witnesses. *Applied Cognitive Psychology*, *14*, 379–392.

Dorn, T., Ceelan, M., Buster, M., Stirbu, I., Donker, G., & Das, K. (2014). Mental health and health-care use of detainees in police custody. *Journal of Forensic and Legal Medicine*, *26*, 24–28.

Eaton, T. E., Ball, P. J., & Callaghan (2001). Child-witness and defendant credibility: Child evidence presentation mode and judicial instructions. *Journal of Applied Psychology*, *31*, 1845–1858.

European Parliament. (2016). *Directive (EU) 2016/800 of European Parliament and the Council on Procedural Safeguards for children who are suspects or accused persons in criminal proceedings*. European Parliament.

Evans, R. (1993). *The conduct of police interviews with young people*. Royal Commission on Criminal Justice Research Study, no. 8. HMSO.

Ewin, R. (2015). The vulnerable and intimidated witness: A socio-legal analysis of special measures. *Journal of Applied Psychology and Social Science*, *1*(2), 31–54.

Farrugia, L. (2021). Identifying vulnerability in police custody: Making sense of information provided to custody officers. *Journal of Forensic and Legal Medicine*, *80*, 102169.

Farrugia, L. (2022). *Interviewing of suspects with mental health conditions and disorders in England and Wales. A paradigm shift*. Routledge.

Farrugia, L. (2023). The appropriate adult: Their perspective working in the criminal justice system. *Criminology and Criminal Justice*. https://doi.org/10.1177/17488958231193126.

Farrugia, L., & Gabbert, F. (2019). The appropriate adult: What they do and what they should do in police interviews with mentally disordered suspects. *Criminal Behaviour and Mental Health*, *29*(3), 134–141.

Fazel, S., & Seewald, K. (2012). Severe mental illness in 33,588 prisoners worldwide: Systematic review and meta-regression analysis. *The British Journal of Psychiatry*, *200*, 364–373.

Forrester, A., Samele, C., Slade, K., Craig, T., & Valmaggia, L. (2016). Suicide ideation amongst people referred for mental health assessment in police custody. *Journal of Criminal Psychology*, *6*, 146–156.

Ghelani, A. (2022). Knowledge and skills for social workers on mobile crisis intervention teams. *Clinical Social Work Journal*, *50*, 414–425.

Giuffrida, J., & Mackay, A. (2021). Extending witness intermediary schemes to vulnerable adult defendants. *Current Issues in Criminal Justice*, *33*(4), 498–516.

Gooding, P., & O'Mahony, C. (2016). Laws on unfitness to stand trial and the UN convention on the rights of persons with disabilities: Comparing reform in England, Wales, Northern Ireland and Australia. *International Journal of Law, Crime and Justice*, *44*, 122–145.

Goodman, G. S., Tobey, A. E., Batterman-Faunce, J. M., Orcutt, H., Thomas, S., Shapiro, C., & Sachsenmaier, T. (1998). Face-to-face confrontation: Effects of closed-circuit technology on children's eyewitness testimony and jurors' decisions. *Law and Human Behavior*, *22*, 165–203.

Gudjonsson, G. H. (2018). *The psychology of false confessions: Forty years of science and practice*. John Wiley & Sons Ltd.

Haines, A., Goldson, B., Haycox, A., Houten, R., Lane, S., McGuire, J., Nathan, T., Perkins, E., Richards, S., & Whittington, R. (2012). *Evaluation of the Youth Justice Liaison and Diversion (YJLD) pilot scheme. Final report*. University of Liverpool.

Hamlyn, B., Phelps, A., Turtle, J., & Sattar, G. (2004). *Are special measures working? Evidence from surveys of vulnerable and intimidated witnesses (home office research study 283)*. Home Office.

Hanna, K., Davies, E., Henderson, E., & Hand, L. (2013). Questioning child witnesses: Exploring the benefits and risks of intermediary models in New Zealand. *Psychiatry, Psychology and Law*, *20*, 527–542.

Hartford, K., Heslop, L., Stitt, L., & Hoch, J. (2005). Design of an algorithm to identify persons with mental illness in a police administrative database. *International Journal of Law and Psychiatry*, *28*, 1–11.

Henderson, E. (2012). Alternative routes: Accusatorial jurisdictions on the slow road to best evidence. In J. Spencer & M. Lamb (Eds.), *Children and cross-examination: Time to change the rules?* Hart.

Henderson, E. (2014). Judges as cross-examiners: The starmer v grieve debate. *Archbold Review*, *5*, 3–4.

Henderson, E. (2015). Bigger fish to fry: Should the reform of cross-examination be expanded beyond vulnerable witnesses? *The International Journal of Evidence & Proof*, *19*(2), 83–99.

Hepner, I., Woodward, M. N., & Stewart, J. (2015). Giving the vulnerable a voice in the criminal justice system: The use of intermediaries with individuals with intellectual disability. *Psychiatry, Psychology, & Law*, *22*, 453–464.

Hiday, V., & Wales, H. (2003). Civil commitment and arrests. *Current Opinion in Psychiatry*, *16*, 575–580.

HM Inspectorate of Constabulary (HMIC). (2015). *The welfare of vulnerable people in custody*. HMIC.

HM Inspectorate of Constabulary and Fire and Rescue Services (HMICFRS). (2018). *Policing and mental health*. HMIC.

Hoff, S., Powell, M., & Plater, D. (2022). When good intentions are not enough: Professionals' perceptions of the South Australian communication partner scheme. *Australian Journal of Social Issues*, *57*, 970–986.

Home Office. (1989). *Report of the advisory group on video evidence*. Home Office.
Home Office. (1998). *Speaking up for justice*. Home Office.
Home Office. (2018). *Police and Criminal Evidence Act (1984) and codes of practice*. Home Office.
Howard, R., Phipps, E., Clarbour, J., & Rayner, K. (2015). "I'd trust them if they understood learning disabilities" support needs of people with learning disabilities in the criminal justice system. *Journal of Intellectual Disabilities and Offending Behaviour*, *6*(1), 4–14.
Hyun, E., Hahn, L., & McConnell, D. (2014). Experiences of people with learning disabilities in the criminal justice system. *British Journal of Learning Disabilities*, *42*, 308–314.
Jacobson, J., & Talbot, J. (2009). *Vulnerable defendants in the criminal courts: A review of provision for adults and children*. Project Report. Prison Reform Trust.
Jessiman, T., & Cameron, A. (2017). The role of the appropriate adult in supporting vulnerable adults in custody: Comparing the perspectives of service users and service providers. *British Journal of Learning Disabilities*, *45*, 246–252.
Jonker, G., & Swanzen, R. (2007). Intermediary services for child witnesses testifying in South African criminal courts. *Journal of Child and Youth Care Work*, *22*, 205–227.
Kane, E., Evans, E., Mitsch, J., & Jilani, T. (2020). Are liaison and diversion interventions in policing delivering the planned impact: A longitudinal evaluation in two constabularies? *Criminal Behaviour and Mental Health*, *30*, 256–267.
Kane, E., Evans, E., & Shokraneh, F. (2018). Effectiveness of current policing-related mental health interventions: A systematic review. *Criminal Behaviour and Mental Health*, *28*(2), 108–119.
Landstrom, S., & Granhag, P. A. (2010). In-court versus out-of-court testimonies: Children's experiences and adults' assessments. *Applied Cognitive Psychology*, *24*, 941–955.
Leggett, J., Goodman, W., & Dinani, S. (2007). People with learning disabilities' experience of being interviewed by the police. *British Journal of Learning Disabilities*, *35*, 168–173.
Libai, D. (1969). The protection of the child victim of a sexual offence in the criminal justice system. *Wayne Law Review*, *15*, 977–984.
Mackay, A., & Giuffrida, J. (2020). Implications of the royal commission into institutional responses to child abuse for the protection of vulnerable witnesses: Royal commission procedures and introduction of intermediaries and ground rules hearings around Australia. *Journal of Judicial Administration*, *29*, 136–153.
Marchant, R. (2016). Age is not determinative': The evidence of very young children in the English justice system. *Criminal Law and Justice Weekly*, *180*, 12–13.
McEwan, J. (2009). The testimony of vulnerable victims and witnesses in criminal proceedings in the European Union. *ERA Forum*, *10*, 369–386.
McKinnon, I., & Finch, T. (2018). Contextualising health screening risk assessments in police custody suites – Qualitative evaluation from the HELP-PC study in London, UK. *BMC Public Health*, *18*, 393–406.
McKinnon, I., & Grubin, D. (2010). Health screening in police custody. *Journal of Forensic and Legal Medicine*, *17*, 209–212.
McKinnon, I., & Grubin, D. (2013). Health screening of people in police custody – Evaluation of current police screening procedures in London, UK. *The European Journal of Public Health*, *23*, 399–405.
McKinnon, I., & Grubin, D. (2014). Evidence-based risk assessment screening in police custody: The HELP-PC study in London, UK. *Policing*, *8*, 174–182.
McKinnon, I., Thomas, S., Noga, H., & Senior, J. (2016). Police custody healthcare: A review of health morbidity, models of care and innovations within police custody in the UK, with international comparison. *Rick Management and Healthcare Policy*, *9*, 213–226.
Medford, S., Gudjonsson, G., & Pearse, J. (2003). The efficacy of the appropriate adult safeguard during police interviewing. *Legal and Criminological Psychology*, *8*(2), 253–266.
Miller, R. (2015). *An exploration of mental health triage and support in the criminal justice system: Attitudes and experiences of professionals supporting people with mental health needs* [Unpublished thesis].

Ministry of Justice. (2023). *Registered intermediary procedural guidance*. https://assets.publishing.service.gov.uk/media/64e4858e4002ee000d560cf5/registered-intermediary-procedural-guidance-manual.pdf

Ministry of Justice. (2021). *The witness intermediary scheme. Annual report 2020/21*.

National Appropriate Adult Network. (2015). *There to help: Ensuring provision of appropriate adults for mentally vulnerable adults detained or interviewed by police*. https://www.appropriateadult.org.uk/policy/research/there-to-help

National Appropriate Adult Network. (2019). *There to Help 2*. https://appropriateadult.org.uk/policy/research/there-to-help-2

National Appropriate Adult Network. (2023). https://www.appropriateadult.org.uk/about-us/our-work

Naylor, B. (2014). Prisoner/patient: Prisons as mental health institutions. In E. Carroll & K. Warner (Eds.), *Re-imagining imprisonment in Europe: Effects, failures and the future* (pp. 195–216). The Liffey Press.

Nemitz, T., & Bean, P. (2001). Protecting the rights of the MD in police stations: The use of the appropriate adult in England and Wales. *International Journal of Law and Psychiatry*, *24*, 595–605.

Newburn, T. (2013). *Criminology*. Routledge.

NHS England. (2014). *Liaison and diversion operating model 2013/14*. https://www.youtube.com/watch?v=TOIIGLI2bP8&t=9s

NHS England. (2020). *About liaison and diversion*. https://www.england.nhs.uk/commissioning/health-just/liaison-and-diversion/about/

O'Mahony, B. M., Smith, K., & Milne, B. (2011). The early identification of vulnerable witnesses prior to an investigative interview. *The British Journal of Forensic Practice*, *13*(2), 114–123.

Orcutt, H. K., Goodman, G. S., Tobey, A. E., Batterman-Faunce, J. M., & Thomas, S. (2001). Detecting deception in children's testimony: Fact finders' abilities to reach the truth in open court and closed-circuit trials. *Law and Human Behavior*, *25*, 339–372.

Parliament of New South Wales. (2014). *Joint Select Committee on Sentencing of Child Sexual Assault Offenders, Report No 1/55*. Retrieved September 2, 2023, from https://www.parliament.nsw.gov.au/ladocs/inquiries/2211/Final%20Report%20of%20the%20Joint%20Select%20Committee%20on%20Sent.PDF

Perks, M. (2010). *Appropriate adult provision in England and Wales*. National Appropriate Adult Network. https://assets.publishing.service.gov.uk/media/5a7adad0e5274a34770e7921/appropriate-adult-report.pdf

Petrosino, A. (2010). *Formal system processing on juveniles: Effects on delinquency*. The Campbell Collaboration.

Pierpoint, H. (2000). How appropriate are volunteers as 'Appropriate Adults' for young suspects? *Journal of Social Welfare and Family Law*, 22, 383–400.

Pierpoint, H. (2001). The performance of volunteer appropriate adults: A survey of call outs. *Howard Journal of Criminal Justice*, *40*(3), 255–271.

Pierpoint, H. (2004). A survey of volunteer appropriate adult services in England and Wales. *Youth Justice*, *4*(1), 33–45.

Pierpoint, H. (2006). Reconstructing the role of the appropriate adult in England and Wales. *Criminology and Criminal Justice*, 6, 219–237.

Plotnikoff, J., & Woolfson, R. (2007). *The 'go-between': Evaluation of intermediary pathfinder projects. Research summary*. Lexicon Limited.

Plotnikoff, J., & Woolfson, R. (2015). *Intermediaries in the criminal justice system. Improving communication for vulnerable witnesses and defendants*. Policy Press.

Powell, M. B., Bowden, P., & Mattison, M. (2014). Stakeholder's perceptions of the benefit of introducing an Australian intermediary system for vulnerable witnesses. *Australian & New Zealand Journal of Criminology*, *48*(4), 1–15.

Punter, H., & Bronitt, S. (2020). New paradigms of policing mental illness in Australia. The future of 'mental health street-sweeping. In J. McDaniel (Ed.), *Policing and mental health: Theory, policy and practice* (pp. 59–82). Taylor & Francis.

R (AS) v Great Yarmouth Youth Court [2011] EWHC 2059 (Admin). https://vlex.co.uk/vid/r-as-v-great-793582753

Ridley, A. M., van Rheede, V., & Wilcock, R. (2015). Interviews, intermediaries and interventions: Mock jurors', police officers' and barristers' perceptions of a child witness interview. *Investigative Interviewing: Research and Practice*, 7, 21–35.

Righarts, S., Jack, F., Zajac, R., & Hayne, H. (2015). Young children's responses to cross- examination style questioning: The effects of delay and subsequent questioning. *Psychology, Crime & Law*, *21*, 274–296.

Roberts, P., & Zuckerman, A. A. S. (2010). *Criminal evidence*. Oxford University Press.

Sanders, A., Creaton, J., Bird, S., & Weber, L. (1997). *Victims with learning disabilities: Negotiating the criminal justice system*. University of Oxford.

Schucan, K., & Shemilt, I. (2019). The crime, mental health, and economic impacts of prearrest diversion of people with mental health problems: A systematic review. *Criminal Behaviour and Mental Health*, *29*(3), 142–156.

Scott, D., McGilloway, S., Dempster, M., Browne, F., & Donnelly, M. (2013). Effectiveness of criminal justice liaison and diversion services for offenders with mental disorders: A review. *Psychiatric Services*, *64*(9), 843–849.

Taggart, J. (2018). Defendant intermediaries in the criminal justice system: Is Northern Ireland leading the way? Social Science Research Network. Policy Briefing Paper No. 30. https://doi.org/10.2139/ssrn.3219987

Taggart, J. (2021). 'I am not beholden to anyone…I consider myself to be an officer of the court': A comparison of the intermediary role in England and Wales and Northern Ireland. *The International Journal of Evidence and Proof*, *25*(2), 141–162.

The Guardian. (2017a). *Two-year-old girl gives evidence in UK abuse case*. https://www.theguardian.com/law/2017/oct/10/two-year-old-girl-gives-evidence-in-uk-abuse-case

The Guardian. (2017b). *Stephen Hawking style eye tracking tech helped convict vicar Cyril Rowe of child abuse*. https://www.theguardian.com/uk-news/2017/feb/13/stephen-hawking-style-eye-tracking-tech-helped-convict-vicar-cyril-rowe-of-child-abuse

Victims Commissioner. (2018). *A Voice for the voiceless: The Victims' Commissioner's review into the provision of registered intermediaries for children and vulnerable victims and witnesses*. https://victimscommissioner.org.uk/document/a-voice-for-the-voiceless-provision-of-registered-intermediaries-for-children-and-vulnerable-victims-and-witnesses/

Watts, A. (2013). To investigate models of intermediaries for child victim and witnesses in the criminal justice system in England, Ireland, Austria and Norway. The Winston Churchill Memorial Trust of Australia. Retrieved September 2, 2023, from https://www.odpp.nsw.gov.au/sites/default/files/2023-02/AmyWatts_ProjectReport.pdf

Williams, G. (1987a). Videotaping children's evidence. *New Law Journal*, *351*, 108–112.

Williams, G. (1987b). Child witnesses. Criminal Law: Essays in Honour of J.C. Smith. *Cambridge Law Journal*, *46*(3), 539–541.

World Health Organisation. (2001). *Mental health: New understanding, new hope*. https://apps.who.int/iris/handle/10665/42390

Wurtzel, D., & Marchant, R. (2017). Intermediaries. In P. Cooper & H. Norton (Eds.), *Vulnerable people and the criminal justice system: A guide to law and practice* (pp. 363–389). OUP.

Young, S., Goodwin, E., Sedgwick, O., & Gudjonsson, G. (2013). The effectiveness of police custody assessments in identifying suspects with intellectual disabilities and attention deficit hyperactivity disorder. *BMC Medicine*, *11*, 248–259.

Youth Justice and Criminal Evidence Act (YJCEA). (1999). London: HMSO.

4 Interviewing Vulnerable Witnesses

Introduction

Over 1 million individuals entered the criminal justice system (CJS) in the year ending 2022 (Ministry of Justice, 2022) with many cases involving victim and witness testimony (hereon referred to as witnesses). Thus, the evidence of witnesses is central to the justice system for successful criminal prosecutions (Farrugia & Maras, 2023). The quality of the evidence provided by witnesses is often relied upon by the prosecution in proving their case and is a fundamental aspect of the CJS. For example, evidence provided by a witness during the early investigation stages can play an essential role in delivering justice later at trial (Association of Chief Police Officers, 2013). As such, being able to elicit reliable information from witnesses during interviews is crucial (Hanway & Akehurst, 2018). Police officers must be able to interview all types of witnesses in the most appropriate manner to ensure that the evidence they obtain is accurate and can further their investigation (Maras & Bowler, 2010).

The reality, however, is that many witnesses providing evidence via a police interview are vulnerable; that is, they are either children or have learning, mental health or physical difficulties that may impede upon their ability to provide information during the police interview, or certainly place them at a disadvantage; thus, requiring assistance in providing their best evidence (Farrugia & Maras, 2023). For example, they may find it more difficult to cope with the demands of a formal police interview and to provide the necessary detailed information, or they may be more susceptible to providing ambiguous information if they have difficulties in their communication or social skills (Gudjonsson, 2018). Consequently, it is vital that their needs are accommodated for and that interviews conducted with vulnerable witnesses are done so in an appropriate manner; it was only following a number of inquiries and revisions of guidance that led to the existing guidance for interviewing vulnerable witnesses (Farrugia & Maras, 2023). This is where the chapter shall start.

Interviewing Vulnerable Witnesses: The Memorandum of Good Practice

In the United Kingdom, the interviewing of vulnerable witnesses is underpinned by Ministry of Justice guidance known as 'Achieving Best Evidence in Criminal Proceedings' (ABE; Ministry of Justice, 2022). However, prior to the development of this guidance, the admissibility of video-recorded interviews with children was considered by an advisory group chaired by His Honour Judge Thomas Pigot KC. The Pigot Report (Home Office, 1989) made recommendations that interviews conducted with such witnesses by a police officer or social worker should be used as examination-in-chief evidence at trial. The report initially recommended that a 'Code of Practice' be developed to govern the way in which interviews should

DOI: 10.4324/9781003386735-4

be conducted. Such recommendations also proposed the use of intermediaries. Following a number of revisions and the involvement of a number of professionals, what emerged was a 'Memorandum of Good Practice'; guidance published by the Home Office in 1992 to assist with conducting video-recording interviews with children and vulnerable witnesses, rather than the set of strict inflexible rules previously in play. Launched to coincide with the implementation of the Criminal Justice Act (1991), which permitted the use of the videotaped interview as evidence-in-chief at trial, the guidance suggested that the interview should be conducted as soon as possible after the reporting of the alleged offence and be conducted in an informal setting to assist with rapport building, and be no longer than one hour in duration. Furthermore, it was recommended that children and other vulnerable witnesses be given the opportunity to provide their account before being asked any questions, that questions should be open in nature and become more direct and specific towards the end of the interview if required, and that the interview should be closed in an appropriate manner (Smith & O'Mahony, 2018).

The impact of the Memorandum of Good Practice has been the focus of much psychological research. For example, early work regarding its use, found that less than a quarter of 15,000 videotaped interviews that had been conducted in the first nine months of its implementation had been submitted to the Crown Prosecution Service (CPS), and only 44 were known to have been played at trial (Butler, 1993). A large variation was also reported by the author between police force areas in terms of video recorded interviews being conducted and submitted. In 1995, an evaluation was commissioned by the Home Office (Davis et al., 1995). Whilst their results suggested that interviewers were not always following the guidance in terms of encouraging a free narrative from a vulnerable witness and not always using open questions during the interview, they reported that 75% of cases at trial included an application to show a video-recorded interview. There was also a general acceptance regarding the value of providing evidence in this way amongst legal professionals, and children were more relaxed when providing their evidence via video-recording than those who gave their evidence-in-chief in Court. Other research has also reported mixed findings in terms of the use and impact of the Memorandum of Good Practice. For example, some research has found support for the principles included in the guidance whilst other work has indicated that it fails to address the needs of children with special needs.

Given the guidance that was incorporated in the Memorandum of Good Practice and given that the Youth Justice and Criminal Evidence Act (YJCEA; 1999) extended the option of using video recorded interviews as evidence-in-chief to all vulnerable witnesses, the UK government set up an interdepartmental working group (including psychologists) to review and draft a new set of interview guidelines relating to interviewing vulnerable adults as well as children. Their recommendations were published a year later in the 'Speaking Up for Justice' report (Home Office, 1998) and included the development of a Memorandum of Good Practice for vulnerable adult witnesses, allowing the use of video-recorded interviews with vulnerable adult witnesses to be played as their evidence-in-chief at trial, and the use of communication aids and intermediaries to assist vulnerable witnesses to give their evidence if required. This collaboration between practitioners and psychologists resulted in the development of the interview guidance for best practice when interviewing all vulnerable witnesses. The 'Achieving Best Evidence in Criminal Proceedings' guidelines (Ministry of Justice, 2022) or as it is frequently regarded, 'ABE guidance' provides information to interviewers to help guide them in managing better the complexities of interviewing vulnerable witnesses (Hanway & Akehurst, 2018). Largely consistent with the Memorandum of Good Practice in that it encourages the use of video recorded interviews to capture vulnerable witnesses' evidence, it also differs as additional guidance is provided to ensure that vulnerable witnesses are supported prior to the police interview and trial. Thus, the guidance is directed towards all professionals involved in the justice system and includes how best to conduct an interview with a vulnerable witness.

Interviewing Vulnerable Witnesses: Achieving Best Evidence

Obtaining detailed and reliable information from witnesses, including those that are vulnerable, is essential for any criminal investigation (Gabbert et al., 2018). It plays a significant role in the directing of resources in the early stages and is crucial for latter decision-making (Ridley et al., 2013). Thus, being able to conduct interviews in the appropriate manner is critical for reliable prosecutions and mitigating the risks of miscarriages of justice (Gabbert et al., 2018). Skilled interviewing is not something that all investigators possess, nor is it intuitive or easily learned on the job (Powell, 2013). It is a skill that requires continuous training and evaluation.

Initially, it was thought that vulnerable witnesses were unable to provide their evidence during interview and at trial given the impact of their vulnerability, for example, age, mental illness, learning disability etc. on their ability to communicate (Davidson & Bifulco, 2009). This was compounded by the fact that vulnerable witnesses were given very little assistance (Macpherson, 2001). However, since the implementation of the ABE guidance, such witnesses are able to effectively participate in the justice system and give their evidence in a way that suits their needs. The ABE framework provides overall guidance on how best to interview witnesses including those that are vulnerable. Predominately, the guidance focuses on four main areas: (i) planning and preparation; (ii) conducting the interview; (iii) witness support and preparation for Court; and (iv) witnesses in Court. For the purposes of this chapter, the focus will be on conducting the interview.

When considering interviewing a vulnerable witness, the ABE guidance emphasises the importance of four phases during the interview. These include rapport, obtaining a free recall, using appropriate questioning, and closure (see Figure 4.1).

Phase 1: Rapport

Developing rapport and empathy is central to an effective interview and is something that is advocated for in all major interviewing and interrogation guidelines in order to achieve best evidence (Fisher & Geiselman, 1992; Gabbert et al., 2021; Lamb et al., 2007). The ABE guidance stresses too, the need to establish rapport and empathy with a witness (see para 2.25). It is a key and critical aspect of any interview and assists in eliciting information. For example, developing rapport and empathy helps to build trust and thus can lead to a more co-operative witness and subsequently more recall (Abbe & Brandon, 2014). This is particularly important should the crime be a serious one, or one that may evoke fear or shame in disclosing information about the alleged offence (Lamb, 2016). Thus, developing and demonstrating rapport and empathy should not be based on specific responses during the interview, but must be evident in a more generic supportive social environment (Walsh & Milne, 2008). There must be a balance, therefore, between ensuring the witness feels comfortable enough to disclose information, but that the interviewer has not been seen to be leading the witness.. The guidance highlights that the development of rapport and empathy should be established by the lead interviewer (see para 2.43) and this can be achieved by the interviewer and witness engaging in neutral topics that are unrelated to the alleged

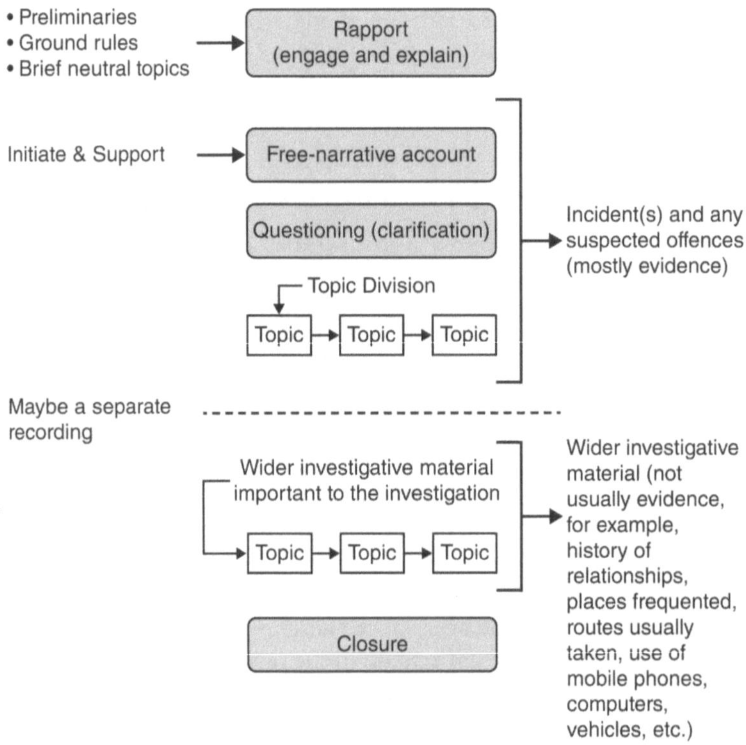

Figure 4.1 Interview phases from ABE guidance (MOJ, 2022)

incident, and which can be answered positively prior to the start of the formal interview (see para 2.103). The ABE guidance also advises that such discussions should be open in nature so that the witness can become familiar with that type of interaction whilst practising providing detailed responses. However, it is important to note that whilst it is critical to develop rapport and empathy prior to the start of the interview, it should not be so long so as to exhaust the witness or confuse the purpose of the interview. If lengthy rapport-building is required, consideration should be given to factoring this into witness planning and preparation.

Once rapport and empathy are developed prior to the start of the interview, it should be maintained throughout. Several methods have been suggested by the ABE guidance to assist with this. For example, the witness should receive an explanation of what will happen during the interview and be provided with the ground rules before they provide their account. This enables the witness to better understand what is expected of them during the interview – for example, given the unusual social interaction that is a police interview, the witness may withhold information that they consider irrelevant, especially if they are insecure about their cognitive abilities (Gabbert, 2015; Maras & Wilcock, 2013). Thus, ground rules encouraging the witness to tell the interviewer everything, even if it seems irrelevant, allows for some understanding in terms of the level and type of detail needed. Furthermore, the ground rules also serve to reassure the witness. For example, by informing the witness that they can say if they do not know an answer or cannot remember a detail, and that they can take a break should they become upset will help maintain rapport and demonstrate empathy whilst preserving the accuracy of the information obtained.

Despite the importance of rapport and empathy being highlighted in the guidance, the ABE framework does not offer any definition of what these constructs are nor how they can be developed and maintained (Farrugia & Maras, 2023). This is also reflected in the psychological literature. For example, those working to define 'rapport' have not yet reached a firm consensus, and the definitions provided already in the literature are often vague and imprecise, leaving much ambiguity to the way in which it should be interpreted and thus developed (see Gabbert et al., 2021 for a full review). Whilst there is no widely shared definition of rapport, Tickle-Degnen and Rosenthal's (1990) tripartite theoretical model of rapport remains the most influential and conceptualises rapport as having three main components relating to mutual attentiveness, positivity, and co-ordination. However, there remains limitations to how this theoretical framework can inform how individuals build rapport in professional settings such as a police interview (Gabbert et al., 2021).

Early research work found the use of rapport and empathy in interviews conducted using the ABE guidance to be variable (Westcott & Kynan, 2006). This has been reported by more recent research. For example, whilst Hill and Davies (2012) reported the positive effects of the ABE guidance on the rapport-building phase of the interview in addition to the setting of ground rules, Bunting et al. (2015) found that the use of practice interviews could be considered as coaching with some reporting that there was not enough time to build rapport or empathy.

Phase 2: Free Recall

Following the initial stage of the interview, the witness should be invited to provide a free recall of the alleged incident using open-ended questions, for example, 'Tell me what happened'. The ABE guidance highlights that the witness must be allowed to provide their free recall without any interruptions and encourages the interviewer to demonstrate active listening and use non-specific prompts to ensure a free narrative is provided. Thus, the type of questioning used is of particular importance.

Phase 3: Questioning

After the witness has provided their free recall, the ABE guidance advises the interviewer to ask questions in order to encourage the witness to expand upon and clarify any necessary points provided during their recall. However, although how question types are classified and defined has received much attention, there remains some discrepancies between academics and practitioners. This was reported in a review conducted by Oxburgh and his colleagues. For example, in their literature review, they reported that an open question is most commonly described as a 'TED' question – 'Tell,' 'Explain,' 'Describe' (Oxburgh et al., 2010). Other scholars have reportedly defined the same type of question in a number of different ways, including, 'open-ended' (Davies et al., 2000), free report (Aldridge & Cameron, 1999), open-ended breadth and depth (Powell & Snow, 2007), invitational (Korkman et al., 2006), or a 5WH ('What,' 'Where,' 'When,' 'Who', 'How'; Centrex, 2004). Similarly, a probing question which is most commonly defined as a 5WH question ('What,' 'Where,' 'When,' 'Who', 'How'), has also been identified as a closed identification question (Myklebust & Bjorklund, 2006), a directive question (Korkman et al., 2006), and a specific question (Milne & Bull, 1999). This is true also for closed questions – those that typically result in a 'yes,' or 'no,' response, have also defined as specific questions (Aldridge & Cameron, 1999) and split into appropriate closed and inappropriate closed questions

Table 4.1 Question types

	Question type	*Description*
Appropriate Questions	Open	Questions that are open-ended and encourage a free recall; known as 'TED' questions, 'Tell,' 'Explain,' 'Describe'
	Probing	Questions that are designed to probe the account; known as the 5WH, 'What,' 'Where,' 'Who,' 'When,' 'How'
	Encouragers / Acknowledgements	Utterances that are designed to encourage the interviewee to continue talking, e.g., 'Uh huh'
Inappropriate Questions	Closed	Questions that are designed to elicit a 'yes' or 'no' response only
	Forced Choice	Questions that provide the interviewee with limited response options, e.g., 'Was the car red or white?'
	Leading	Questions that mention new pieces of information that have not been previously mentioned by the interviewee, typically quite leading in nature
	Opinion/Statements	An opinion or statement offered rather than a question being asked
	Multiple	A number of questions asked in one instance
	Echo	The interviewer repeats the response of the interviewee

Oxburgh et al. (2010).

(Fiengo, 2007). In England and Wales, the College of Policing identify only five key question types; (i) open-ended – defined as 'TED' questions, (ii) specific-closed – known as the 5WH, (iii) forced-choice – those that provide the interviewee with a limited response, for example, 'was the car red or blue?', (iv) multiple – a number of questions that are asked in one instance, and (v) leading – questions that either implies the answer or assumes facts that are likely to be disputed (College of Policing, 2023). Table 4.1 provides an overview of the most commonly used question types amalgamated from the literature base and thus used within the current textbook.

Although there has been much work conducted in classifying and defining question types (see Oxburgh et al., 2010 for a full review), when considering the types of questions that should be used in witness interviews, the gold standard is the use of open questions, commonly known as 'TED' questions (Tell, Explain, Describe). These types of questions have been consistently shown to elicit more detailed and more accurate responses (Myklebust, 2009; Phillips et al., 2011; Snook et al., 2012) and the ABE guidance advocates for these types of questions to be used (see para 3.29). Should the witness' response to these types of questions be vague, the ABE guidance encourages interviewers to move to 'WH' questions; these types of questions can be useful for focusing on and clarifying information. If these types of questions fail to produce sufficient information or clarify a point, then the guidance suggests moving to closed questions, although caution is provided given that these question types can lead to limited responses and may lead a witness to acquiesce – that is, the witness may simply respond 'yes' to these types of questions irrespective of their content (Roberts et al., 2020). However, much like the psychological literature, the ABE guidance too has various definitions for question types. What are commonly known as the 5WH questions in the literature (see Oxburgh et al., 2010), are defined as 'specific-closed questions' in the ABE guidance, and no reference is made to a 'how' question. Furthermore, the guidance refers to specific-closed questions as open questions (see para 3.56) and so there remains some confusion in what constitutes various types of questions.

Whilst the ABE guidance highlights a range of questions that could be used in this phase of the interview, there is some conflict with what exists in the psychological literature. For example, multiple questions contain multiple parts, and thus make it difficult for the witness to understand which part they are meant to answer (Snook et al., 2012). Tag and leading questions may lead to memory contamination, thus impacting upon the accuracy and reliability of the information provided and can be difficult for any type of witness (Airaksinen et al., 2005), especially those who are vulnerable (Roberts et al., 2020). However, the ABE guidance makes reference to forced-choice questions and leading questions being used as a last resort (para 3.51). This contradicts existing literature that indicates that a vulnerable individual may exhibit an increased risk of suggestibility, compliance, and acquiescence if interviewed using such inappropriate question types (Farrugia, 2022; Gudjonsson, 2018).

When completing the questioning phase with a witness, the ABE guidance highlights that the interviewer must ensure that the witness is not rushed and that they have sufficient time to process and respond to the question. This is particularly important for those that are vulnerable. Research has documented the impact of rapid-fire closed questions on witnesses; witnesses tend to become passive in their responses rather than providing information rich answers (Hope & Gabbert, 2019).

Phase 4: Closure

The ABE guidance highlights that the closure phase of the interview should only occur once the free narrative and questioning phases are finished. During the closure phase of the interview, a summary of the witness' account is provided by the interviewer back to the witness to ensure that what the interviewer has recorded is accurate. In doing so, it allows the witness the opportunity to correct any inaccuracies and can lead to further information being remembered by the witness. The guidance indicates also that the interviewer may return back to the more neutral topics that were being discussed between the interviewer and witness in the rapport-building phase (see para 3.90). Whilst there is no exact science on how to best complete the closure phase, the ABE guidance documents the importance of doing so that the witness feels that their interview is now completed and feels that they have fulfilled what was required of them during the interview. It also provides an opportunity for the witness to ask any questions about subsequent stages of the investigation. However, research continues to suggest that this phase of the interview is completed on a variable level (Bunting et al., 2015; Hill & Davies, 2012).

Although the ABE guidance has recently been updated, there still remains limitations within the framework, particularly regarding how key concepts relating to rapport and empathy, and question types are explained in the guidance and the techniques that are suggested for vulnerable witnesses (Farrugia & Maras, 2023). Furthermore, research has suggested mixed findings in terms of the four phases being followed as set out in the ABE guidance (Robinson, 2008). For example, when Hill and Davies (2012) compared interviews conducted under the Memorandum of Good Practice and interviews conducted as per the ABE guidance, they found very few differences and reported a failure to include all four phases of the interview. This has been echoed by more recent research (Bunting et al., 2015).

Generally, the ABE guidance highlights that witnesses should be interviewed using a phased interview approach that incorporates the phases described above. One such interview model that is suggested in the ABE guidance is that of the Cognitive Interview (Fisher & Geiselman, 1992).

The Cognitive Interview

The Cognitive Interview (Fisher & Geiselman, 1992) was initially developed over 25 years ago in response to the need for an interview method that helps improve witness recall (Memon et al., 2010). Based upon well-established psychological principles relating to human memory and information retrieval, the Cognitive Interview comprises a series of stages to increase the amount of information that can be obtained from a witness by engaging the witness in a detailed retrieval of the alleged incident. In line with Tulving's (1983) concept of memory being a joint product of stored memory traces and cues that can become available at retrieval, the original Cognitive Interview consists of four techniques to enhance witness recall.

Four Techniques of the Cognitive Interview

The first technique, *context reinstatement* encourages the witness to mentally reconstruct the physical and personal context that existed at the time of the alleged incident. This is based upon research that suggests this enhances recall (Tulving & Thomson, 1973). Thus, the witness is encouraged to re-experience the external, emotional, and cognitive factors that were present. For example, the weather, smells and other sensory factors, feelings, and thoughts.

The second technique, *report everything*, instructs the witness to recall as much information as possible even if the information is partial or incomplete, or may be deemed irrelevant by the witness. This allows for as much information as possible to be collated and is based on the premise that reporting even incomplete information may lead to other information being remembered.

Technique three, *variety of perspectives*, is based upon the notion that different retrieval cues may access different aspects of a complex event (Anderson & Pichert, 1978). Thus, witnesses are instructed to recall from their own perspective but also that of others, for example, being encouraged to recall what they think another witness may have seen.

The final technique, *temporal order*, encourages witnesses to recall information in a variety of orders, for example, from the start, from the end and then working backwards in time, or from the middle or any other point that may be salient to the witness (Memon, 2006). This has two primary aims: (i) some information may be more accessible when memory is interrogated in this way; and, (ii) memories may be more accurate when reporting in reverse order for example, as interviewers are less likely to fill in details based on their own expectations and biases (see Schank & Abelson, 1977 for their work on schema theory).

In 1992, the authors of the Cognitive Interview published an enhanced version of the Cognitive Interview (Enhance Cognitive Interview) which included a framework for building rapport and enhancing effective communication. For example, much like the ABE guidance, the interviewer is discouraged from interrupting the witness and encouraged to demonstrate active listening. Ground rules such as not guessing and witnesses indicating if they do not know the answer are also incorporated (Fisher & Geiselman, 1992).

Since the introduction of the Cognitive Interview and the enhanced version, there has been a substantial amount of psychological research conducted in testing its efficacy. Laboratory research has shown that using the Cognitive Interview with participants dramatically improves the number of correct details recalled, whilst only slightly increasing the number of incorrect details (Köhnken et al., 1999; Memon, 2006; Schreiber & Fisher, 2006). Field work involving police officers trained in its techniques have also shown that they gain more information overall and more detailed information from witnesses in interviews (Clifford & George, 1996; Fisher et al., 1989), and the Cognitive Interview and Enhanced Cognitive Interview has been shown to be useful in other contexts where information gathering is the goal; the investigation of accidents (Flin et al., 2008) for example, or gathering information about attitudes and opinions from respondents in non-investigative contexts (see Köhnken, 1995, for a full review).

More recently, other versions of the Cognitive Interview have been developed and labelled as the Modified Cognitive Interview (an adaptation of the Enhanced Cognitive Interview). For example, some researchers changed the interview technique so that it is suitable for children aged 4–9 years old. In her work, Holliday (2003a, 2003b) maintained the procedure of building rapport as per the Enhanced Cognitive Interview but removed the variety of perspectives technique. Similarly, Davis et al. (2005) omitted the use of variety of perspectives and temporal order and replaced them with an additional prompt to recall the event once more in a chronological order. In their study, Davis and colleagues compared their version with the Cognitive Interview and with a structured interview. They found that their Modified Cognitive Interview was statistically as good as the Cognitive Interview in eliciting correct information and took less time to complete (a concern that has previously been raised by police officers when conducting Cognitive Interviews – see Kebbell et al., 1999). More recently, Dando et al. (2009b) produced another modified version of the Cognitive Interview whereby participants were asked to sketch the event being recalled – she and her colleagues found that this led to similarly high levels of recall and to a reduction in time needed compared to the standard Cognitive Interview.

The range of participants/witnesses that the Cognitive Interview, the Enhanced Cognitive Interview, and the various Modified Cognitive Interviews have been tested with has also been explored – for example, the Cognitive Interview has been found to elicit more information in children (Memon et al., 1997), adult witnesses (Davis et al., 2005), and with older adults (Wright & Holliday, 2007). However, the use of these interview techniques and the phased interview guidance and question types suggested in the ABE framework may not always be completely suitable for the vulnerable witness. This is where the focus of the chapter shall now turn.

Interviewing Vulnerable Witnesses: The Impact of Vulnerability on Current Interview and Questioning Techniques

The development of the Memorandum of Good Practice, the ABE guidance in interviewing vulnerable witnesses and the development of interview techniques to enhance witness recall shows how far interviewing witnesses has come. Undoubtedly, these methods and the implementation of appropriate questioning techniques have assisted and led to interviewers now having the tools and skills necessary to obtain accurate and reliable information. However, such interview techniques and question types are proving not to be as effective with vulnerable witness.

The ABE guidance recommends that vulnerable witnesses be interviewed using the Cognitive Interview (Mattison et al., 2015). This interview method is based on principles concerning how memory typically operates; that is the retrieval of the alleged incident will be enhanced if the context experienced at recall matches that experienced during encoding (Fisher & Geiselman, 1992; Tulving & Thomson, 1973) and that memories are stored as interconnected nodes that provide multiple retrieval routes (Tulving, 1974). The effectiveness of this strategy, however, is dependent on how an individual stores a memory in the first instance, with a substantial amount of evidence suggesting that individuals with particular vulnerabilities, for example, an Autism Spectrum Condition may do so rather differently than a neurotypical individual (Bowler & Gaigg, 2008).

Individuals with an Autism Spectrum Condition may not encode, store, or retrieve contextual information surrounding an event or alleged incident in the same way as neurotypical individuals (Maras & Bowler, 2010), and may not bind elements of an experience in memory like typical individuals do (Bowler & Gaigg, 2008). Individuals with an Autism Spectrum Condition may also experience impairments in temporal cognition (Boucher, 2001) and interpersonal difficulties characterised by social impairments and difficulties in domains such as face processing and gaze perception (Blair et al., 2002). Research has consistently documented, for example, that individuals with an Autism Spectrum Condition typically spend less time viewing people and faces in social situations (Riby & Hancock, 2009). Furthermore, those with an Autism Spectrum Condition are known to have difficulties adopting a frame of reference other than their own and have difficulties on spatial working memory tasks (Williams et al., 2006). In addition, they typically experience certain difficulties when trying to recall a witnessed crime (Maras & Bowler, 2010, 2014) and in the episodic recollection of a personally experienced event (Bruck et al., 2007), as well as their source monitoring; that is, the ability to recall where, when, how, or from whom they have learnt something (Bowler et al., 2004). Individuals with an Autism Spectrum Condition may have an increased tendency to confabulate given the neuropathology of the frontal lobes in such individuals (Turner et al., 2008). Thus, the various techniques employed in the Cognitive Interview may not be effective strategies to enhance memory recall in witnesses with an Autism Spectrum Condition. Conducting a content-reinstatement technique assumes that memories about details of the alleged incident are somehow bound to memories of the context. That is, the underlying presumption is that by using a context reinstatement technique, a direct route to memories of other elements of the alleged event is provided. However, given the difficulties that those with an Autism Spectrum Condition experience in binding elements of an experience in memory, context reinstatement may fail to enhance the recall in this type of vulnerable witness and recall may be limited. This is also true for other techniques used in the Cognitive Interview such as temporal order and variety of perspectives.

Research has explored the use of the Cognitive Interview with witnesses that have an Autism Spectrum Condition. Maras and Bowler (2010) found that those with an Autism Spectrum Condition are as accurate and detailed in their reports compared to typical individuals when interviewed using a standard interview (e.g., one that is based on ABE guidance). They also found that using the Cognitive Interview fails to increase the number of correct details reported by such vulnerable individuals, and in fact when individuals with an Autism Spectrum Condition were interviewed using the Cognitive Interview, they reported significantly more incorrect details, thus resulting in being significantly less accurate than their neurotypical counterparts. Further work has also highlighted the ineffectiveness of the context reinstatement technique specifically for those with an Autism Spectrum Condition (Maras & Bowler, 2012). Similar findings concerning the effectiveness of the Cognitive Interview have been found in adults with an intellectual disability (Robinson & McGuire, 2005).

The consideration of such interview techniques is not just limited to adults with vulnerabilities. Interviewing techniques used with children have also been examined. Mattison and

Dando (2020) reported that children typically recall less episodic information than adults; this is in line with other research (Barlow et al., 2011). Furthermore, techniques that rely on a free recall that draws on episodic memory can also prove difficult for children as they tend to employ less exhaustive retrieval strategies when compared to adults (Lloyd et al., 2009). Thus, although such interview techniques have been developed on psychological principles and have undoubtedly improved the state of play in interviewing witnesses, they may not be completely suitable for vulnerable witnesses.

As well as the interview method used, the type of questioning is also important when considering vulnerable witnesses. Bowles and Sharman (2014) found that witnesses' level of accuracy is very much dependent on the types of questions they are asked. Their review found that compared with other question types, open and closed questions that presumed certain information to be true elicited the greatest number of errors in children and adults with intellectual disabilities. Other research has reported similar findings. For example, some scholars have reported that children with an intellectual disability provided fewer correct responses when compared to their typically developing counterparts when asked to provide a free recall (Henry & Gudjonsson, 2003, 2007), were less accurate when answering closed questions, and more likely to agree with leading questions (Henry & Gudjonsson, 2007). Similarly, research has found that children with an intellectual disability were more suggestible to misleading open specific questions and that open specific questions produced the greatest number of errors (Agnew & Powell, 2004). Scholars have also reported that young typically developing children recall less episodic information in response to open questions (Arnold & Lindsay, 2002; Hershkowitz et al., 2012); they report that this may be due to the open nature of the question, for example, 'Tell me everything you remember about XXX' inviting multiple types of responses and thus offer no retrieval support. Whilst episodic recall to open questions improves with age in typically developing children (Brown & Lamb, 2015), for children with additional needs, free recall performance is not only significantly reduced (Brown et al., 2018; Wyman et al., 2018), it does not improve with age. Thus, even though open questions are considered the gold standard in that they have been consistently shown to elicit more detailed and more accurate responses (Myklebust, 2009; Phillips et al., 2011; Snook et al., 2012) and are recommended in interview guidance and psychological literature, there is a growing body of research that indicates they may not be wholly suitable for vulnerable witnesses, with free recall questions proving to be particularly difficult. This is problematic because witnesses should be invited to provide a free recall at the start of the interview, upon which subsequent questions are based. If the free recall is reduced, then there is less for the interviewer to follow up on (Farrugia & Maras, 2023) which has implications for the quality of the interview conducted and the nature of recall obtained.

Whilst research suggests that vulnerable adults and children may not perform as well in typical interview situations as those without any vulnerabilities, there is a substantial amount of evidence that vulnerable witnesses can produce accurate and reliable information when questioned using appropriate techniques (Maras & Bowler, 2014). The development of new interview methods for vulnerable witnesses is starting to emerge.

Interviewing Vulnerable Witnesses: Achieving *New* Best Evidence?

Whilst many interview models and techniques have improved the way that witnesses provide their evidence, they do not necessarily cater for the needs of vulnerable witnesses; this is no easy feat! However, for vulnerable witnesses to be able to provide their best evidence, interview techniques must be adapted, or new ones created to ensure their effective participation in the justice system. Progress is starting to be made with the modification and introduction of new interview techniques that try to cater to witnesses with specific vulnerabilities.

Sketch Reinstatement of Context (Sketch-RC)

Whilst children are interviewed with reference to the ABE guidance, there does not exist any practical guidance on how best to support episodic free recall in children with an Autism Spectrum Condition. As highlighted earlier in the chapter, individuals with this type of vulnerability experience cognitive impairments including deficits in episodic memory (Maras & Bowler, 2010). Although the ABE guidance promotes the use of the Cognitive Interview (Fisher & Geiselman, 1992) with vulnerable witnesses, it does not provide specific retrieval techniques for those with an Autism Spectrum Condition. One of the techniques in the Cognitive Interview is the context reinstatement which supports a witness to mentally recreate both the psychological and physical environment that existed at the time of the alleged incident; whilst this has proven beneficial to support episodic memory in typically developing adults (Dando et al., 2011), there have been mixed results with typically developing children. That is, some studies have found this technique to be beneficial compared to standard interview formats (Dietze et al., 2010), whilst others have reported to find a positive effect in relation to recall (Darwinkel et al., 2014). There has been little to no research investigating the impact of context reinstatement with children that have an Autism Spectrum Condition.

Mattison et al.'s (2015) work sought to investigate the context reinstatement technique within the Cognitive Interview by comparing it to a new technique, 'sketch reinstatement of context' in children that have an Autism Spectrum Condition. Initially developed as a replacement for the context reinstatement technique for use by less experienced interviewers, the Sketch-RC technique starts by supplying the witness with drawing materials and then providing drawing instructions. Witnesses are asked to draw about the alleged incident and encouraged to draw as much as possible in any way that they want. Witnesses are also encouraged to tell the interviewer what they are drawing as they draw it and are given unlimited time to complete their sketch. Once the drawing is completed, the witness is asked to provide a free recall. Previous work has tested the Sketch-RC using mock witness paradigms involving adult populations and results have consistently indicated the efficacy of this technique; participants have typically performed equal to or better than those interviewed using the context reinstatement technique in terms of the amount of correct information elicited (Dando, 2013; Dando et al., 2009a, 2009b). In Mattison and colleague's (, 2015) work, they tested the Sketch-RC technique with children with and without an Autism Spectrum Condition and in comparison to the context reinstatement technique typically used in the Cognitive Interview. They found that children with an Autism Spectrum Condition were 25% more accurate in the Sketch-RC than their counterparts in the context reinstatement technique and that all participants in the latter condition reported more errors than in the Sketch-RC condition. Their results highlight that the recall of a child with an Autism Spectrum Condition is markedly improved when supported by sketching.

The success of the Sketch-RC technique for such vulnerable witnesses may be because it is a flexible retrieval strategy that encourages spontaneous self-directed drawing; this allows those using it to draw on their own retrieval cues rather than those directed by the interviewer (Mattison et al., 2015). This technique also reduces the demand on working memory and negates the need to follow numerous complex instructions – difficulties that are associated with having an Autism Spectrum Condition (Maras & Bowler, 2010). Whilst there are a number of practical and theoretical implications from this work, and further research is needed, when appropriately supported, this type of vulnerable witness can provide an accurate and reliable account in a police interview. Another modification to the Cognitive Interview in vulnerable witnesses has also been explored; the Self-Administered Interview.

The Self-Administered Interview (SAI)

The Self-Administered Interview (SAI; Gabbert et al., 2009) was developed to assist with gathering evidence quickly from many witnesses at large-scale incidents (e.g., terrorist attacks, road traffic accidents). It is an interviewing technique that is based on the Cognitive Interview but is completed by the witness themselves rather than by an interviewer. The SAI is a standardised protocol of instructions, open-ended questions and cues that enable witnesses to provide a detailed statement independently without the presence of a police officer (Gabbert et al., 2022). The witness works their way through a structured recall attempt, following detailed written instructions that have been developed based on current psychological understanding of memory and retrieval support. Whilst it incorporates the report everything and context reinstatement techniques from the Cognitive Interview, the witness is also prompted to report any additional information that they can remember, is encouraged to sketch the scene and provide any details that they may not have thought to mention in the free recall stage (e.g., weather conditions or restriction of view).

The evidence base for the efficacy of the SAI is growing; many studies have reported the amount of correct information is higher when using the SAI compared to other reporting formats such as a standard free recall (Gabbert et al., 2009; Hope et al., 2014). Furthermore, witnesses who complete the SAI are more resistant to post-event misinformation (Gittins et al., 2015) and forgetting is reduced. In a more recent meta-analysis Horry et al. (2021) found that the SAI results in more correct details being elicited from witnesses than other reporting formats, with only a slight cost to overall accuracy. The SAI has since been translated into multiple languages and adopted by police forces all over the world, including the Netherlands, Sweden, and Germany and is recommended for use in England and Wales by the College of Policing.

The vast majority of the research exploring the SAI has focused on neurotypical adult witnesses, although some studies have explored older adults (Dando et al., 2020). However, given that the SAI includes several cognitive components that do not necessarily require social interaction, it may be useful for vulnerable witnesses – in particular, those that have an Autism Spectrum Condition or experience similar impairments in their social and cognitive functioning. This is because the SAI removes the social component of the interview and instructions are delivered via a sensory modality with the witness being in control at the pace of which they complete the interview and provide their recall (Maras et al., 2014). As such, Maras and her colleagues (, 2014) aimed to examine the effectiveness of the SAI in witnesses that have an Autism Spectrum Condition. They reported that the SAI failed to elicit more correct details in vulnerable witnesses when compared to a written interview although the SAI sketch plan component did elicit more correct details from those with an Autism Spectrum Condition. Such mixed findings are consistent with the growing research that highlights that the techniques used in the Cognitive Interview (many upon which the SAI is based) are not effective for some vulnerable witnesses in their standard form (Maras & Bowler, 2010). Thus, emerging research concerning a new interview technique is well underway.

Witness-Aimed First Account (WAFA)

Despite the emerging research that suggests that current interview techniques may not always be entirely effective for vulnerable witnesses, there does not exist an alternative theoretically driven and legally appropriate framework to assist with this type of witness (Maras et al., 2020). This is concerning given that vulnerable witnesses are disproportionately more likely to be questioned by police officers about what they have experienced or witnessed (Cooper et al., 2022). Consequently, scholars have started working on developing a new interview technique aimed specifically at witnesses that have an Autism Spectrum Condition. Coined the Witness-Aimed First Account (WAFA; Maras et al., 2020), it was created to better support this type of vulnerable witness through diminishing the socio-cognitive and executive demands placed on the witness by encouraging them to generate and direct their own topics. The WAFA interview procedure asks each witness to create their own topic or segment area by directing them to think about the most important event that happened. The interviewer records the event on a post-it note and displays it in front of the witness before asking the witness to think about something else that has happened as part of the alleged incident. The post-it note serves as a reminder of the structure of the event, thus reducing the amount of event information that the witness has to remember and the cognitive demand this involves. Each time the witness recalls a new segment, this is recorded on a post-it note. Once the witness has recalled everything they can, the interviewer revisits each of the self-directed topics in turn and in the order in which they were recalled. The witness is encouraged to provide a free recall based on the topic after which they are prompted to provide further detail where possible.

Research into the efficacy of the WAFA is developing. Maras and her colleagues (2020) found that the WAFA interviews resulted in more detailed and accurate recall from witnesses with and without an Autism Spectrum Condition when compared to a standard best practice interview. Further work is continuing to explore the use of the WAFA in improving witnesses' accounts and ensuring that best evidence can be achieved.

Summary

The evidence of witnesses is central to the justice system for successful criminal prosecutions (Farrugia & Maras, 2023). Thus, the quality of the evidence that is relied upon is a fundamental part of the justice system in England and Wales, and further afield. Being able to elicit accurate and reliable information during witness interviews, therefore, is crucial and police must be able to interview all types of witnesses as part of their investigations, including those that are vulnerable. This is no easy task; vulnerable witnesses may find it difficult to cope with the demands of a formal police interview and can become susceptible to providing inaccurate or ambiguous information (Gudjonsson, 2018), especially given the impact of their vulnerabilities on their communication and social skills. Interview models and questioning techniques used by interviewing officers must accommodate the needs of the vulnerable witness.

Initially, the Memorandum of Good Practice was developed to assist with this; recommendations included interviews to be used as evidence-in-chief at trial and the use of intermediaries to assist in communication. The use of open questions was also recommended. Following some initial research work, mixed findings were reported regarding the use and impact of the Memorandum of Good Practice. What followed, was an interdepartmental working group to review and draft a new set of guidelines relating to interviewing vulnerable adults as well as children and the development of the ABE guidance which focuses on how best to interview vulnerable witnesses. The interview guidance suggests the use of a phased approach and details the importance of rapport, obtaining a free recall, using appropriate questioning and closure of the interview. There have been mixed findings as to the success of each phase with psychological literature providing much needed insights.

The ABE guidance also refers to interview techniques developed by psychologists; namely that of the Cognitive Interview (Fisher & Geiselman, 1992). Initially developed over 25 years ago, the interview model has been enhanced and modified based on its efficacy for different witness groups. Research has consistently documented that the Cognitive Interview is not entirely suitable for those that are vulnerable (Maras & Bowler, 2010). The type of questioning strategies used in interviews conducted with vulnerable witnesses has also been examined with key pieces of research indicating that many vulnerable witnesses struggle with an unsupported free recall (Brown et al., 2018; Wyman et al., 2018). This is concerning given that the guidance indicates that all witnesses should be invited to provide a free recall at the start of the interview upon which subsequent questions are based. There are implications for the quality of the interview and the nature of recall obtained if the initial free recall is reduced.

Subsequently, scholars are now looking to adapt or modify existing interview techniques and/or create new interview models for specific groups of vulnerable witnesses. The Sketch-RC (Mattison et al., 2015) for example, encourages children with an Autism Spectrum Condition to use sketching as part of their recall. Findings to date highlight that the recall of this type of witness is markedly improved when supported by sketching. Furthermore, the SAI (Gabbert et al., 2009) has been adapted from the Cognitive Interview and provides witnesses involved in large-scale incidents the tools to provide their evidence independently without the presence of a police officer, thus protecting their recall from forgetting and post-event misinformation (Gittens et al., 2015). However, when used with a vulnerable population, it failed to elicit more correct details in those that have an Autism Spectrum Condition, although the SAI sketch plan element was successful in eliciting correct recall in this witness type (Maras et al., 2014). Finally, the WAFA (Maras et al., 2020) is a new interview technique that has been developed specifically for adult witnesses who have an Autism Spectrum Condition. Witnesses here are encouraged to produce their own topic or segment area which is recorded on a post-it note. This technique has proven successful in initial research, although further work must be done.

Thus, whilst there is now an acknowledgement that vulnerable witnesses' needs must be met in order to achieve their best evidence, and an emerging research base that is exploring how interview techniques can be adapted or created for the needs of vulnerable witnesses, there remains more work to be done. However, the challenges faced when interviewing vulnerable individuals is not limited to just vulnerable witnesses. Vulnerability is a common thread that is woven throughout the justice system and includes those that enter custody as a vulnerable suspect. How they are interviewed is equally as important in ensuring that the evidence they provide is reliable and accurate too. This is where the next chapter shall focus.

Key Learning Points

- The quality of the evidence provided by witnesses is paramount within the justice system and is often relied upon for successful prosecutions.
- The Memorandum of Good practice developed as a result of the Pigot Report which made recommendations that interviews should be used as examination-in-chief at trial. The Memorandum of Good Practice was published in 1992 to assist with the video-recording of interviews conducted with children and vulnerable witnesses.
- The ABE guidance was subsequently developed as a result of an interdepartmental working group. The guidance is for all professionals involved in the justice system and includes how best to conduct an interview with a vulnerable witness; it encourages four key phases (rapport, free recall, appropriate questioning, and closure).
- The Cognitive Interview is one type of interview model that is recommended by the ABE guidance and is based upon well-established psychological principles relating to memory and information retrieval.
- Consisting of four main techniques, the Cognitive Interview has been enhanced and modified since its development. However, research has shown that this interview model is not effective in eliciting reliable and accurate information from some vulnerable witnesses.
- Psychological research has also documented that current best practice questioning techniques, namely the encouragement of a free recall, may be problematic for some vulnerable witness, particularly those with an Autism Spectrum Condition (Brown et al., 2018; Wyman et al., 2018).
- Scholars are continuing to modify and create new interview models that address specific witness vulnerabilities. For example, the use of the Sketch-RC (Mattison et al., 2015), the SAI (Gabbert et al., 2009), and the WAFA (Maras et al., 2020).
- Research work into the modified and new interview models is at preliminary stages with some mixed findings.

References

Abbe, A., & Brandon, S. E. (2014). Building and maintaining rapport in investigative interviews. *Police Practice and Research*, *15*(3), 207–220.

Agnew, S. E., & Powell, M. B. (2004). The effect of intellectual disability on children's recall of an event across different question types. *Law & Human Behaviour*, *28*, 273–293.

Airaksinen, E., Larsson, M., & Forsell, Y. (2005). Neuropsychological functions in anxiety disorders in population-based samples: Evidence of episodic memory dysfunction. *Journal of Psychiatric Research*, *39*, 207–214.

Aldridge, J., & Cameron, S. (1999). Interviewing child witnesses: Questioning techniques and the role of training. *Applied Developmental Science*, *3*, 136–147.

Anderson, R. C., & Pichert, J. W. (1978). Recall of previously unrecallable information following a shift in perspective. *Journal of Verbal Learning & Verbal Behavior*, *17*, 1–12.

Arnold, M. M., & Lindsay, D. S. (2002). Remembering remembering. *Journal of Experimental Psychology: Learning, Memory & Cognition*, *28*, 521–529.

Association of Chief Police Officers, National Investigative Interviewing Strategic Steering Group. (2013). *Advice on the structure of visually recorded witness interviews* (2nd ed.). http://library.college.police.uk/docs/APPREF/ACPO-WitnessInterview-Structure-2013.pdf

Barlow, C. M., Jolley, R. P., & Hallam, J. L. (2011). Drawing as memory aids: Optimising the drawing method to facilitate young children's recall. *Applied Cognitive Psychology*, *25*(3), 480–487.
Blair, R. J. R., Frith, U., Smith, N., Abell, F., & Cipolotti, L. (2002). Fractionation of visual memory: Agency detection and its impairment in autism. *Neuropsychologia*, *40*, 108–118.
Boucher, J. (2001). Lost in a sea of time': Time parsing and autism. In C. Hoel & T. McCormack (Eds.), *Time and memory: Issues in philosophy and psychology* (pp. 111–135). Oxford University Press.
Bowler, D. M., & Gaigg, S. B. (2008). Memory in ASD: Enduring themes and future prospects. In J. Boucher & D. M. Bowler (Eds.), *Memory in autism* (pp. 330–349). Cambridge University Press.
Bowler, D. M., Gardiner, J. M., & Berthollier, N. (2004). Source memory in adolescents and adults with Asperger's syndrome. *Journal of Autism and Developmental Disorders*, *34*, 533–542.
Bowles, P., & Sharman, S. (2014). A review of the impact of different types of leading interview questions on child and adult witnesses with intellectual disabilities. *Psychiatry, Psychology, and Law*, *21*(2), 205–217.
Brown, D. A., Brown, E. J., Lewis, C. N., & Lamb, M. E. (2018). Narrative skill and testimonial accuracy in typically developing children and those with intellectual disabilities. *Applied Cognitive Psychology*, *32*(5), 550–560.
Brown, D. A., & Lamb, M. E. (2015). Can children be useful witnesses? It depends how they are questioned. *Child Development Perspectives*, *9*(4), 250–255.
Bruck, M., London, K., Landa, R., & Goodman, J. (2007). Autobiographical memory and suggestibility in children with autism spectrum disorder. *Development and Psychopathology*, *19*, 73–95.
Bunting, L., Carr, N., Hayes, D., & Marshall, J. (2015). *Good practice in achieving best evidence interview with child witnesses in Northern Ireland – Criminal justice perspectives*. Northern Ireland Department of Justice.
Butler, A. (1993). Spare the child. *Police Review*, *14–15*.
Centrex (2004). *Management of volume crime*. Centrex.
Clifford, B. R., & George, R. (1996). A field evaluation of training in three methods of witness and victim investigative interviewing. *Psychology, Crime, & Law*, 2, 231–248.
College of Policing. (2023). *Investigative interviewing*. https://www.college.police.uk/app/investigation/investigative-interviewing/investigative-interviewing
Cooper, D., Uppal, D., Railey, K., Wilson, A., Maras, K., Zimmerman, E., Bornman, J., & Shea, L. (2022). Policy gaps and opportunities: A systematic review of autism spectrum disorder and criminal justice intersections. *Autism*, *26*(5), 1014–1031.
Criminal Justice Act. (1991). https://www.legislation.gov.uk/ukpga/1991/53/contents
Dando, C. (2013). Drawing to remember: External support of older adults' eyewitness performance. *PLOS ONE*, *8*, Article e69937.
Dando, C., Gabbert, F., & Hope, L. (2020). Supporting older eyewitnesses' episodic memory: The self-administered interview and sketch reinstatement of context. *Memory*, *28*(6), 712–723.
Dando, C. J., Wilcock, R., Behnkle, C., & Milne, R. (2011). Modifying the cognitive interview: Countenancing forensic application by enhancing practicability. *Psychology, Crime, & Law*, *17*, 491–511.
Dando, C. J., Wilcock, R., & Milne, R. (2009a). Novice police officers' application of the cognitive interview procedure. *Psychology, Crime & Law*, *15*, 679–696.
Dando, C. J., Wilcock, R., & Milne, R. (2009b). The efficacy of a modified mental reinstatement of context procedure for frontline police investigators. *Applied Cognitive Psychology*, *23*, 138–147.
Darwinkel, E. C., Powell, M. B., & Sharman, S. J. (2014). Does extensive free narrative prompting minimise the effect of mental reinstatement on children's recall of events? *Psychiatry, Psychology and Law*, *21*(3), 351–359.
Davidson, J., & Bifulco, A. (2009). Investigating police practice in the UK: Achieving best evidence in work with young victims of abuse. *Pakistan Journal of Criminology*, *1*(3), 19–46.
Davies, G., Westcott, H., & Horan, N. (2000). The impact of questioning style on the content of investigative interviews with suspected child sexual abuse victims. *Psychology, Crime and Law*, 6, 81–97.

Davies, G., Wilson, C., Mitchell, R., & Milsom, J. (1995). *Videotaping of childrens' evidence: An evaluation*. Home Office.

Davis, M. R., McMahon, M., & Greenwood, K. M. (2005). The efficacy of mnemonic components of the cognitive interview: Towards a shortened variant for time-critical investigations. *Applied Cognitive Psychology*, *19*, 75–93.

Dietze, P. M., Powell, P. B., & Thomson, D. M. (2010). Mental reinstatement of context with child witnesses: Does it matter whether context is reinstated 'out loud'? *Psychology, Crime and Law*, *16*, 439–448.

Farrugia, L. (2022). *Interviewing of suspects with mental health conditions and disorders in England and Wales: A paradigm shift*. Routledge.

Farrugia, L., & Maras, K. (2023). Achieving best evidence from victims and witnesses. In G. Oxburgh, T. Myklebust, M. Fallon, & M. Hartwig (Eds.), *Interviewing and interrogation: A review of research and practice since World War II*. Torkel Opsahl Academic EPublisher.

Fiengo, R. (2007). *Asking questions: Using meaningful structures to imply ignorance*. Oxford University Press.

Fisher, R. P., & Geiselman, R. E. (1992). *Memory-enhancing techniques for investigative interviewing: The cognitive interview*. Charles C. Thomas.

Fisher, R. P., Geiselman, R. E., & Amador, M. (1989). Field test of the cognitive interview: Enhancing the recollection of actual victims and interviewees of crime. *Journal of Applied Psychology*, *74*, 722–727.

Flin, R., O'Connor, P., & Crichton, M. (2008). *Safety at the sharp end: A guide to non technical skills*. Ashgate.

Gabbert, F. (2015). The role of initial witness accounts within the investigative process. In G. Oxburgh, T. Myklebust, T. Grant, & R. Milnes (Eds.), *Communication in investigative and legal contexts: Integrated approaches from forensic psychology, linguistics and law enforcement* (pp. 107–132). Wiley-Blackwell.

Gabbert, F., Hope, L., & Confrey, M. (2018). Witness testimony. In A. Griffiths & R. Milne (Eds.), *The psychology of criminal investigation: From theory to practice* (pp. 113–132). Routledge.

Gabbert, F., Hope, L., & Fisher, R. (2009). Protecting eyewitness evidence: Examining the efficacy of a self-administered interview tool. *Law and Human Behaviour*, *33*, 298–307.

Gabbert, F., Hope, L., Horry, R., Drain, T., & Hughes, C. (2022). Examining the efficacy of a digital version of the self-administered interview. *Computers in Human Behaviour Reports*, *5*, 100159.

Gabbert, F., Hope, L., Luther, K., Wright, G., Ng, M., & Oxburgh, G. (2021). Exploring the use of rapport in professional information-gathering contexts by systematically mapping the evidence base. *Applied Cognitive Psychology*, *35*(2), 329–341.

Gittins, C. B., Paterson, H. M., & Sharpe, L. (2015). How does immediate recall of a stressful event affect psychological response to it? *Journal of Behaviour Therapy and Experimental Psychiatry*, *46*, 19–26.

Gudjonsson, G. (2018). *The psychology of false confessions: Forty years of science and practice*. John Wiley & Sons Ltd.

Hanway, P., & Akehurst, L. (2018). The voice from the front line: Police officers' perceptions of real-world interviewing with vulnerable witnesses. *Investigative Interviewing: Research and Practice*, *9*(1), 14–33.

Henry, L. A., & Gudjonsson, G. H. (2003). Eyewitness memory, suggestibility, and repeated recall sessions in children with mild and moderate intellectual disabilities. *Law and Human Behaviour*, *5*, 481–505.

Henry, L. A., & Gudjonsson, G. H. (2007). Individual and developmental differences in eyewitness recall and suggestibility in children with intellectual disabilities. *Applied Cognitive Psychology*, *3*, 361–381.

Hershkowitz, I., Lamb, M. E., Orbach, Y., Katz, C., & Horowitz, D. (2012). The development of communicative and narrative skills among preschoolers: Lessons from forensic interviews about child abuse. *Child Development*, *83*, 611–622.

Hill, E. S., & Davies, G. M. (2012). Has the quality of investigative interviews with children improved with changes in guidance? An exploratory study. *Policing*, *7*(1), 63–71.

Holliday, R. (2003a). Reducing misinformation effects in children with cognitive interviews: Dissociating recollection and familiarity. *Child Development*, *74*, 728–751.

Holliday, R. (2003b). The effect of a prior cognitive interview on children's acceptance of misinformation. *Applied Cognitive Psychology*, *17*, 443–457.

Home Office. (1989). *Report of the advisory group on video evidence*. Home Office.

Home Office. (1992). *Memorandum of good practice*. His Majesty's Stationary Office.

Home Office (1998). *Speaking up for justice: Report of the interdepartmental working group on the treatment of vulnerable or intimidated witnesses in the criminal justice system*. Home Office Procedures and Victims Unit.

Hope, L., & Gabbert, F. (2019). Interviewing witnesses and victims. In N. Brewer & A. Douglass (Eds.), *Psychological science and the law* (pp. 56–74). The Guildford Press.

Hope, L., Gabbert, F., Fisher, R. P., & Jamieson, K. (2014). Protecting and enhancing eyewitness memory: The impact of an initial recall attempt on performance in an investigative interview. *Applied Cognitive Psychology*, *28*, 304–313.

Horry, R., Hughes, C., Sharma, A., Gabbert, F., & Hope, L. (2021). A meta-analytic review of the self-administered interview: Quantity and accuracy of details reported on initial and subsequent retrieval attempts. *Applied Cognitive Psychology*, *35*(2), 428–444.

Kebbell, M., Milne, R., & Wagstaff, G. (1999). The cognitive interview: A survey of its forensic effectiveness. *Psychology, Crime and Law*, *5*, 101–115.

Köhnken, G. (1995). Interviewing adults. In R. Bull & D. Carson (Eds.), *Handbook of psychology in legal contexts* (pp. 215–233). Wiley.

Köhnken, G., Milne, R., Memon, A., & Bull, R. (1999). The cognitive interview: A meta- analysis. *Psychology, Crime and Law*, *5*, 3–27.

Korkman, J., Santtila, P., & Sandnabba, N. (2006). Dynamics of verbal interaction between interviewer and child in interviews with alleged victims of child sexual abuse. *Scandinavian Journal of Psychology*, *47*, 109–119.

Lamb, M. (2016). Difficulties translating research on forensic interview practices to practitioners: Finding water, leading horses, but can we get them to drink? *American Psychologist*, *71*(8), 710.

Lamb, M. E., Orbach, Y., Hershkowitz, I., Esplin, P. W., & Horowitz, D. (2007). A structured forensic interview protocol improves the quality and informativeness of investigative interviews with children: A review of research using the NICHD investigative interview protocol. *Child Abuse & Neglect*, *31*(11), 1201–1231.

Lloyd, M. E., Doydum, A. O., & Newcombe, N. S. (2009). Memory binding in early childhood: Evidence for a retrieval deficit. *Child Development*, *80*(5), 1321–1328.

Macpherson, C. (2001). The Youth Justice and Criminal Evidence Act 1999: Achieving best evidence? *Medicine, Science and the Law*, *41*(3), 230–236.

Maras, K., & Bowler, D. (2012). Context reinstatement effects on eyewitness memory in autism spectrum disorder. *British Journal of Psychology*, *103*(3), 330342.

Maras, K. L., & Bowler, D. M. (2010). The cognitive interview for eyewitnesses with autism spectrum disorder. *Journal of Autism and Developmental Disorders*, *40*, 1350–1360.

Maras, K. L., & Bowler, D. M. (2014). Eyewitness testimony in autism spectrum disorder: A review. *Journal of Autism and Developmental Disorders*, *44*(11), 2682–97.

Maras, K., Dando, C., Stephenson, H., Lambrechts, A., Anns, S., & Gaigg, S. (2020). The witness-aimed first account (WAFA): A new technique for interviewing autistic witnesses and victims. *Autism*, *24*(6), 1449–1467.

Maras, K., Mulcahy, S., Memon, A., Picariello, F., & Bowler, D. (2014). Evaluating the effectiveness of the self-administered interview for witnesses with autism spectrum disorder. *Applied Cognitive Psychology*, *28*, 693–701.

Maras, K., & Wilcock, R. (2013). Suggestibility in vulnerable groups: Witnesses with intellectual disability, autism spectrum disorder, and older people. In A. Ridley, F. Gabbert, & D. La Rooy (Eds.), *Investigative suggestibility: Theory, research and applications* (pp. 149–170). Wiley-Blackwell.

Mattison, M., & Dando, C. (2020). Police officers' and registered Intermediaries' use of drawing during investigative interviews with vulnerable witnesses. *Psychology, Crime and Law*, *26*(2), 167–185.

Mattison, M., Dando, C., & Ormerod, T. (2015). Sketching to remember: Episodic free recall task support fort child witnesses and victims with autism spectrum disorder. *Journal of Autism and Developmental Disorders*, *45*, 1751–1765.
Memon, A. (2006). The cognitive interview. In O. Hargie (Ed.), *A handbook of communication skills* (3rd ed.). Routledge.
Memon, A., Meissner, C. A., & Fraser, J. (2010). The cognitive interview: A meta-analytic review and study space analysis of the past 25 years. *Psychology, Public Policy, and Law*, *16*, 340–372.
Memon, A., Wark, L., Bull, R., & Koehnken, G. (1997). Isolating the effects of the cognitive interview techniques. *British Journal of Psychology*, *88*, 179–197.
Milne, R., & Bull, R. (1999). *Investigative interviewing: Psychology and practice*. Wiley.
Ministry of Justice (MOJ). (2022). *Achieving best evidence in criminal proceedings*. Home Office.
Ministry of Justice (MOJ). (2022). *Criminal Justice Statistics Quarterly: Year ending December 2022*. https://www.gov.uk/government/statistics/criminal-justice-system-statistics-quarterly-december-2022
Myklebust, T. (2009). *Analysis of field investigative interviews of children conducted by specially trained police investigators* [Unpublished PhD thesis]. University of Oslo.
Myklebust, T., & Bjorklund, R. (2006). The effect of long-term training on police officers' use of open and closed questions in field investigative interviews of children (FIIC). *international. Journal of Investigative Psychology and Offender Profiling*, *3*, 165–181.
Oxburgh, G., Myklebust, T., & Grant, T. (2010). The question of question types in police interviews: A review of the literature from a psychological and linguistic perspective. *International Journal of Speech, Language and the Law*, *17*, 45–66.
Phillips, E., Oxburgh, G., & Myklebust, T. (2011). Investigative interviews with victims of child sexual abuse: The relationship between question and investigation relevant information. *Journal of Police and Criminal Psychology*, *27*, 45–54.
Powell, M. (2013). An overview of current initiatives to improve child witness interviews about sexual abuse. *Current Issues in Criminal Justice*, *25*, 711–720.
Powell, M., & Snow, P. (2007). Guide to questioning children during the free-narrative phase of an investigative interview. *Australian Psychologist*, *42*(1), 57–65.
Riby, D., & Hancock, P. J. B. (2009). Looking at movies and cartoons: Eye-tracking evidence from Williams syndrome and autism. *Journal of Intellectual Disability Research*, *53*, 169–181.
Ridley, A., Gabbert, F., & La Rooy, D. (2013). *Investigative suggestibility: Theory, research and applications*. Wiley-Blackwell.
Roberts, J., Lightbody, R., Low, R., & Elstub, S. (2020). Experts and evidence in deliberation: Scrutinising the role of witnesses and evidence in mini-publics, a case study. *Policy Sciences*, *53*, 3–32.
Robinson, B. (2008). ABE interviews: Is the child's 'best evidence' being achieved in alleged sexual abuse cases? *Family Law Week*.
Robinson, J., & McGuire, J. (2005). Suggestibility and children with mild learning disabilities: The use of the cognitive interview. *Psychology, Crime & Law*, *12*, 537–556.
Schank, R. C., & Abelson, R. P. (1977). *Scripts, plans, goals and understanding: An inquiry into human knowledge structures*. Lawrence Erlbaum.
Schreiber, N., & Fisher, R. P. (2006). Evaluating police training. In *Cognitive interview techniques: Possibilities and difficulties*. Paper presented at the American Psychology and Law Society Conference, St. Petersburg, FL.
Smith, K., & O'Mahony, B. (2018). Vulnerability and criminal investigations. In A. Griffiths & R. Milne (Eds.), *The psychology of criminal investigation. From theory to practice* (pp. 91–112). Routledge.
Snook, B., Luther, K., Quinlan, H., & Milne, R. (2012). Let 'em talk! A field study of police questioning practices of suspects and accused persons. *Criminal Justice and Behaviour*, *39*(10), 1328–1339.
Tickle-Degnen, L., & Rosenthal, R. (1990). The nature of rapport and its nonverbal correlates. *Psychological Inquiry*, *1*, 285–293.
Tulving, E. (1974). Cue-dependent forgetting. *American Scientist*, *62*, 74–82.

Tulving, E. (1983). *Elements of episodic memory*. Oxford University Press.
Tulving, E., & Thomson, D. M. (1973). Encoding specificity and retrieval processes in episodic memory. *Psychological Review*, *80*, 352–373.
Turner, M. S., Cipolotti, L., Yousry, T. A., & Shallice, T. (2008). Confabulation: Damage to a specific inferior medial prefrontal system. *Cortex*, *44*, 637–648.
Walsh, D., & Milne, R. (2008). Keeping the PEACE? A study of investigative interviewing practices in the public sector. *Legal and Criminological Psychology*, *13*, 39–57.
Westcott, H., & Kynan, S. (2006). Interviewer practice in investigative interviews for suspected child sexual abuse. *Psychology, Crime and Law*, *12*(4), 367–388.
Williams, D. L., Goldstein, G., & Minshew, N. J. (2006). The profile of memory function in children with autism. *Neuropsychology*, *20*, 21–29.
Wright, A. M., & Holliday, R. E. (2007). Interviewing cognitively impaired older adults: How useful is a cognitive interview? *Memory*, *15*, 17–33.
Wyman, J. D., Lavoie, J., & Talwar, V. (2018). Best practices for interviewing children with intellectual disabilities in maltreatment cases. *Exceptionality*, *27*(3), 167–184.
Youth Justice and Criminal Evidence Act. (1999). London: HMSO.

5 Interviewing Vulnerable Suspects

Introduction

Vulnerable suspects are becoming increasingly over-represented in the justice system (Sirdifield & Brooker, 2012), and the impact of vulnerability on the investigative interview is becoming increasingly documented. However, this was not well considered in an era when police officers in England and Wales used interrogative practices to elicit false confessions. What followed was an array of miscarriages of justice highlighting that, in fact, innocent individuals do confess, and the risk of doing so is heightened if the suspect is vulnerable. Thus, those interviewing vulnerable suspects must have an awareness of the specific needs of the vulnerable suspect, particularly as this population do not respond well to traditional methods of policing.

Prior to the 1980s in England and Wales, and other countries around the world, police officers received little or no training in interviewing suspects, including those that were considered vulnerable. This led to police officers frequently using coercive and manipulative techniques with the onus on seeking a confession (Walkley, 1987). Indeed, even as recently as the turn of the century, it was still thought that 'you don't obtain a confession by asking the suspect questions. You have to convince a suspect to confess by the use of persuasive interrogational techniques' (Holmes, 2002, p. 3). Such an ethos was encouraged by influential training manuals at the time which drew on inappropriate interview tactics; thus, early police interrogation manuals in England and Wales in particular encouraged police officers to 'interrogate' rather than 'interview' suspects (Farrugia & Milne, 2012). Perhaps, one of the most well-known interrogation techniques that is still used in some parts of the world is known as the Reid Interrogation Technique (Inbau et al., 2013).

Interviewing Vulnerable Suspects: Early Methods

The concept of 'interrogation' describes a heuristic approach which focuses heavily on coercive and manipulative techniques when interviewing suspects. Originally developed in the 1970s, the Reid Interrogation Technique is designed to elicit a confession from the suspect involved. This is encouraged via a two-stage approach during the investigation; the Behaviour Analysis Interview (BAI) subsequently followed by the nine-step interrogation process.

The Behaviour Analysis Interview

The general principles of the BAI focuses primarily on nonverbal behaviour being more reliable than verbal behaviour, nonverbal behaviour being responsible for over half of total communication and being able to interpret a suspect's innocence or guilt through their

DOI: 10.4324/9781003386735-5

nonverbal behaviour, as well as a suspects' behaviour being influenced by the interrogator. The BAI is conducted prior to the main interrogation process and involves 'interviewing' the suspect to explore their version of events, and to ascertain any independent sources who may be able to corroborate the suspects' version of events. During this stage, interviewing officers will also examine any potential motive or opportunity the suspect had to commit the crime by asking standard investigative questions and 'behaviour provoking' questions. For example, the interviewing officer may present a 'bait question' whereby they present a plausible possibility of the existence of some evidence that implicates the suspect in the crime or make attempts to evaluate the memory of the suspect by asking for a detailed account before, during, and after the crime period and requesting that the suspect retell their account in a reverse order. Such questions during the BAI stage are designed to elicit behaviour symptoms within the suspect that indicate innocence or guilt; Inbau and colleagues (2013) believe that when evaluating the memory of the suspect for example, should the suspect not be able to retell their account in a reverse order, then they are being deceptive. They also suggest that liars are more likely to cross their legs or shift about in their chair and be less helpful than truth-tellers.

Advocates for the BAI describe this stage as a non-accusatory question and answer session (Inbau et al., 2013). Others suggest that those who conduct the BAI are instructed to try and differentiate between innocent and truthful suspects and those who are being deceptive (Masip & Herrero, 2013). Although it is often claimed that it is possible to detect when an individual is telling the truth or lying based on nonverbal behaviour (Inbau et al., 2013), there has been a large body of research work that has suggested that such behaviours are unreliable indicators of deception (see, e.g., Granhag et al., 2015). Furthermore, the verbal and nonverbal behaviours that Inbau and his colleagues endorse as indicators of guilt, have been shown to be exhibited by innocent suspects (Vrij et al., 2006). In addition, research has indicated that when police officers follow the guidance regarding cues to detecting deception, they actually become worse at distinguishing between truth and lies (Mann et al., 2004) and certainly no better than chance level (Vrij et al., 2007). More recently, scholars have found that should the verbal and nonverbal behaviour indicators endorsed by Inbau and colleagues be used, the likelihood of incorrect judgements and miscarriages of justice are significantly increased (Synnott et al., 2015). This has implications for suspects being subjected to the BAI.

The Reid Interrogation Technique is considered the gold standard of law enforcement across many states in America and some other countries worldwide (Gudjonsson & Pearse, 2011). The aim of the interrogation technique is to obtain a confession. Thus, once the BAI has been conducted and if it is believed that the suspect's behaviour suggests guilt, then they are subjected to the nine-step interrogation. In fact, Inbau and colleagues (2013) advocate for an immediate interrogation given that the suspect is '...most vulnerable to interrogation immediately following the interview because of his concern that the investigator detected his deception' (p. 169). The first step of the interrogation involves the interrogator presenting real or fictional evidence of the suspect's involvement in the crime whilst continuously enforcing the need for the truth. Step two provides the opportunity to develop moral excuses for the suspect's involvement in the crime; this includes using coercive and manipulative techniques such as minimisation (playing down the seriousness of the crime). Steps three and four consists of procedures for handling the suspect's initial denial of guilt and secondary line of defence often returning to the moral excuse developed previously. Advocates for this technique believe that only guilty suspects provide excuses. In steps five and six, the interrogator seeks to maintain the suspect's attention and handle the passive mood of

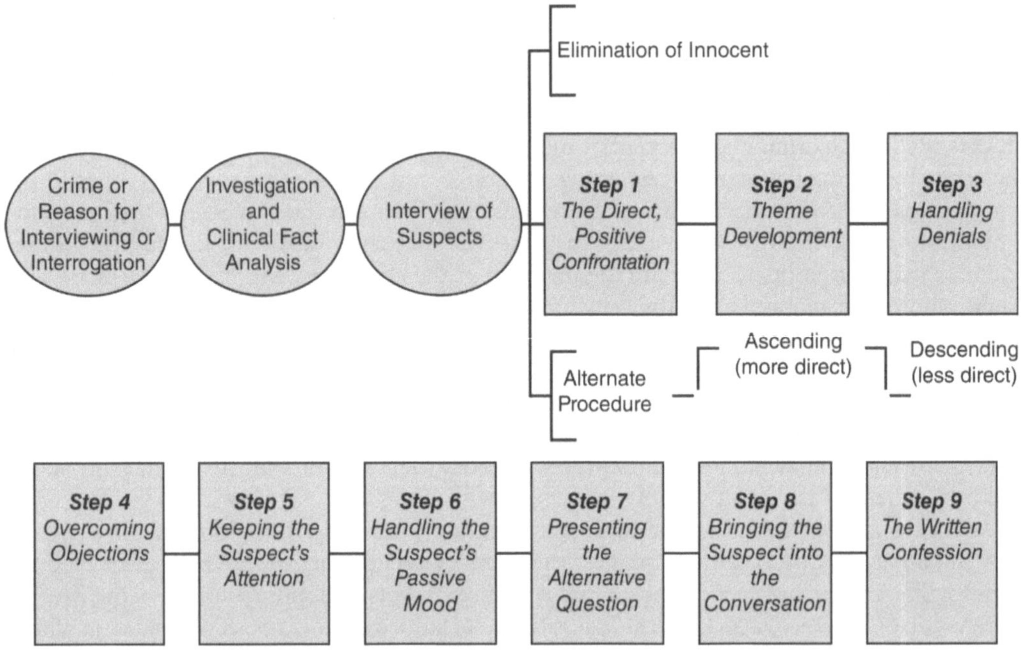

Figure 5.1 The nine-step Reid Interrogation Technique (Inbau et al., 2013)

the suspect – in doing so, the interrogator is taught to display sincerity towards the suspect whilst focusing their attention on possible reasons for committing the crime. In step seven, the interrogator presents the alternative question – that is, they give the suspect an opportunity to explain their involvement in the crime. Step eight involves obtaining an oral confession; this is reinforced by the interrogator. The final step involves converting the oral confession into a written one (see Figure 5.1).

Those who engage in such interrogation techniques believe that such an accusatory approach is a successful one for gaining a confession. However, the Reid Interrogation Technique has been heavily criticised throughout the academic and psychological literature for the use of psychological tactics including repetitive questioning and the fabrication of evidence. Indeed, these tactics have been shown to lead to a heightened risk of the suspect providing misleading and inaccurate information (Meissner et al., 2014). Furthermore, the use of such an interrogation technique leads to an environment whereby it is psychologically and emotionally more appealing to confess in order to escape the hostile environment (Kelly & Meissner, 2016) – it is only when the suspect has confessed, that the interrogation (which can last several hours, if not longer) ends. This particular approach has been viewed as a major contributory cause in a number of miscarriages of justice involving a false confession (Gudjonsson, 2018).

False Confessions and Miscarriages of Justice

Anecdotally, individuals believe that we would not provide a confession to something we did not to. However, in the 1970s particularly, there was a series of high-profile miscarriages of justice in England and Wales and further afield internationally. Perhaps one of the most well-known ones is that concerning Judith Ward.

> Judith Ward was arrested in early 1974 for the M62 coach explosion in which 12 soldiers and their families were murdered, as well as the IRA bombings at Euston station and the National Defence College. She was sentenced to 12 life terms and 30 years' imprisonment. Her conviction was based on evidence from the same Home Office forensic scientist whose methods had been discredited in an earlier miscarriage of justice case.
>
> When she was arrested, Judith was homeless and had been sheltering in a Liverpool shop doorway. Initially, police intended to charge her with placing the M62 bomb at Manchester's Chorlton Street bus station. However, irrefutable evidence emerged that she was 150 miles away at the time of the bombing. Instead, the police charged her with planning and organising the explosion instead. During her arrest and detention, Judith was held under oppressive and disorienting conditions where she was repeatedly moved from one location to another and deprived of sleep. As a result, she signed numerous confessions that contained multiple anomalies and contradictions. During her trial, evidence confirming that she had a serious psychotic illness was deliberately concealed by the defence. It was not until June 1992 that her conviction was quashed.

It is hard to believe that an innocent individual would knowingly confess to a crime that they have not committed, especially given the subsequent likelihood of receiving a criminal record and custodial sentence. However, false confessions and miscarriages of justice are not new in the justice system and are well documented throughout the academic literature (see, e.g., Gudjonsson, 2018). For example, some scholars report that approximately 30% of all miscarriages of justice involve a false confession as a contributing factor (Garrett, 2010). As a result, there is now a substantial literature base with organisations including the Innocence Project in the United Kingdom and United States of America (USA) reporting on wrongfully convicted individuals who have since been exonerated. The reasons why innocent individuals falsely confess will now be explored.

False Confessions – Why Do People Falsely Confess?

It was not until the 1980s that false confessions started to become widely discussed, despite early insights from a Harvard psychology professor, Hugo Münsterberg (1908). A number of scholars have defined false confessions since. For example, Ofshe (1989) identified that 'a confession is considered false if it is elicited in response to a demand for a confession and is either intentionally fabricated or is not based on actual knowledge of the facts that form its content' (p. 13). Similarly, Ofshe and Leo (1997) described a false confession as a '...detailed admission to a criminal act that the confessor either did not commit or is, in fact, ignorant of having committed' (p. 24). What is clear is that the most central criterion in defining a false confession is that an *innocent* individual confesses to a crime that they did not commit (Gudjonsson, 2018).

There has been much research work and classification systems to explain why innocent individuals falsely confess, but perhaps the most well-known is that of Kassin and Wrightsman's (1985) taxonomy on false confessions. They highlight that there are three main types of false confessions:

1 Voluntary: innocent individuals volunteer self-incriminating information without any coercion or pressure from the interviewing officer. There may be several reasons for doing so including protecting the real perpetrator (e.g., a parent confessing to a crime that their

child committed) or for a morbid desire for notoriety (e.g., Henry Lee Lucas confessed to over 600 murders in the 1980s to attract more attention). Those who are vulnerable may also provide voluntary false confessions as they may have experienced a breakdown in reality monitoring and thus have the inability to distinguish between fact and fiction.

2 Coerced-compliant: these types of false confessions occur due to the interrogative or coercive pressures experienced during the interrogation or interview, or to serve the individual's own self-interest. Importantly, the individual providing the false confession knows that they are doing so for some immediate instrumental gain, for example, the individual believes if they provide a false confession, the interrogation will end, and they can go home and thus avoid further conflict (Gudjonsson, 2018). Thus, the key element is the desire to escape from what is perceived to be an intolerable situation and so the short-term perceived immediate gains far outweigh the potential long-term consequences. The individual is likely to maintain the false confession for as long as is perceived necessary for the instrumental gain – for example, the confession is likely to be retracted once the individual feels safe and is no longer in custody.

The Central Park Jogger Case (1989)

In 1989, a female jogger, Trisha Meili, was assaulted and raped in New York City's Central Park. Following interrogations that lasted between 14 and 30 hours, five teenage males aged 14–16 years old confessed to being involved in the violent attack and were subsequently convicted. However, in 2002, a convicted murderer confessed to the attack and with the help of DNA evidence, the five teenage males were exonerated. They claimed that they had simply told investigators what they wanted to hear and believed that they would be allowed to go home once they had done so.

3 Coerced-internalised: this type of false confession occurs when the innocent individual comes to question their own innocence and subsequently believes that they are responsible for the crime. This occurs because of highly misleading claims about the evidence presented to them, for example, the evidence may be fictional, and so the individual comes to accept the allegations presented to them by the police. In some cases, such individuals may come to confabulate memories to support their confession. There are two main facilitating factors that can lead to this type of false confession; (i) the conditions of the interrogation or interview produce a trance-like state leading to distortions in reality, heightened capacity for imagination, and increased suggestibility and confabulation, and (ii) reiterating a lie can lead to some individuals believing it, especially if it comes from an individual in a position of power. Evidence also suggests that this type of false confession is directly linked to memory distrust – 'a condition where people develop profound distrust of their memory recollections, as a result of which they are particularly susceptible to relying on external cues and suggestions' (Gudjonsson, 2003, p. 196). Whilst memory distrust can be generated internally, it is often developed through prolonged and persuasive interrogations or interviews and may be prevalent in individuals who are highly prone to fantasy or confabulation (Horselenberg et al., 2006).

Ofshe and Leo (1997) provided the most vocal critique of Kassin and Wrightsman's false confession classification system. They highlighted that there is no need for separate systems for true and false confessions because they are both driven by the same underlying logic and arise from interrogations. They have also indicated that the classification system fails to take into account police-induced confessions that do not involve coercion, for example, false confessions that occur in the absence of police threats or inducements, and that the concept of internalisation is misapplied by suggesting it can permanently distort memory – Ofshe and Leo (1997) in fact indicate that internalisation is temporary, unstable, and may change depending on the situation. More recently, Gudjonsson (2003) also highlighted that compliant or internalised confessions may not always be coerced.

However, despite the critique, the Kassin and Wrightsman (1985) model of false confessions remains a useful framework and has since been extended and refined by others (see, e.g., Gudjonsson, 2003). It also provides some understanding as to the human decision-making involved in providing a false confession and the impact of a coercive and manipulative interrogation. For example, early research found that individuals will make decisions that they perceive to maximise their wellbeing given the constraints they may face (Herrnstein et al., 1997), and that individuals are impulsive, preferring immediate outcomes rather than delayed ones (Rachlin, 2000). This is evident in the coerced-compliant false confession outlined previously and has been supported by more recent work. Madon et al. (2012) found that individuals tended to make admissions of misconduct to avoid the short-term consequence of denial even though it increased the risk of the larger long-term consequence. Thus, when short-sighted decision-making is used to characterise what suspects may face in an interrogation or interview, even suspects that refuse to confess at first will eventually become exhausted over time and lose their will to resist (Davis & Leo, 2012). The risk of providing a false confession increases and leads to a miscarriage of justice (Gudjonsson, 2018; Vrij et al., 2017). In England and Wales, this was particularly prevalent when police were using similar interrogational methods and led to perhaps one of the most important inquiries in changing the direction of policing to date.

The Fisher Inquiry and the Royal Commission

On 22 April 1972, the fire brigade was called to an address in South-East London. Upon their arrival, the body of Maxwell Confait was found in an upstairs bedroom behind a locked door. The fire was extinguished, and the police were called shortly afterwards. Maxwell Confait's lips were blue and there were marks on Maxwell's neck indicating strangulation with a rope or cord. The coroner ruled the cause of death to have been asphyxia.

The home where Maxwell Confait's body was found belonged to the landlord, Winston Goode, whom Maxwell had started renting a room from earlier that year. Two days later, a number of fires in the area led to the arrest of an 18-year-old male, Colin Lattimore, who admitted to lighting the fires with his friends, 15-year-old Ronnie Leighton, and 14-year-old Ahmet Salih. All three males were arrested and interrogated without the presence of a parent or guardian.

During the interrogations, all three males admitted to starting the fire where Maxwell Confait was found, and both Colin Lattimore and Ronnie Leighton also confessed to the murder of Maxwell Confait. In late 1972, Colin Lattimore was found guilty of manslaughter on the grounds of diminished responsibility in addition to two counts of arson. Similarly, Ronnie Leighton was convicted for murder, arson, and burglary at a nearby address and Ahmet Salih was found guilty of burglary and arson. In 1973, the Court of Appeal rejected an appeal by their legal representatives, however, it was referred back to the Court of Appeal in 1974. In late 1975, the Court of Appeal quashed their convictions, labelling them as unsafe and unsatisfactory, with the police being heavily criticised for the handling of the case. The case remains unsolved.

Although miscarriages of justice relating to coercive interrogatory practices did not begin with the Maxwell Confait case, a full inquiry chaired by Sir Henry Fisher was ordered following the three youths' acquittals in 1975. Thus, it was this case that highlighted the impact of the interview process in causing false confessions and miscarriages of justice (Price & Caplan, 1977). After the convictions were quashed, the Court of Appeal had in fact identified that the confessions obtained had been done so from the males under improper police pressure (Williamson, 2007). Thus, the mission of the inquiry was to make recommendations about the current Judges' Rules stipulating how suspects, especially those who were children and/or vulnerable, should be treated by the police. His findings suggested procedural issues with the investigation into the Maxwell Confait case, and issues concerning the protections of suspects' rights. Furthermore, he found that a flawed interview process coupled with the psychological vulnerabilities of the three teenage males led to them falsely confessing (Fisher, 1977). Such judicial concerns led to the Royal Commission on Criminal Procedure in England and Wales (RCCP; Home Office, 1981). The Commission examined and made recommendations for policy change relating to police powers when investigating crimes, the rights of suspects and the responsibility for the prosecution of criminal offences. Thus, the Judges' Rules that previously governed police interviews prior to 1984 were found to be inadequate, with the police being viewed as prioritising the need for a confession, usually through the use of oppressive and coercive questioning techniques, over searching for the truth. The police were also identified as taking advantage of suspects' vulnerabilities (Irving, 1980). These findings, taken together with the increased attention being paid to police procedure, paved the way for new legislation to be introduced. It is here that the chapter now turns.

Interviewing Vulnerable Suspects: PACE and PEACE

The introduction of the Police and Criminal Evidence Act (PACE, 1984; Home Office, 2018) and its associated Codes of Practice, provided a legislative framework for the use of police powers including arrest, detention, investigation, and interviewing of all suspects, including those that were vulnerable. This ensured that interviews were now audio-recorded and that all suspects were offered the right to free legal advice in an attempt to ensure fairness and transparency in the investigative process. Despite this, suspect interviewing remained poor; miscarriages of justice were still occurring in spite of their importance in driving reform. Thus, whilst PACE had increased suspects' rights and introduced transparency to the investigative process, the same confession-seeking ethos was still in place (Baldwin, 1992). Scholars frequently reported the impact this had on public confidence; for example, Williamson (1993) highlighted how, 'unethical behaviour by interrogators has undermined public confidence and left the police service with a serious skills deficit in its ability to obtain evidence through questioning' (p. 107). Consequently, there remained a need to shift from the ineffective use of coercive and manipulative questioning techniques towards a more information-seeking style of interviewing.

In the early 1990s, Shepherd (1991) advocated for the move towards using the term, 'investigative interviewing' to describe how police should be interviewing victims, witnesses, and suspects (Gudjonsson, 1992). In 1991, amid such concerns over ineffective interrogation practices, the Home Office set up a steering group on investigative interviewing comprising of members from the police service, the Home Office, and the Crown Prosecution Service (CPS) in order to coordinate work on interviewing, and the delivery of training. The steering group came up with an interviewing model aimed at offering a more effective and ethical alternative to the interrogation techniques previously used. Thus, the PEACE model of investigative interviewing (a mnemonic for each stage of the model; Planning and preparation, Engage and explain, Account, clarify and challenge, Closure, and Evaluation) was developed and introduced to police officers in England and Wales (Williamson, 2006; see Figure 5.2).

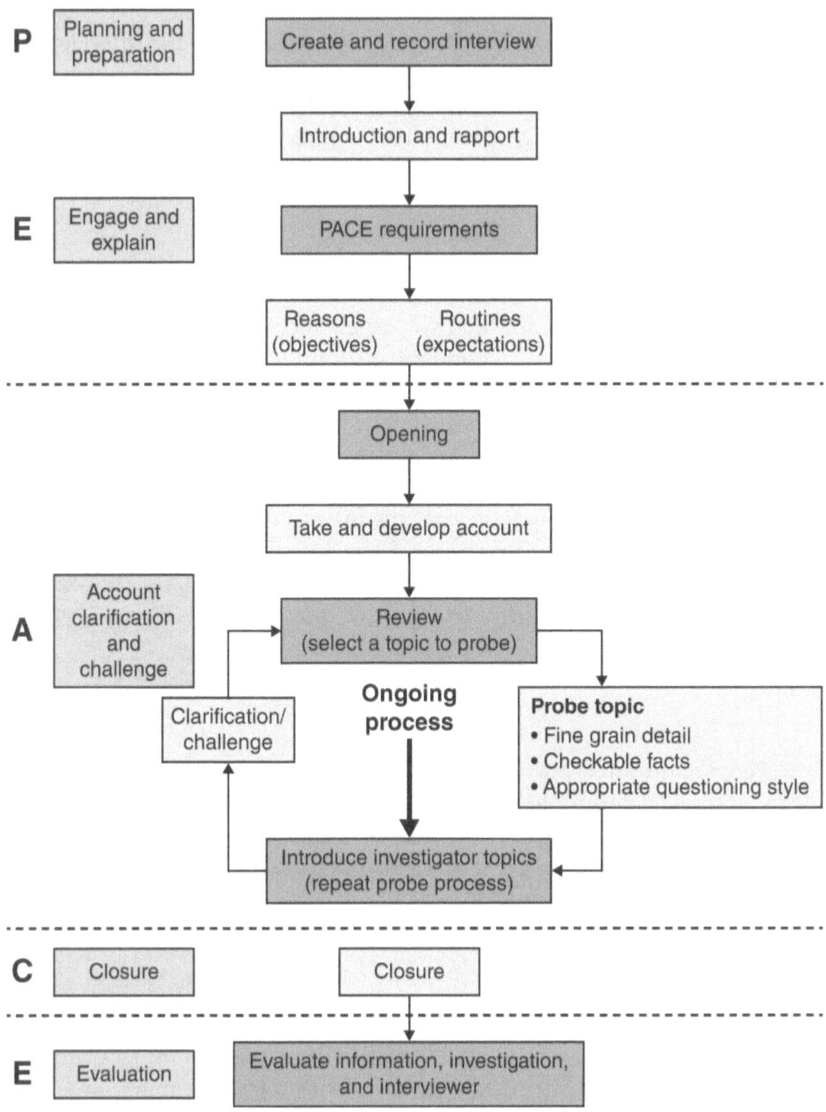

Figure 5.2 The PEACE model of interviewing (College of Policing, 2020)

Planning and Preparation

The first step of the model, the planning and preparation, is considered one of the most important. Interviewers are encouraged to consider all available information and identify key objectives for the purpose of the interview; in doing so, the use of an interview plan outlining interview topics, necessary points to prove the potential offence or those that may be a defence should be considered, as well as any exhibits, possibilities of prepared statements, special warnings or significant comments or silences. The characteristics of the interviewee should also be considered including age, gender, cultural background, domestic circumstances, and any disabilities or vulnerabilities.

Engage and Explain

The importance of rapport in conducting interviews is increasingly recognised (see Gabbert et al., 2020 for a full review). Thus, this stage should involve the interviewer trying to engage with the interviewee by demonstrating active listening and building rapport. In addition, clear reasons for the interview and interview objectives should be explained to the interviewee at the start of the interview, as well as informing the interviewee that the interview is an opportunity to explain their involvement (or non-involvement) of the alleged offence.

Account, Clarify and Challenge

Within this stage, interviewers are encouraged to obtain as much information as possible through the use of appropriate questioning strategies, including open-ended questions that are designed to elicit a free recall (see Chapter 4 for a full discussion of question typology). Elements used in the previous stage, such as active listening and maintaining rapport, are also encouraged in this stage, as well as prompting the interviewee to report a full and complete account. After the free recall, interviewers are directed to clarify and explore each topic area in turn by systematically probing for further details until the whole account has been fully explored. It is during this stage that the interviewee's account may be challenged with evidence identified during the planning phase. In order to do this, interviewers can employ one of two interview styles; (i) the Conversation Management Approach (see Shepherd, 2007 for a full discussion) or (ii) the Cognitive Interview (see Fisher et al., 1987 for a full discussion).

Closure

Once the interviewer and interviewee are satisfied that a full account has been obtained, a summary of the interview should be provided to ensure that the information provided has been interpreted accurately. The interviewer should then formally end the interview and turn the recording off. Next steps in the investigation should be explained and any questions from the interviewee should be dealt with.

Evaluation

After the conclusion of the interview, the interviewer is encouraged to reflect upon and evaluate what information has been obtained with a view to determining whether any additional action is necessary, such as further interviews with the same interviewee or other victims, witnesses or suspects, or the obtaining of further evidence. How the account fits with

Table 5.1 Seven key principles of investigative interviewing

Principle	*Description*
Principle 1	The aim of investigative interviewing is to obtain accurate and reliable accounts from victims, witnesses, or suspects about matters under police investigation.
Principle 2	Investigators must act fairly when questioning victims, witnesses, or suspects. They must ensure that they comply with all the provisions and duties under the Equality Act 2010 and the Human Rights Act 1998.
Principle 3	Investigative interviewing should be approached with an investigative mindset.
Principle 4	Investigators are free to ask a wide range of questions in an interview in order to obtain material which may assist an investigation and provide sufficient evidence or information.
Principle 5	Investigators should recognise the positive impact of an early admission in the context of the criminal justice system.
Principle 6	Investigators are not bound to accept the first answer given. Questioning is not unfair merely because it is persistent.
Principle 7	Even when a suspect exercises the right to silence, investigators have a responsibility to put questions to them.

College of Policing (2021).

the rest of the investigation should also be considered. Furthermore, the interviewer's own performance should be evaluated and whether they adhered to current policy and practice (see Farrugia et al., 2019, 2022, for a full discussion of evaluation techniques).

Alongside the introduction of the PEACE model of interviewing, the national strategic steering group developed seven key principles to assist with the application of good investigative interviewing techniques and to guide interviewers on how best to implement the PEACE model framework. The principles are listed in Table 5.1.

The Efficacy of the PEACE Model of Interviewing

The implementation of the PEACE model of interviewing and its core principles were to ensure that all police officers were provided with the necessary skills and training to conduct effective, information-seeking investigative interviews. Since its introduction, scholars have investigated its efficacy. McGurk et al. (1993) were one of the first to evaluate the impact of the PEACE model on interviewing behaviour; they used a combination of knowledge tests, interviews involving hypothetical offences under simulated conditions, and examined real-life suspect interviews. They found that once training had been delivered on the PEACE model of interviewing, police officers displayed more open-mindedness, better listening and communication skills and their overall questioning techniques and interview structure improved. Less than ten years later, a national evaluation of the PEACE model of interviewing was conducted in 2001. Clarke and Milne analysed 177 taped suspect interviews and found that generally the overall interviewing style had improved with good communication skills reported. However, they also found that the interviews were still interviewer driven and confirmatory, rather than allowing the interviewee to provide their free recall, that whilst there was some evidence of planning and preparation and closure, this was limited, as was the delivery of the caution and explanation regarding rights to legal advice and interview format. Furthermore, they reported that whilst there were some open questions used, this was limited, and the emphasis remained on using closed questions. More recent research has reported a similar mixed picture. For example, whilst ethical interviewing techniques emphasised by the PEACE model have been commonly found in police interviews (Soukara et al., 2009), other scholars have reported that poor practices still exist indicating that police officers are reverting back to old interview techniques and using a high level of inappropriate questioning strategies (Oxburgh et al., 2010a, 2010b; Wright & Powell, 2006). Thus, research into the effectiveness of the PEACE model continues to appear mixed.

Since the introduction of the PEACE model of interviewing, psychologists have continuously assessed its efficacy and thus developed an understanding as to what constitutes best practice based on scientific knowledge. As a result, there now exists a large amount of literature which has led to the development of several protocols when conducting investigative interviews. However, these largely relate to child and adult witness interviewing (see Benia et al., 2015 for a full discussion on the NICHD protocol for example). Typically, any suspect interview in England and Wales and further afield will start by cautioning the suspect and informing them of their rights, as well as the reason for the interview and the objectives and expectations (College of Policing, 2020). A free recall is then sought followed by a series of more probing questions concerning the details provided and the evidence already gained. In doing so, the use of appropriate questioning techniques must be utilised to ensure that accurate and reliable information can be obtained without influencing the suspect's memory – this is particularly crucial for those who may be at a heightened risk of falsely implicating themselves, due to age and/or vulnerability. Whilst some psychological enquiry has explored the ability to detect deception (Hartwig & Bond, 2011), and the efficacy of suspect interrogation approaches including the prevalence of false confessions (Meissner et al., 2014; Stewart et al., 2018), which has led to a large and growing body of scientific knowledge that has established that rapport-based, non-coercive methods for interviewing are the most effective, and the subsequent development of a set of international standards for investigative interviews (see Mendez, 2021, for a full discussion regarding 'Principles on Effective Interviewing for Investigation and Information Gathering'), the PEACE model of interviewing is the only theoretically driven interview framework in England and Wales for interviewing suspects.

The interviewing of suspects has come a long way from early interrogation techniques to the investigative mindset now encouraged and employed by police officers in England and Wales and around the world. Information-gathering during the interview must be based on appropriate questioning techniques, however, there is an emerging branch of research that suggests that current interviewing methods, primarily the techniques concerning the free recall and the use of open questions, may not be suitable for the vulnerable suspect. The chapter now turns to the impact of vulnerability within the suspect interview.

Interviewing Vulnerable Suspects: The Impact of Vulnerability on Current Interview and Questioning Techniques

It is well established that conducting interviews with suspects (including those that are vulnerable) is an integral and crucial part of the evidence gathering process (Oxburgh & Ost, 2011). However, research has only started to explore the impact of the interview and questioning techniques on vulnerable suspects, particularly those with mental health conditions and disorders. Of the work that has been conducted, research findings have cast doubt upon the appropriateness of open questions for all vulnerable suspect populations. For example, three independent studies have found that adults with intellectual disability report fewer correct details than those without an intellectual disability when asked open questions that invite a free recall (Bowles & Sharman, 2014; Perlman et al., 1994; Ternes & Yuille, 2008). In addition, police officers in England and Wales have highlighted that open questions are not always suitable for suspects with mental health conditions or disorders as they can be 'too broad', and thus indicated their preference for using more specific questions that can aid a vulnerable suspects' understanding (Oxburgh et al., 2016). Thus, this has implications for how the vulnerable suspect should and is being interviewed.

More recent work conducted by Farrugia and Gabbert (2019) sought to explore this. Using a sample of 66 real-life suspect interviews that had been conducted in England and Wales with vulnerable and non-vulnerable suspects, they sought to examine whether current interview practices with a particular focus on procedures, questioning techniques and the impact on information elicited were appropriate for suspects with mental health conditions and disorders. The sample included suspects who reportedly had mental health issues ranging from anxiety and mood disorders to more serious and complex conditions such as schizophrenia and dissociative identity disorder, and who had been implicated in serious crimes such as murder/attempted murder and a range of sexual offences. They found that whilst procedural differences were minimum in terms of elements of 'engage and explain' and the 'closure' stages, there were differences in the way the two groups of suspects were questioned. The vulnerable suspects were asked significantly more inappropriate questions than appropriate questions. Furthermore, the suspects with mental health conditions and disorders were found to seek significantly more clarification to open questions and tended to provide more investigation relevant information to closed questions. The work of Farrugia and Gabbert (2019) therefore suggests that current best practice interviewing techniques endorsing the use of open questions, may not be suitable for those with mental health conditions and disorders. Explanations for this can be found when examining specific vulnerabilities.

The Impact of Mood and Anxiety Disorders on Current Interview and Questioning Techniques

Mood disorder is an umbrella term that covers all types of depression and bipolar disorders. Approximately one in six adults worldwide will experience at least one episode of a mood disorder, the most common being depression (Office for National Statistics, 2021). Such disorders are characterised by behavioural, emotional, and cognitive symptoms including weight loss or gain, insomnia, feelings of guilt or worthlessness, difficulties in concentration and emotion regulation and an overall negative affect (Gotlib & Joorman, 2010). Given such high prevalence rates, it seems likely that at least some individuals with a mood disorder will come into contact with the justice system at some point in their lives (Burki, 2017) and so an understanding of the impact of this vulnerability on the investigative interview is paramount.

Generally, individuals with a mood disorder, particularly depression, tend to have depression-related deficits in control of attention, level of engagement, and free recall tasks (Hertel, 1998). Research has documented that those with depression can perform at the same level as individuals without a mood disorder when they are provided with structured instructions (Hertel, 2004) as the opportunity to ruminate (a key characteristic in depression) is eliminated. Furthermore, it has been found that individuals with a mood disorder tend to have a higher recall and encoding of negative stimuli rather than positive material (Mathews & MacLeod, 2005) and tend to display an attentional bias towards emotional stimuli, known as a cognitive bias congruent with their mood (Lemogne et al., 2006). In addition, individuals with a mood disorder tend to interpret ambiguous information in a negative manner (Rude et al., 2002) and have a negative bias in all types of their information processing (Beevers & Carver, 2003).

Such cognitive impairments can impact upon their performance in a suspect interview. For example, those with depression have impairments typically found in 'free recall' tasks and so it is likely that they will find a free recall at the start of an interview difficult to complete; the wide nature of the open question used to request the free recall may allow for opportunities for rumination and not provide the necessary structured instructions required to control the attention of the suspect with depression. Furthermore, they may be more likely to falsely implicate themselves during the suspect interview, given the tendency to selectively attend to emotional cues, particularly if the alleged offence being discussed is distressing or emotional.

Similar impairments have also been found in those with an anxiety disorder. This type of mental health condition is a worldwide health concern (Robinson et al., 2013) with a high prevalence rate reported in the UK offender population (Tyler et al., 2019). Characterised by excessive anxiety and worry and physical and cognitive symptoms such as feeling on edge, impaired concentration and difficulty sleeping, individuals with this condition may also be at a heightened risk of providing unreliable or misleading information during the suspect interview. For example, those with this type of condition may experience intrusive thoughts and emotions (Eysenck et al., 2007); these symptoms have been linked to an attentional bias for threat. Thus, much like those with depression, individuals with an anxiety disorder may show a predisposition to threat-related information which subsequently impacts upon their performance to attend to other tasks (Macleod & Mathews, 2012). Such anxious worry impacts upon cognitive resources needed to engage in free recall tasks that draws upon episodic memory – indeed, those with an anxiety disorder have been shown to exhibit impairments in episodic memory (Airaksinen et al., 2005) – as well as being able to retain information provided to them in a question, process the question and provide a response, thus drawing upon working memory, an area of the memory that is also affected by anxious worry (Lindstrom & Bohlin, 2012). Thus, the questioning style used in an interview involving a vulnerable suspect must be considered. This is also true when one considers a suspect with a learning disability.

The Impact of Learning Disability on Current Interview and Questioning Techniques

A learning disability or intellectual disability can be defined as 'a disorder with onset during the developmental period that includes both intellectual and adaptive functioning deficits in conceptual, social and practical domains' (APA, 2013). Intellectual functioning deficits can include challenges in reasoning, problem solving and planning, abstract thinking, and judgement, as well as academic and experiential learning. Deficits relating to adaptive functioning can result in a failure to meet developmental standards for independence and social responsibility (Drizin & Leo, 2004).

Research has frequently documented that those with a learning disability are over-represented in police custody (Murphy, 2019; Young et al., 2013) and within the prison system (Gulati et al., 2018) when compared to general prevalence rates within the community (Mencap, 2020). Like many vulnerable individuals, those with a learning disability do not form a homogenous group – however it is generally acknowledged that those with a learning disability encounter significant challenges in communication and their cognitive abilities, particularly within the context of a suspect interview (Morrison et al., 2019). For example, those with a learning disability have been found to have broad deficits in memory encoding, storage, and retrieval (Ternes & Yuille, 2008), and thus may find it difficult to spontaneously recall specific events. Furthermore, research has indicated that such individuals are more likely to report unclear generic details about an alleged incident such as names, dates, and times (Beail, 2002) and will typically demonstrate a final-option bias in response to multiple questions or forced choice questions. Numerous studies have also reported heightened levels of suggestibility and acquiescence in those that have a learning disability, as well as increased rates of confabulation and nay-saying (Gudjonsson & Joyce, 2011). All of these difficulties make it much more challenging for a suspect with a learning disability to provide an accurate account during a police interview (Cusack, 2020); indeed, those with learning disabilities are over-represented in cases of miscarriages of justice involving unreliable and false confessions (Kassin et al., 2010). This is echoed internationally – a retrospective analysis of the US register of exonerations revealed that over 25% of exonerations arising from false confessions involved individuals with a learning disability (Schatz, 2018).

The Impact of Age on Current Interview and Questioning Techniques

Police interviewing of juvenile suspects is a particularly challenging task especially if one considers the developmental role of the child (Cleary, 2014). For example, whilst it has been suggested that adolescents are equally as capable as adults in making rational choices about risk under laboratory conditions (see, e.g., Steinberg, 2004), in real-world scenarios, this may not be the case. That is '...much depends on the particular situation in which a decision is made...on the spur of the moment, in unfamiliar situations, when trading off risks and benefits favours bad long-term outcomes, and when behavioural inhibition is required for good outcomes, adolescents are likely to reason more poorly than adults do' (Reyna & Farley, 2006, p. 1). This is particularly important during the police interview, especially when the appropriate safeguards may not always be implemented.

There has not been a great deal of research recently that has explored juvenile suspect interviews; instead the work has tended to focus on the psychosocial capabilities of children when understanding their legal rights (Goldstein et al., 2003; Grisso et al., 2003), or experimental methods that have been conducted to explore the capabilities of children in simulated interviews or hypothetical situations (Redlich & Goodman, 2003; Woolard et al., 2008). That said, Feld's (2006a, 2006b) research which explored 66 interrogation videos and transcripts conducted with juveniles in America represents one of the first modern observations of child interviewing. Followed up by a second study in 2013, Feld obtained a much larger sample of child interrogations and examined youths' responses during their interrogations. The results suggested that juvenile suspects were presented with fabricated or hypothetical evidence in over half of the interrogations, youths were accused of lying in over a third of the interrogations and information was withheld from the juvenile suspect to increase anxiety and uncertainty. Furthermore, their findings highlighted that over half of juveniles confessed within the first few minutes of the interrogation. This is not surprising given that other research has documented that police obtained more than one-third of proven false confessions from suspects younger than the age of 18 years (Drizin & Leo, 2004), and that the younger the suspect, the greater risk of false confession (Tepfer et al., 2010). This is also supported by more recent research (Cleary, 2014).

Psychologists attribute children's over-representation amongst false confessors to their reduced cognitive ability, developmental immaturity, and increased susceptibility to manipulation (Redlich, 2004). Differences in knowledge, experience, time-perspective, attitudes towards risk, impulsivity and appreciation of consequences contribute to youths' poor decision-making (Scott & Steinberg, 2008). That is, in comparison to adults, children underestimate the amount and likelihood of risks and focus on gains rather than losses (Grisso, 2000); this is particularly prevalent when a youth is mid-teens (Scott & Steinberg, 2008). Such differences are attributed to brain development and the increased ability of the prefrontal cortex to perform executive functions and control impulses (Maroney, 2009). This is important should a youth find themselves involved in a suspect interview. Generally, children have fewer life experiences or psychological resources with which to cope with the demands of an interrogation or interview (Drizin & Luloff, 2007) and higher levels of societal expectations of obedience to authority (Leo, 2009); that is juveniles are more likely than adults to comply with authority figures, such as the police, and tell them what they think they want to hear and respond to negative feedback, for example, being told that their account is not true (Gudjonsson, 2003). The impulsive decision-making of a juvenile and limited ability to consider the long-term consequences of their decisions heighten their risk to provide a false confession in a bid to remove themselves from the stress and anxiety of a police interview (Birckhead, 2008; Maroney, 2009). This has implications for justice outcomes and miscarriages of justice.

The Impact of General Vulnerabilities on Current Interview and Questioning Techniques

In addition to the impact of specific mental health conditions and disorders, and the impact of age within the suspect interview, there are general factors that may arise within vulnerable suspects. An overgeneral memory may be one of these. This relates to the issue that vulnerable individuals recall generic memories or repeated events, rather than specific events or single episodes (Williams et al., 2007) and is particularly prevalent in individuals who have a mood disorder or post-traumatic stress disorder (Lemogne et al., 2006). The underlying mechanism related to an overgeneral memory is emotion regulation; Williams (1996) explained that negative emotions attached to distressing memories are minimised thus blocking access to details of those memories or by retrieving them in a less specific way. Consequently, the vulnerable suspect may find it difficult to recall specific events and in the correct order and may, therefore, purposefully appear vague or difficult (Kingdon & Turkington, 2005).

Other general vulnerabilities can relate to suggestibility, compliance, and acquiescence, and those with mental health conditions and disorders, as well as juvenile suspects, may be particularly prone to heightened levels (Gudjonsson, 2018). Suggestibility is defined as 'the extent to which, within a closed social interaction, people come to accept messages communicated during formal questioning, as a result of which their subsequent behavioural response is affected' (Gudjonsson & Clark, 1986, p. 84). What this means is that during the suspect interview, the vulnerable suspect has to cognitively process the question and the context in which it is taking place and in doing so, deal with uncertainty, interpersonal trust, and expectations within the formal interaction. It is these three components that are essential prerequisites for suggestibility which can be manipulated during the interview process. Furthermore, levels of suggestibility have been reported to be affected by factors such as intelligence, memory, and language as well as anxiety and self-esteem (Bruck & Melnyk, 2004), and are heightened in individuals who have experienced adverse life events (Drake, 2014) resulting in subsequent mental health conditions or disorders (Vagni et al., 2021).

Similarly, vulnerable suspects may display heightened levels of compliance. Describe as 'the tendency of the individual to go along with propositions, requests, or instructions for some immediate instrumental gain' (Gudjonsson, 1992, p. 137), key components include an eagerness to please and an avoidance of conflict; this is relevant during a suspect interview if one thinks about the potential criminal justice outcomes of a suspect interview. Research has frequently reported a link between attention deficit hyperactivity disorder and compliance; components of inattention and hyperactivity/impulsivity being most correlated with heightened levels of compliance (Gudjonsson & Sigurdsson, 2010).

Gudjonsson (1990) describes being acquiescent as involving three stages; the first is having the ability to listen to the question which involves paying attention and interest, the second is being able to understand the question which requires understanding of the vocabulary used, having some general knowledge about the topic area and having an overall comprehension of the conversation – should the individual not understand the question, then the third stage occurs and uncertainty develops and the individual may guess in their response, or simply agree. Thus, 'the tendency of the person to answer questions affirmatively irrespective of content' (Gudjonsson, 1990, p. 34) assists the individual in restoring their self-esteem. Those who are vulnerable are more likely to display heightened levels of acquiescence, particularly if the question is ambiguous or where the individual has limited cognitive ability to understand the question structure, grammar, or complexity of the question (Gudjonsson, 2018). Thus, those who acquiesce during a police interview may not be fully aware of the consequences of their responses.

It is clear that suspects who are vulnerable are placed at a disadvantage during the police interview given the impact of their difficulties on their ability to effectively engage with the formal questioning they may face. As such, interviewer questions must match the cognitive abilities of those they are interviewing. Emerging work is starting to explore how vulnerable suspects, particularly those with mental health conditions and disorders should best be interviewed.

Interviewing Vulnerable Suspects: Developing Insights

Despite the acknowledgement that vulnerable individuals face challenges when completing a suspect interview, there remains a lack of research that has explored alternative interview techniques for this population, especially when one considers the research work exploring this with vulnerable witnesses (see Chapter 4). The work of Farrugia and Gabbert (2020) is perhaps one of the first attempts in England and Wales to consider the use of an alternative or modified interview model with adult suspects that have mental health conditions and disorders. Their work aimed to experimentally test two different interview models with a vulnerable population; a best practice interview containing largely open questions, and a modified interview that contained largely specific and closed questions. The focus was to explore which interview model elicited the most amount of investigation relevant information and the most accurate, and thus which one was the most appropriate for suspects with mental health conditions and disorders. By experimentally placing 108 participants within a suspect context, and obtaining the services of a serving police officer, the researchers were able to somewhat replicate a real-life suspect interview and analyse the findings. Results highlighted that those with mental health conditions and disorders tended to provide more information during the modified interview than the best practice interview, whereas the non-vulnerable participants provided more information when asked open questions during the best practice interview. Furthermore, the vulnerable suspects also provided more accurate information during the modified interview compared to the best practice interview. In addition, and in line with previous research, those with vulnerabilities sought more clarification when asked open questions.

Thus, the findings from Farrugia and Gabbert (2020) are interesting and challenge what currently constitutes best practice interviewing in England and Wales for vulnerable suspects. Whilst the general consensus is that the use of open and probing questions elicit more detailed and accurate information when compared to closed questions (Oxburgh et al., 2010a; Snook et al., 2012), vulnerable suspects in their sample tended to provide a higher level of information and more accurate information to the modified interview, which contained closed questions. This is not surprising given that it is becoming increasingly clear that vulnerable suspects do not respond well to traditional policing tactics (Farrugia & Gabbert, 2019; Gudjonsson, 2018), and is line with earlier pieces of work (Bowles & Sharman, 2014; Perlman et al., 1994; Ternes & Yuille, 2008). This is also the case when one considers vulnerable witnesses (see Chapter 4). Further work is continuing to explore this with vulnerable suspects based on specific difficulties, such as those with an Autism Spectrum Condition, and is yet to be published.

Summary

Interviewing a vulnerable suspect is not an easy task (Herrington & Roberts, 2012), but is an important one given the implications that their account may have for criminal justice outcomes. Initially, police officers in England and Wales endorsed popular interrogation techniques such as those used in the United States. The Reid Interrogation Technique (Inbau et al., 2013) encourages investigators to use manipulative and coercive techniques to seek a confession rather than a search for the truth. Given the lack of training and guidance in England and Wales prior to the 1980s, these were also the methods used for interviewing suspects, including those who were vulnerable.

Unsurprisingly, what followed was a number of false confessions and miscarriages of justice; it was the acquittal of the three youths' in the Maxwell Confait case that triggered a full inquiry chaired by Sir Henry Fisher into the impact of the interview process in causing false confessions and miscarriages of justice (Price & Caplan, 1977). What followed soon after was the introduction of a legislative framework for all police powers in England and Wales (as per PACE, 1984; Home Office, 2018) and a new interview model designed to search for the truth and move away from the confession seeking ethos previously encouraged.

Those trained in the PEACE model of interviewing are encouraged to following the five stages and use an 'investigative mindset' when conducting interviews with all victims, witnesses, and suspects. To date, research findings have been mixed although they suggest an overall improvement in interview style compared to previously used interrogation techniques.

However, there remains work to be done when one considers vulnerable suspects. Depending on the type of vulnerability the individual may present with can depend on the difficulties they may encounter during the police interview. Whilst the current interview model encourages the use of open questions as best practice, there is an emerging branch of research that suggests this may not be entirely suitable for vulnerable suspects. Whilst this research, however, is in its primacy, the implications for the police interview must be acknowledged and considered; best practice may not always be best practice for those who are vulnerable. The investigative interviewing of vulnerable individuals is not the only stage where consideration must be given to how vulnerable individuals are treated; the vulnerable witness and the vulnerable defendant at trial is the focus of the subsequent two chapters.

Key Learning Points

- Vulnerable suspects do not respond well to traditional methods of policing; their vulnerabilities during the interview must be considered in light of their communicative abilities and the impact on the interview and justice outcomes.
- Prior to the 1980s in England and Wales, police officers frequently used coercive and manipulative techniques, similar to those used in interrogation practices around the world.
- The Reid Interrogation Technique is one of the most influential and common methods still used in parts of the world. It includes a Behaviour Analysis Interview (BAI) used to determine if a suspect is guilty, before moving onto the nine-step interrogation technique. This has led to a number of high-profile false confessions and miscarriages of justice.
- False confessions were not widely discussed until the early 1980s. The work of Kassin and Wrightsman (1985) is commonly used when classifying false confessions.
- The impact of the interview process in causing false confessions and miscarriages of justice was highlighted within the Maxwell Confait case. This led to the Fisher Inquiry (1977) and the subsequent Royal Commission on Criminal Procedure in England and Wales (1981).
- The introduction of the Police and Criminal Evidence Act (PACE, 1984; Home Office, 2018) and its associated Codes of Practice provided a legislative framework for the use of police powers in England and Wales; these included arrest, detention and the investigation and interviewing of all suspects, including those that are vulnerable.
- Amid concerns over ineffective interviewing, a steering group developed an interview model aimed at offering a more effective and ethical alternative to the interrogation techniques previously used; known as PEACE, the model was developed and introduced to police officers in England and Wales.
- Whilst much progress has been made in interviewing vulnerable suspects, there remains a lack of research in examining alternative interview models for this population. Further work must address the fact that best practice may not always be the best practice for vulnerable suspects.

References

Airaksinen, E., Larsson, M., & Forsell, Y. (2005). Neuropsychological functions in anxiety disorders in population-based samples: Evidence of episodic memory dysfunction. *Journal of Psychiatric Research*, *39*, 207–214.

American Psychiatric Association (APA). (2013). *Diagnostic and Statistical Manual of Mental Disorders (DSM-5)*. https://www.psychiatry.org/psychiatrists/practice/dsm

Baldwin, J. (1992). *Video-taping police interviews with suspects – An evaluation*. Home Office.

Beail, N. (2002). Interrogative suggestibility, memory and intellectual disability. *Journal of Applied Research in Intellectual Disabilities*, *15*, 129–137.

Beevers, C., & Carver, C. (2003). Attentional bias and mood persistence as prospective predictors of dysphoria. *Cognitive Therapy and Research*, *27*, 619–637.

Benia, L., Hauck-Filho, N., Dillenburg, M., & Stein, L. (2015). The NICHD investigative interview protocol: A meta-analytic review. *Journal of Child Sexual Abuse*, *24*(3), 259–279.

Birckhead, T. (2008). The age of the child: Interrogating juveniles after *roper v. Simmons. Washington and Lee Law Review*, *65*, 385–450.
Bowles, P., & Sharman, S. (2014). A review of the impact of different types of leading interview questions on child and adult witnesses with intellectual disabilities. *Psychiatry, Psychology and Law*, *21*(2), 205–217.
Bruck, M., & Melnyk, L. (2004). Individual differences in children's suggestibility: A review and synthesis. *Applied Cognitive Psychology*, *18*, 947–996.
Burki, T. (2017). Crisis in UK prison mental health. *The Lancet Psychiatry*, *4*(12), P904.
Clarke, C., & Milne, R. (2001). *National evaluation of the PEACE investigative interviewing course. Police research award scheme, report no. PRAS/149*. Institute of Criminal Justice Studies.
Cleary, H. (2014). Police interviewing and interrogation of juvenile suspects: Descriptive examination of actual cases. *Law and Human Behaviour*, *38*(3), 271–282.
College of Policing. (2020). *Investigative interviewing*. https://www.college.police.uk/app/investigation/investigative-interviewing/investigative-interviewing
College of Policing. (2021). *Principles and ethics*. https://www.college.police.uk/app/investigation/investigation-introduction#pip
Cusack, A. (2020). Beyond special measures: Challenging traditional constructions of competence and cross-examination for vulnerable witnesses in Ireland. *Irish Judicial Studies Journal*, *4*(2), 98–115.
Davis, D., & Leo, R. (2012). Interrogation-related regulatory decline: Ego depletion, failures of self-regulation, and the decision to confess. *Psychology, Public Policy, and Law*, *18*(4), 673–704.
Drake, K. (2014). The role of trait anxiety in the association between the reporting of negative life events and interrogative suggestibility. *Personality and Individual Differences*, *60*, 54–59.
Drizin, S. A., & Luloff, G. (2007). Are juvenile courts a breeding ground for wrongful convictions? *Northern Kentucky Law Review*, *34*, 257–322.
Drizin, S., & Leo, R. (2004). The problem of false confessions in the post-DNA world. *North Carolina Law Review*, *82*, 891–1007.
Eysenck, M., Derakshan, N., Santos, R., & Calvo, M. (2007). Anxiety and cognitive performance: Attentional control theory. *Emotion*, *7*, 336–353.
Farrugia, L., & Gabbert, F. (2019). Vulnerable suspects in police interviews: Exploring current practice in England and Wales. *Journal of Investigative Psychology and Offender Profiling*, *17*(1), 17–30.
Farrugia, L., & Gabbert, F. (2020). Forensic interviewing of mentally disordered suspects: The impact of interview style on investigation outcomes. *Current Psychology*, *41*(11). https://www.researchgate.net/publication/342107311_Forensic_interviewing_of_mentally_disordered_suspects_the_impact_of_interview_style_on_investigation_outcomes
Farrugia, L., & Milne, R. (2012). Suspect interviewing and mental health in the UK: An overview. *Investigative Interviewing: Research and Practice*, *4*(2), 25–42.
Farrugia, L., Oxburgh, G., & Gabbert, F. (2019). Effective evaluation of forensic interviews: The Forensic Interview Trace (FIT)©. *Investigative Interviewing: Research and Practice*, *10*(1), 20–31.
Farrugia, L., Oxburgh, G., & Gabbert, F. (2022). Evaluating process. *Police Professional*. https://www.policeprofessional.com/feature/evaluating-process/
Feld, B. C. (2006a). Juveniles' competence to exercise *Miranda* rights: An empirical study of policy and practice. *Minnesota Law Review*, *91*, 26–100.
Feld, B. C. (2006b). Police interrogation of juveniles: An empirical study of policy and practice. *Journal of Criminal Law and Criminology*, *97*, 219–316.
Feld, B. C. (2013). *Kids, cops, and confessions: Inside the interrogation room*. NYU Press.
Fisher, H. (1977). *Report of an inquiry by the Hon. Sir Henry Fisher into the circumstances leading to the trial of three persons on charges arising out of the death of Maxwell Confait and the fire at 27 Doggett Road, London, SE6*. HMSO.
Fisher, R., Geiselman, R., & Raymond, D. (1987). Critical analysis of police interview techniques. *Journal of Police Science and Administration*, *3*, 177–185.
Gabbert, F., Hope, L., Luther, K., Wright, G., Ng, M., & Oxburgh, G. (2020). Exploring the use of rapport in professional information-gathering contexts by systematically mapping the evidence base. *Applied Cognitive Psychology*, *35*(2), 329–341.

Garrett, B. (2010). The substance of false confessions. *Stanford Law Review, 62*, 1051–1119.
Goldstein, N. E., Condie, L. O., Kalbeitzer, R., Osman, D., & Geier, J. L. (2003). Juvenile offenders' *Miranda* rights comprehension and self-reported likelihood of offering false confessions. *Assessment, 10*, 359–369.
Gotlib, I., & Joorman, J. (2010). Cognition and depression: Current status and future directions. *Annual Review of Clinical Psychology, 6*, 285–312.
Granhag, P., Vrij, A., & Verschuere, B. (2015). *Detecting deception: Current challenges and cognitive approaches*. Wiley-Blackwell.
Grisso, T. (2000). What we know about youths' capacities as trial defendants. In T. Grisso & R. G. Schwartz (Eds.), *Youth on trial: A developmental perspective on juvenile justice* (pp. 139–1711). University of Chicago Press.
Grisso, T., Steinberg, L., Woolard, J., Cauffman, E., Scott, E., Graham, S., Lexcen, F., Reppucci, N. D., & Schwartz, R. (2003). Juveniles' competence to stand trial: A comparison of adolescents' and adults' capacities as trial defendants. *Law and Human Behaviour, 27*(4), 333–363.
Gudjonsson, G. (1990). The relationship of intellectual skills to suggestibility, compliance and acquiescence. *Personality and Individual Differences, 11*(3), 227–231.
Gudjonsson, G. (1992). *The psychology of interrogations, confessions and testimony*. Wiley.
Gudjonsson, G. (2003). *The psychology of interrogations and confessions. A handbook*. Wiley.
Gudjonsson, G. (2018). *The psychology of false confessions: Forty years of science and practice*. John Wiley & Sons Ltd.
Gudjonsson, G., & Clark, N. (1986). Suggestibility in police interrogation: A social psychological model. *British Journal of Psychiatry, 41*, 624–627.
Gudjonsson, G. H., & Joyce, T. (2011). Interviewing adults with intellectual disabilities. *Advances in Mental Health and Intellectual Disabilities, 5*, 16–21.
Gudjonsson, G., & Pearse, J. (2011). Suspect interviews and false confessions. *Current Directions in Psychological Science, 20*(1), 33–37.
Gudjonsson, G., & Sigurdsson, J. (2010). The relationship of compliance with inattention and hyperactivity/impulsivity. *Personality and Individual Differences, 49*(6), 651–654.
Gulati, G., Murphy, V., Clarke, A., Delcellier, K., Meagher, D., Kennedy, H., Fistein, E., Bogue, J., & Dunne, C. P. (2018). Intellectual disability in Irish prisoners: Systematic review of prevalence. *International Journal of Prisoner Health, 14*(3), 188–196.
Hartwig, M., & Bond Jr (2011). Why do lie-catchers fail? A lens model meta-analysis of human lie judgments. *Psychological Bulletin, 137*(4), 643–659.
Herrington, V., & Roberts, K. (2012). Addressing psychological vulnerability in the police suspect interview. *Policing, 6*, 1–10.
Herrnstein, R., Rachlin, H., & Laibson, D. (1997). *The matching law. Papers in psychology and economics*. Harvard University Press.
Hertel, P. (1998). Relation between rumination and impaired memory in dysphoric moods. *Journal of Abnormal Psychology, 107*, 166–172.
Hertel, P. (2004). Memory for emotional and nonemotional events in depression: A question of habit. In D. Reisberg & P. Hertel (Eds.), *Memory and emotion* (pp. 186–216). Oxford University Press.
Holmes, J. (2002). Interpersonal expectations as the building blocks of social cognition: An interdependence theory perspective. *Personal Relationships, 9*, 1–26.
Home Office. (1981). *Royal commission on criminal procedure*. HMSO.
Home Office. (2018). *Police and Criminal Evidence Act (1984)*. Home Office.
Horselenberg, R., Merckelbach, H., Sweets, T., Franssens, D., Peters, G., & Zeles, G. (2006). False confessions in the lab: Do plausibility and consequences matter? *Psychology, Crime and Law, 12*, 61–75.
Inbau, F., Reid, J., Buckley, J., & Jayne, B. (2013). *Criminal interrogation and confessions*. Jones & Bartlett Learning.
Irving, B. (1980). *Police interrogation: A case study of current practice. Royal Commission on Criminal Procedure, Research Study no. 2*. HMSO.
Kassin, S., Drizin, S., Grisso, T., Gudjonsson, G., Leo, R., & Redlich, A. (2010). Police induced confessions: Risk factors and recommendations. *Law and Human Behaviour, 34*, 3–38.

Kassin, S., & Wrightsman, L. (1985). Confession evidence. In S. Kassin & L. Wrightsman (Eds.), *The psychology of evidence and trial procedure* (pp. 67–94). Sage.

Kelly, C., & Meissner, C. (2016). Interrogation and investigative interviewing in the United States: Research and practice. In D. Walsh, G. Oxburgh, A. Redlich, & T. Myklebust (Eds.), *International developments and practices in investigative interviewing and interrogation: Volume 2, suspects* (pp. 255–266). Routledge.

Kingdon, D., & Turkington, D. (2005). *Cognitive therapy for schizophrenia.* Guildford.

Lemogne, C., Piolino, P., Friszer, S., Claret, A., Girault, N., Jouvent, R., Allilaire, J., & Fossati, P. (2006). Episodic autobiographical memory in depression: Specificity, autonoetic consciousness, and self-perspective. *Consciousness and Cognition, 15*, 258–268.

Leo, R. A. (2009). False confessions: Causes, consequences, and implications. *The Journal of the American Academy of Psychiatry and the Law, 37*, 332–343.

Lindstrom, B., & Bohlin, G. (2012). Threat-relevance impairs executive functions: Negative impact on working memory and response inhibition. *Emotion, 12*, 384–393.

Macleod, C., & Mathews, A. (2012). Cognitive bias modification approaches to anxiety. *Annual Review of Clinical Psychology, 8*, 189–217.

Madon, S., Guyll, M., Scherr, K., Greathouse, S., & Wells, G. (2012). Temporal discounting: The differential effect of proximal and distal consequences on confession decisions. *Law and Human Behaviour, 36*(1), 13–20.

Mann, S., Vrij, A., & Bull, R. (2004). Detecting true lies: Police officers' ability to detect deceit. *Journal of Applied Psychology, 89*, 137–149.

Maroney, T. (2009). The false promise of adolescent brain science in juvenile justice. *The Notre Dame Law Review, 85*, 89–176.

Masip, J., & Herrero, C. (2013). What would you say if you were guilty? Suspects strategies during a hypothetical behaviour analysis interview concerning a serious crime. *Applied Cognitive Psychology, 27*(1), 60–70.

Mathews, A., & MacLeod, C. (2005). Cognitive vulnerability to emotional disorders. *Annual Review of Clinical Psychology, 1*, 167–195.

McGurk, B. J., Carr, M. J., & McGurk, D. (1993). *Investigative interviewing courses for police officers: An evaluation* (Police Research Series Paper 4). Police Research Group, The Home Office.

Meissner, C., Kelly, C., & Woestehoff, S. (2014). Improving the effectiveness of suspect interrogations. *Annual Review of Law & Social Science, 11*(1), 211–233.

Mencap. (2020). *How common is learning disability?* Retrieved November 1, 2023, from https://www.mencap.org.uk/learning-disability-explained/research-and-statistics/how-common-learning-disability

Mendez, J. (2021). *Principles on effective interviewing for investigations and information gathering.*

Morrison, J., Forrester-Jones, R., Bradshaw, J., & Murphy, G. (2019). Communication and cross-examination in court for children and adults with intellectual disabilities: A systematic review. *International Journal of Evidence and Proof, 23*(4), 366–398.

Münsterberg, H. (1908). *On the witness stand: Essays on psychology and crime.* Forgotten Books.

Murphy, G. (2019). People with intellectual and/or developmental disabilities in the criminal justice system. *Journal of Intellectual Disability Research, 63*(7), 631.

Office for National Statistics (2021). *Coronavirus and depression in adults, great Britain: July to August 2021.* Office for National Statistics.

Ofshe, R. (1989). Coerced confessions: The logic of seemingly irrational action. *Cultic Studies Journal, 6*, 1–15.

Ofshe, R., & Leo, R. (1997). The social psychology of police interrogation. The theory and classification of true and false confessions. *Studies in Law, Politics and Society, 16*, 189–251.

Oxburgh, L., Gabbert, F., Milne, R., & Cherryman, J. (2016). Police officers' perceptions and experiences with MD suspects. *International Journal of Law and Psychiatry, 49*, 138–146.

Oxburgh, G., Myklebust, T., & Grant, T. (2010a). The question of question types in police interviews: A review of the literature from a psychological and linguistic perspective. *International Journal of Speech, Language and the Law, 17*, 45–66.

Oxburgh, G., & Ost, J. (2011). The use and efficacy of empathy in police interviews with suspects of sexual offences. *Journal of Investigative Psychology and Offender Profiling*, *8*, 178–188.

Oxburgh, G., Ost, J., & Cherryman, J. (2010b). Police interviews with suspected child sex offenders: Does use of empathy and question type influence the amount of investigation relevant information obtained? *Psychology, Crime and Law*, 1–15.

Perlman, N., Ericson, K., Esses, V., & Isaacs, B. (1994). The developmentally handicapped witness: Competency as a function of question format. *Law and Human Behaviour*, *18*, 171–187.

Price, C., & Caplan, J. (1977). *The Confait confessions*. Boyars.

Rachlin, H. (2000). *The science of self-control*. Harvard University Press.

Redlich, A. (2004). Mental illness, police interrogations, and the potential for false confession. *Law and Psychiatry*, *55*, 19–21.

Redlich, A. D., & Goodman, G. S. (2003). Taking responsibility for an act not committed: The influence of age and suggestibility. *Law and Human Behaviour*, *27*, 141–156.

Reyna, V. F., & Farley, F. (2006). Risk and rationality in adolescent decision making: Implications for theory, practice, and public policy. *Psychological Science in the Public Interest*, *7*, 1–44.

Robinson, O., Vytal, K., Cornwell, B., & Grillon, C. (2013). The impact of anxiety upon cognition: Perspectives from human threat of shock studies. *Frontiers in Human Neuroscience*, *7*, 1–20.

Rude, S., Wenzlaff, R., Gibbs, B., Vane, J., & Whitney, T. (2002). Negative processing biases predict subsequent depressive symptoms. *Cognition and Emotion*, *16*, 423–440.

Schatz, S. J. (2018). Interrogated with intellectual disabilities: The risks of false confession. *Stanford Law Review*, *70*(2), 643–690.

Scott, E., & Steinberg, L. (2008). *Rethinking juvenile justice*. Harvard University Press.

Shepherd, E. (1991). Ethical interviewing. *Policing*, 7(1), 42–60.

Shepherd, E. (2007). *Investigative interviewing: The conversation management approach*. Oxford University Press.

Sirdifield, C., & Brooker, C. (2012). Detainees in police custody: Results of a health needs assessment in Northumbria, England. *International Journal of Prisoner Health*, *8*, 60–67.

Snook, B., Luther, K., Quinlan, H., & Milne, R. (2012). Let 'em talk! A field study of police questioning practices of suspects and accused persons. *Criminal Justice and Behaviour*, *39*(10), 1328–1339.

Soukara, S., Bull, R., Vrij, A., Turner, M., & Cherryman, J. (2009). What really happens in police interviews of suspects? Tactics and confessions. *Psychology, Crime and Law*, *15*, 493–506.

Steinberg, L. (2004). Risk taking in adolescence: What changes, and why? *Annals of the New York Academy of Sciences*, *1021*, 51–58.

Stewart, J., Woody, W., & Pulos, S. (2018). The prevalence of false confessions in experimental laboratory simulations: A meta-analysis. *Behavioural Sciences and the Law*, *36*(1), 12–31.

Synnott, J., Dietzel, D., & Ioannou, M. (2015). A review of the polygraph: History, methodology, and current status. *Crime Psychology Review*, *1*, 59–83.

Tepfer, J., Nirider, L., & Tricarico, L. (2010). Arresting development: Convictions of innocent youth. *Rutgers Law Review*, *62*, 887–941.

Ternes, M., & Yuille, J. (2008). Eyewitness memory and eyewitness identification performance in adults with intellectual disabilities. *Journal of Applied Research in Intellectual Disabilities*, *21*, 519–531.

Tyler, N., Miles, H., Karadag, B., & Rogers, G. (2019). An updated picture of the mental health needs of male and female prisoners in the UK: Prevalence, comorbidity, and gender differences. *Social Psychiatry and Psychiatric Epidemiology*, *54*, 1143–1152.

Vagni, M., Maiorano, T., & Giostra, V. (2021). The relationship between suggestibility, fabrication, distortion, and trauma in suspected sexually abused children. *Social Sciences*, *10*, 37–52.

Vrij, A., Fisher, R., & Blank, H. (2017). A cognitive approach to lie detection: A meta- analysis. *Legal and Criminological Psychology*, *22*(1), 1–21.

Vrij, A., Mann, S., & Fisher, R. (2006). Information-gathering vs accusatory interview style: Individual differences in respondents' experiences. *Personality and Individual Differences*, *41*, 589–599.

Vrij, A., Mann, S., Kristen, S., & Fisher, R. (2007). Cues to deception and ability to detect lies as a function of police interview styles. *Law and Human Behaviour*, *31*, 499–518.

Walkley, J. (1987). *Police interrogation: A handbook for investigators*. Police Review Publication.
Williams, J. (1996). Depression and the specificity of autobiographical memory. In D. Rubin (Ed.), *Remembering our past: Studies in autobiographical memory* (pp. 244–267). Cambridge University Press.
Williams, J., Barnhofer, T., Crane, C., Herman, D., & Raes, F. (2007). Autobiographical memory specificity and emotional disorder. *Psychological Bulletin*, *133*, 122–148.
Williamson, T. (1993). Review and prospect. In P. Matias (Ed.), *Aspects of police interviewing* The British Psychological Society.
Williamson, T. (2006). *Investigative interviewing: Rights, research, regulation*. Willan.
Williamson, T. (2007). Psychology and criminal investigation. In T. Newburn, T. Williamson, & A. Wright (Eds.), *Handbook of criminal investigation* (pp. 68–91). Willan.
Woolard, J. L., Cleary, H. M. D., Harvell, S., & Chen, A. S. (2008). Examining adolescents' and their parents' conceptual and practical knowledge of police interrogation: A family dyad approach. *Journal of Youth and Adolescence*, *37*, 685–698.
Wright, R., & Powell, M. (2006). Investigative interviewers' perceptions of their difficulty to adhere to open-ended questions with child witnesses. *International Journal of Police Science and Management*, *8*, 316–325.
Young, S., Goodwin, E., Sedgwick, O., & Gudjonsson, G. (2013). The effectiveness of police custody assessments in identifying suspects with intellectual disabilities and attention deficit hyperactivity disorder. *BMC Medicine*, *11*, 248–259.

6 Vulnerable Witnesses at Trial

Introduction

Traditionally, children were not seen as being reliable victims or witnesses (herein referred to as witnesses) – indeed, they were so mistrusted that that juries were warned of relying on their evidence at trial, especially if their evidence was uncorroborated (Burton et al., 2006). Other vulnerable groups of witnesses such as those with physical disabilities, a Learning Disability or mental health conditions were similarly regarded by the criminal justice system (CJS). However, it is also these groups of individuals that are particularly vulnerable to being victims of crime and are likely to experience heightened stress when giving their evidence at trial (Morris, 1999; Sanders et al., 1997). Despite being met with untrustworthiness at trial, in the earlier stages of the investigation, police officers were being urged to recognise the special needs of such vulnerable groups in order to obtain their evidence (Burton et al., 2006). In addition to vulnerable witnesses, it was being recognised that some groups of witnesses were being particularly badly treated within the justice system. For example, victims of sexual offences, frequently experienced re-traumatisation during the process of being cross-examined and by having their ordeals being made public at trial (Burton et al., 2006). Thus, it was regularly observed that the CJS took little heed of the needs and concerns of vulnerable witnesses (Burton et al., 2006).

However, from around the 1970s onwards, concerns for vulnerable witnesses started to grow. For example, Victim Support services developed to provide support and specialised services to all witnesses, and the Witness Service is now situated in all Magistrates and Crown Courts in England and Wales and have played a pivotal role in policy-making and lobbying to improve the services provided to all witnesses (Rock, 2004). Thus, considerations for how best to treat vulnerable witnesses (including intimidated witnesses) were being acknowledged and have come a long way from the early 1970s. This is where the chapter shall focus. Starting with the development and implementation of Special Measures, the chapter shall consider how each Special Measure can assist a vulnerable or intimidated witness at trial and explore the move away from traditional cross-examination to the use of Special Measures at trial. The recently implemented s.28 pre-recorded cross-examination will be considered and key pieces of research and governmental reports will be examined when exploring if Special Measures are effective for the vulnerable witness at trial. Case examples will be used throughout.

The Introduction of Special Measures

Decisions to prosecute in England and Wales (and similar international jurisdictions) are made by law enforcement agencies; in England and Wales, those decisions lie with the police and the Crown Prosecution Service (CPS). In order to decide if a case is to be continued,

DOI: 10.4324/9781003386735-6

the CPS consider whether the prosecution is in the best interests of the public, and whether there is a reasonable likelihood of success. The government is under constant pressure to help secure and increase rates of conviction, whilst also ensuring that miscarriages of justice are avoided (Burton et al., 2006). Thus, it is imperative that those who are vulnerable are able to contribute to the justice system in an effective manner in order to provide their best evidence.

It was not until the late 1990s, that the new government made a commitment to those who are vulnerable to provide them with greater support and assistance. Consequently, an inter-departmental working group was set up to undertake a wide-ranging review. Their report, 'Speaking Up for Justice' (Home Office, 1998) highlighted that 2–3% of all adult prosecutions would be intimidated and that 5–7% would be vulnerable, resulting in a total of approximately 10% of all adult prosecutions involving a vulnerable or intimidated witness in some sense. The report made 78 recommendations in order to improve the way in which vulnerable or intimidated witnesses were dealt with by the justice system and to ensure that they are provided with assistance to give their best evidence at trial. The report also endorsed the arguments that many of the earlier reforms made for children could be equally applicable to other vulnerable and intimidated groups, and the report identified three models on which to found the basis of support. The categorical approach by which specific categories, such as those who have a Learning Disability or a mental health condition, are defined as eligible, although there have been many discussions regarding the rigidity of this model (see, e.g., Sanders et al., 1997). The second model is to assess whether a witness has characteristics such as communication difficulties, and thus provide them with the support that they need. However, such an open-ended approach, whilst allowing for inclusiveness, could lead to delays and an ever-widening pool of eligible witnesses (Burton et al., 2006). The third model is to combine the previous two – that is, with some vulnerable groups such as those with a Learning Disability, or mental health condition or disorder, there would be a presumption of vulnerability, but with other groups, they would need to meet a threshold determined by a Judge. That threshold is based on a three-stage test:

1. Is the witness potentially vulnerable or intimidated?
2. If so, is that vulnerability or intimidation likely to affect their ability and willingness to give their best evidence in Court, and to cause them undue stress?
3. If so, what type of support is most likely to assist?

The 'Speaking Up for Justice' report recommended the third model, and the Government later adopted it in the Youth Justice and Criminal Evidence Act (1999). The aim was to help secure convictions whilst reducing the stress of vulnerable witnesses giving their evidence (Home Office, 1998).

However, before the vulnerable or intimidated witness can receive the assistance they require when going to trial, they must first be identified as vulnerable. Whilst estimates were made in the inter-departmental working group regarding vulnerable and intimidated witnesses, the reality is that this is likely to be much higher. For example, the report identifies that between five to ten times those numbers may be involved in a police interview (Home Office, 1998), with earlier research indicating that the vast majority of vulnerable witnesses are in fact victims (Sanders et al., 1997). Furthermore, the estimates provided in the report are provided by the criminal justice agencies, in particular the police. It is well established that the police have difficulties in identifying vulnerability and that there is no accepted or consistent approach to the assessment of a vulnerable witness and their competence to engage in the justice process in England and Wales (Farrugia & Maras, 2023). Indeed, one of the most significant problems in the justice system is the difficulty in identifying vulnerable witnesses (see Cooper & Roberts, 2005; Ewin, 2015; McLeod et al., 2010; Tekin & Tekin, 2015). Thus, this can lead to vulnerable individuals being left without the necessary support when giving their evidence (Asquith, 2012). For a full discussion of identifying vulnerability, see Chapter 2.

Many scholars highlight how the justice system is heavily reliant on the ability of a trust between the witness and the trial process (Cook & Tattersall, 2010; Ewin, 2016). The Youth Justice and Criminal Evidence Act (YJCEA, 1999) was created to assist in developing that trust. Many of the recommendations in the 'Speaking Up for Justice' report included measures to assist vulnerable witness – these were introduced under the YJCEA (1999) and are known as 'Special Measures' (Ewin, 2016). Such measures are a support mechanism designed to alleviate the fear and distress associated with giving evidence, which is exacerbated by vulnerability, and to enable vulnerable witnesses to give their best evidence using measures to assist them, when they may have been too afraid to do so in ordinary circumstances (Birch, 2000). In order for a vulnerable witness to receive Special Measures, an application is made to the Court (Durston, 2011) and is considered on an individual basis. The Special Measures available for vulnerable and intimidated witnesses include:

- Screening from the defendant (s.23)
- Evidence by video live link (s.24)
- Evidence given in private (s.25)
- Removal of wigs and gowns (s.26)
- Video recorded evidence-in-chief (s.27)
- Video recorded cross-examination (s.28)
- Examination of witness through intermediary (s.29)
- Aids to communication (s.30)

In addition, a number of administrative measures are included in the YJCEA (1999) and are available to vulnerable and intimidated witnesses. These include the completion of a pre-trial familiarisation visit, presence of a support in Court, the use of escorts to and from Court, Liaison officers, separate waiting areas (typically handled by the Witness Service team) and the use of pagers. These will now be explored in further detail.

Administrative Measures

> 'I was scared about it until I went to look round and then it made me feel more comfortable' (14-year-old witness; Plotnikoff & Woolfson, 2009).

The Witness Charter entitles all witnesses to visit the Court they are giving their evidence at before trial (Ministry of Justice, 2013). Visits are usually conducted by the Witness Service team; the vulnerable or intimidated witness meet the usher who is likely to be assisting them on the day they give their evidence, and they are shown around the courtroom and any facilities they will be using, for example, the use of a video link room, whilst being provided with a full explanation of what to expect when they attend trial to give their evidence. Research has shown that 67% of vulnerable and intimidated witnesses found pre-trial familiarisation visits to be the most useful form of support (Burton et al., 2006). This has been echoed by more recent work (Plotnikoff & Woolfson, 2015).

The right to a fair trial under the European Convention on Human Rights under Article 6, includes the right of defendants to examine witnesses against him/her. Thus, the idea of being confronted by the defendant, their family or supporters before, during and after the trial has been noted to be one of the biggest fears of all witnesses (Tekin & Tekin, 2015). In order to prevent the negative effects and consequences of these kinds of confrontations, and the trauma resulting from giving evidence in the courtroom, the use of separate waiting areas was introduced (Kirby et al., 2013). In addition, vulnerable and intimidated witnesses are able to access the Court building from which they will give their evidence from separate entrances to ensure that there is no contact with the defendant or their family and supporters. Typically, these administrative measures work well in conjunction with the Special Measures granted by the Court.

Special Measures

Although a witness may have been identified as vulnerable or intimidated and is, therefore, eligible for Special Measures, the application must be made by prosecution counsel to the Court and be approved by the Judge (Burton et al., 2006). One of the Special Measures available to this group of witnesses is being screened from the defendant (YJCEA, 1999, s.23). This ensures that should the witness wish to give their evidence from the courtroom, they are screened from the defendant whilst they provide their evidence and thus cannot be seen. The purpose of the screens, therefore, is to provide a suitable environment for the witness whilst they give their evidence in a courtroom, thus reducing the impact of the defendant and their presence on the witness giving their evidence (Tekin & Tekin, 2015). Whilst this is a Special Measure under the YJCEA (1999), screening arrangements can vary from Court to Court. For example, in some Courts, the screens are permanent which ensure that the witness is protected from the sight of the defendant on entering and exiting the courtroom in addition to being in the witness box and giving their evidence. In other Courts, the screen may be a curtain and so may not protect the witness from the sight of the defendant once outside of the witness box. In these circumstances, the witness is often placed into the witness box and protected with the use of the screen prior to the defendant entering the dock; once the witness has concluded their evidence, the defendant will be removed from the dock before the screen is removed from the witness to ensure that the witness and defendant do not see each other. Research exploring the use of screens for vulnerable and intimidated witnesses is minimal; however, of the work that has been conducted, it appears that this Special Measure is rarely used. Hamlyn et al. (2004) found that in phase 1 of their work exploring the use of Special Measures, only 8% of vulnerable and intimidated witnesses used this measure, with only a slight increase to 15% in phase 2 of their work a short whilst later.

Giving evidence by video live link is another Special Measure available to vulnerable and intimidated witnesses (YJCEA, 1999, s.24). This allows the witness to give their evidence in a trial from outside of the courtroom through a video link to the courtroom, thus all those present in the courtroom (including the defendant) will be able to see the witness, but the witness is only likely to see the Judge and counsel asking them questions. In using this Special Measure, the witness is normally in a room in another part of the Court building, although there are some provisions whereby Courts have a 'remote' video link outside of the building, from which the witness can provide their evidence (Burton et al., 2006). Thus, by using this method, the witness is not exposed to the defendant's verbal or non-verbal reactions and the witness is in an environment much less intimidating than the courtroom (Tekin & Tekin, 2015). This method of providing evidence has been reported as preferable by child witnesses, although findings overall have been mixed. For example, in early research, Davies and Noon (1991) conducted an evaluation of the video link Special Measure in England and Wales. They reported that those children who were giving evidence via video live link were happier, more audible, and more forthcoming in their evidence, compared to child witnesses who provided their evidence without the use of a video live link. However, other research has suggested that some child witnesses did not find it helpful (Hamlyn et al., 2004), and that others would have preferred to have given their evidence in the courtroom (Plotnikoff & Woolfson, 2004). That said, the use of the video live link is used significantly more by vulnerable and intimidated witnesses than the use of screens; 38% compared to 8% respectively (Home Office, 2004). Thus, whilst it may not always be to the satisfaction of the witness, it is this Special Measure that is more frequently used.

Another Special Measure involves the witness giving their evidence in private (YJCEA, 1999, s.25). Whilst many Courts allow for members of the public and press to be in the public gallery during the trial, where this Special Measure is granted, the Judge will vacate the courtroom's public gallery except for one nominated press member (Tekin & Tekin, 2015). This measure is typically allowed when the witness is victim of a sexual offence or where the witness feels intimidated by another individual other than the defendant. However, research has reported an 'unease' with this Special Measure, as it is seen to conflict with the principle of 'open justice' (Burton et al., 2006). Furthermore, whilst this ensures that very few individuals can hear the evidence given by the witness, and thus they may feel less embarrassment and intimidation, vacating the public gallery means that the vulnerable or intimidated witness will not have their own supporters present when they give their evidence (Smith & Tilney, 2007) and therefore, may feel under-supported. Hamlyn et al. (2004) found that the public gallery was cleared in approximately 10% of the cases they examined, although a further 26% of vulnerable and intimidated witnesses indicated that they would have liked this when they were giving evidence. Furthermore, Hamlyn et al. (2004) also reported that those who were not afforded this Special Measure but would have liked it, were frequently more dissatisfied than those witnesses who opted not to have the public gallery cleared; 49% compared to 28% respectively.

The removal of wigs and gowns is a significant Special Measure (YJCEA, 1999, s.26) and is often granted to minimise the formality of the Court environment and the subsequent pressure and distress as a result. Whilst this measure is typically used with children given that research has suggested the negative impact that formality can have on their ability to provide their best evidence (Flin, 1990), other groups of vulnerable and intimidated witnesses are also eligible for this measure and find it helpful (Tekin & Tekin, 2015). However, removing the wigs and gowns from the trial Judge and counsel is not always helpful. Research has suggested that for individuals with a Learning Disability for example, *not* seeing the wigs and gowns can be disappointing, as the formality of Court may be preferred so that witness can feel that they have had 'their day in a proper court' (Smith & Tilney, 2007, p. 66). In addition, this Special Measure, was reported by many criminal justice agencies to be the most ineffective measure (Burton et al., 2006). Such practitioner views are consistent with the findings of earlier research (Sanders et al., 1997). However, the same scholars reported that for some vulnerable and intimidated witnesses, the removal of wigs and gowns was found to be helpful in reducing stress (Sanders et al., 1997). This was reported by later research (Hamlyn et al., 2004) and thus paints a mixed picture as to how helpful this Special Measure may be.

Using a video recorded interview as evidence-in-chief is becoming commonplace in the CJS when a case involves a vulnerable or intimidated witness (YJCEA, 1999, s.27), thus, the traditional forms of evidence and cross-examination have been changed by the implementation of this Special Measure. As such, written statements can be replaced with video recorded evidence which then becomes orally testified evidence (McDermott, 2013). At odds with the principle of orality, this measure is deemed necessary to allow vulnerable or intimidated witnesses to participate in way that is appropriate and considerate of their needs (Hoyano, 2005). When using this Special Measure, the previously completed Achieving Best Evidence video-recorded interview conducted by the police with the witness will be played to the Court and thus submitted as evidence-in-chief. This ensures that the Court hears the evidence of the witness without the witness having to repeat themselves and thus experience re-traumatisation (Tekin & Tekin, 2015). Early work found strong support for the use of video recorded evidence-in-chief particularly when the witness involved was a child (Burton et al., 2006; Davies et al., 1995), resulting in a more detailed and accurate account than would otherwise be produced at trial. However, some have highlighted that the video interview is designed to perform multiple functions and that an interview that has been conducted to investigate and provide evidence of an offence will never be carried out in the same way that a barrister at trial will construct a credible narrative (Ellison, 2001). However, this Special Measure goes a long way to ensure that vulnerable and intimidated witnesses are not disadvantaged in giving their evidence (Baber, 1999) and can be the difference between engaging with the justice system and/or refusing to give their evidence at trial.

Despite the fact that cross-examination is inevitable within most criminal proceedings in England and Wales and around the world, it has a negative impact upon witnesses (Tekin & Tekin, 2015) and has been reported to be the most stressful experience than anything else for vulnerable and intimidated witnesses (Burton et al., 2007; Hamlyn et al., 2004). Indeed, work conducted by the Home Office reported that 71% of witnesses felt upset during cross examination due to the style of questioning and reliving the trauma experienced (Home Office, 2004). To assist with the impact of cross-examination on vulnerable and intimidated witnesses, pre-trial video-recorded cross-examination has recently been implemented (YJCEA, 1999, s.28). This Special Measure provides such witnesses with the option to pre-record their cross-examination prior to the trial, so that the s.28 recording can be presented (usually along with the video recorded evidence-in-chief, s.27) during trial without the witness needing to attend (Ward et al., 2023). The intentions of this measure are to reduce the burden on the witness, and to enhance the quality of their evidence (Ward et al., 2023). This Special Measure was first piloted in 2014 and following a number of reviews and evaluations, the final phase of the rollout was completed in September 2022; the s.28 measure is now available across all Crown Courts in England and Wales. Research has documented the improved experience for witnesses giving their evidence in this manner, compared to live cross-examination at trial, although some concerns from practitioners in criminal justice agencies remain (see Ward et al., 2023 for a full discussion of the s.28 Special Measure).

Another Special Measure available to vulnerable and intimidated witnesses is the examination of the witness through an intermediary (YJCEA, 1999, s.29). The role of the intermediary is to communicate 'questions put to the witness, and to any persons asking such questions, the answers given by the witness in reply to them, and to explain such questions or answers so far as necessary to enable them to be understood by the witness or person in question' (section 29(2)). Thus, the intermediary's duty is to explain questions or answers to the witness without altering the substance of the evidence (Smith & Tilney, 2007). Whilst it falls outside of the scope of this book to explain in significant detail the role and work of the intermediary, typically, the intermediary is involved in the process when the witness is providing their Achieving Best Evidence video interview to the police (see Plotnikoff & Woolfson, 2015, for a full review of the intermediary role). When a vulnerable witness is identified as such, the intermediary will conduct an assessment of their communication abilities and provide guidance to the police (during the interview stage) and to the Court (during the trial stage) on how best to communicate with the witness. When the vulnerable person is required to give their evidence at trial, the intermediary is usually present to assist with this and to alert the Court to any communication difficulties the witness may be having. Usually the intermediary is used in conjunction with a number of Special Measures. This can include the use of communication aids (YJCEA, s.30) to ensure that best evidence can be achieved. Communication aids can include the use of photographs, body maps and dolls, and other devices to ensure effective participation in the justice system.

The majority of Special Measures for vulnerable and intimidated witnesses in England and Wales were introduced in 2002 in Crown Courts and in 2004 in Magistrates Courts, respectively (Tekin & Tekin, 2015). As described in the description of each Special Measure, they have been designed to allow vulnerable and intimidated witnesses to give their best evidence in Court whilst ensuring their needs are met. However, research regarding the effectiveness of this measure paints a mixed picture – this is where the chapter shall now turn.

The Effectiveness of Special Measures

Not all witnesses are physically or mentally capable of giving their evidence at trial in the traditional manner, especially those who are vulnerable and intimidated (Ewin, 2015). However, to ensure that Special Measures are effective and meet the needs of such witness groups, there must be considerable psychological research that evaluates the impact that they have when they are in use in terms of helpfulness for the witness and on justice outcomes. There have been a number of key studies examining the implementation and use of Special Measures. The earliest evaluation conducted examined the views of vulnerable and intimidated witnesses before and after Special Measures were used. Hamlyn et al. (2004) recruited participants via the Witness Service and conducted face-to-face interviews in two phases. Their results suggested that the use of Special Measures increased between the two phases (phase 1 was conducted between November 2000 and February 2001 and phase 2 was conducted between April and June 2003) particularly where the measure assisted with the vulnerable or intimidated witness not having to see the defendant. Overall, satisfaction rose regarding the use of Special Measures between the two phases, especially in intimidated witnesses. However, although some witnesses were consulted about the various types of Special Measures, there were still a significant number (68%) that had not been consulted and thus not able to choose which Special Measures would suit them best.

Around a similar time, Plotnikoff and Woolfson (2004) conducted a qualitative piece of work exploring the use of Special Measures. After speaking with 50 young witnesses in England, Wales, and Northern Ireland, the authors highlighted ongoing difficulties in the implementation of Special Measures and the support available to child witnesses. They found that there had been a lack of pre-trial support (less than half received a pre-trial Court familiarisation visit and 14 witnesses did not have any contact with a supporter prior to the trial date, with 13 indicating that they were not kept informed about the progression of the case), significant delays in their cases coming to trial and inadequate facilities. Furthermore, several young witnesses were discouraged from receiving pre-trial therapy despite there being a clear policy to the contrary. Overall, the researchers concluded that only a few of the young witnesses in their sample had been able to give their evidence in 'optimum circumstances' despite the policies and procedures intended to facilitate their evidence. In later work, Plotnikoff and Woolfson (2009) conducted interviews with more young witnesses. They found that whilst Special Measures were becoming more frequently used (e.g., 75% of their sample had given their evidence via video live link), there remained problems with other Special Measures. For example, they reported issues with the use of video-recorded evidence being used as evidence-in-chief, a lack of pre-trial support, and confusing and misleading questions during cross-examination. Such issues were reported in participants from England, Wales, and Northern Ireland and were not limited to methods of giving evidence. Research work exploring the use of an intermediary found that almost all those who encountered their work had a positive experience (Plotnikoff & Woolfson, 2007). Such benefits included increased access to justice (e.g., participants within this piece of work highlighted that at least half of the cases would not have reached the trial stage had it not been for the involvement of an intermediary), and input into the most effective way to interview/cross-examine a vulnerable or intimidated witness. However, similar procedural issues were reported – that is, operational difficulties pertaining to obtaining an intermediary within a suitable timescale, and cultural resistance amongst some professionals working in the justice system.

The majority of research that has been conducted examining the effectiveness of Special Measures have typically explored one or two Special Measures at a time with child witnesses, with a predominant focus on the mode of giving evidence, such as the use of screens, live video link and giving evidence in an open courtroom, rather than other Special Measures pertaining to pre-trial preparation, or the formality of wigs and gowns. Specific barriers to the use of Special Measures such as the use of screen or giving evidence via video live link have also been reported. For example, Bunting et al. (2013) highlighted that one of the biggest barriers to the use of Special Measures is the impact it may have on jury perception, and the subsequent negative impact on justice outcomes. Davies and Noon's work in the early 1990s was one of the first to highlight that video evidence may not have the same impact upon the jury as providing evidence in the courtroom. Subsequent research has continued to flag this concern, although findings have been mixed in studies conducted internationally. An early piece of work conducted in the United States during which mock jury members watched a 3-hour video of a simulated child sexual abuse trial involving a child testifying in Court or providing their evidence via a video link, found that the mode of providing evidence did not significantly impact upon juror's perceptions of the witness (Swim et al., 1993). Similarly, research conducted around a similar time in the United States found similar results. Ross et al. (1994) used 300 university students as mock jurors; they were required to watch a 2-hour videotaped child sexual abuse trial based on a real Court transcript. The child witness giving their evidence did so in one of three ways: (i) in an open courtroom, (ii) in an open courtroom but shielded by the use of screen, and (iii) via a video live link in a separate room in the Court building. The mock jurors were required to rate the credibility of the child witness on a variety of characteristics. Their results suggested that the mode in which the child witness gave their evidence bore no impact on the perceived credibility of the child witness. Findings have been repeated by further work (Lindsay et al., 1995).

However, other research has suggested that the mode in which a vulnerable or intimidated witness gives their evidence can impact upon witness credibility. Eaton et al. (2001) used mock jurors in Australia whereby they were required to watch one of three videotaped versions of a simulated child sexual abuse trial. The methodology was similar to previous research in that the child witness gave evidence in a number of ways; live in an open courtroom, by pre-recorded video or by a video live link. The mock jurors were then required to rate their perceptions relating to the credibility of the child witness. They found that child witnesses were rated as more credible when they gave their evidence live in Court or by pre-recorded video rather than by video live link, although there were no significant differences between perceptions of credibility when evidence was given live in Court or by a pre-recorded video. Thus, these findings suggest that a witness may be perceived to be less credible should they give their evidence by video live link. These findings have also been replicated in three other similar studies conducted in the United States. That is, child witnesses giving evidence by video live link were judged more negatively in mock juror experiments compared to those giving evidence live in Court; the latter being rated as more accurate, believable, and honest (see Goodman et al., 1998; Orcutt et al., 2001; Tobey et al., 1995). More recent research conducted in Sweden has also found that a child witness giving evidence live in an open courtroom was viewed more favourably and more convincing by mock jurors compared to video live link or pre-recorded video evidence (Landstrom & Granhag, 2010; Landstrom et al., 2007).

Although the majority of research work to date has focused on the child witness, there have been some scholars that have explored the use of Special Measures with adult witnesses. For example, a study conducted in the United Kingdom compared mock jurors' perceptions of a witness giving evidence in relation to a fictitious domestic violence incident. The witness gave evidence either live in Court, via video live link or by video live link after an initial face-to-face meeting with the mock jurors. The mock jurors were required to rate the evidence and witness credibility; they indicated that the evidence was less believable when it was given via the video live link compared to face-to-face (Fullwood et al., 2008). However, similarly to the research work conducted with child witnesses, other studies have found there to be no significant differences in juror perceptions of witness credibility based on the mode in which the evidence is provided. An Australian study conducted by Taylor and Joudo (2005) and a UK study conducted by Ellison (2012) explored the use of Special Measures by adult victims of sexual offences in similar experimental methods previously used. Taylor and Joudo (2005) concluded that, 'the findings in this study do not suggest that mode of presentation per se impacts detrimentally in any meaningful or consistent way on jury outcomes for either the complainant or the accused' (p. 66). Similar findings were reported by Ellison (2012) in that they reported that the mode of evidence did not substantially impact upon mock jurors' perceptions of witness credibility, with no clear or consistent evidence of reduced emotional impact should the video live link or pre-recorded video be used instead of live evidence in an open courtroom.

Whilst the research reports such mixed findings, the results appear to be counterintuitive to the purpose of Special Measures. For example, the same research has also shown that when vulnerable or intimidated witnesses use Special Measures such as the video live link, pretrial anxiety is reduced, and such witnesses are more relaxed when providing their evidence and thus able to provide a more complete and detailed account compared to those who gave their evidence in an open courtroom (e.g., Goodman et al., 1998). However, this appears at odds with research findings that suggest that 'as the visibility of the child increased, jurors were more likely to perceive the child as credible, to feel sympathetic towards the child, and to rate the trial as fair to the child' (Goodman et al., 2006, p. 386), and 'the more proximal the presentation mode, the more positive the observers' evaluation of a child witness' (Landstrom & Granhag, 2010, p. 952). Furthermore, concerns regarding the use of video-recorded evidence-in-chief have been identified by lawyers in that, compared to evidence given live in Court, the use of video-mediated testimony distances the witness from the jury and thus lessens the impact of the evidence and affects the overall jury verdict (Davies & Pezdek, 2010). Thus, the complexities in ensuring a vulnerable and intimidated witness are identified as such and can give their best evidence using Special Measures to assist them in order to do so and ensuring the best possible justice outcomes remain. This is evidenced in the following two cases.

Case 1: R v Iqbal (Imran) & anr [2011]

The witness was aged 17-years-old when, walking back from his College for those with special education needs, he was physically assaulted. During the initial investigation stages, the police failed to identify the witness as vulnerable; he provided a written statement to the police regarding the assault. The case progressed to trial and the witness was required to give his evidence and be cross-examined at Crown Court. The first trial in 2010 was halted as the Judge became concerned about the learning and communication difficulties the witness displayed. Following a submission that the witness has a significant impairment in social functioning, intelligence, and communication, he was allowed Special Measures to assist him – this included the use of screen and the use of an intermediary.

The case highlights the impact of not identifying vulnerability early enough in the process, and the positive impact that using Special Measures can have on a vulnerable or intimidated witness. Scholars have identified the 'missed opportunities' regarding the witness' vulnerability – for example, the witness could have completed a video recorded interview which could have been used as evidence-in-chief at trial (Ewin, 2015). Undoubtedly, the stressful experience that this would have been for the witness could have been avoided.

Case 2 (from Charles, 2012)

The female witness reported allegations of domestic violence from her partner; she indicated that her partner had been violent towards her and in the presence of her child. It was confirmed that no enquiries or concerns were raised about any vulnerability, and she was not considered an intimidated witness; indeed, there was no information to suggest that this had been discussed between the officer on the case and the charging lawyer. There was also no information regarding the witness' views on prosecution and/or the present state of the relationship between the witness and her partner. Once the case progressed to trial, the witness made a retraction statement which cast doubt on the accuracy of her original statement. Thus, the reviewing lawyer offered no evidence at trial and the defendant was not prosecuted.

Summary

The witness plays a key role in the trial process, and thus it is imperative that they are protected and supported, especially when they are vulnerable or intimidated (Tekin & Tekin, 2015). However, vulnerable witnesses, in particular, were traditionally viewed as unreliable witnesses. Despite this, police officers were still urged to recognise the needs of vulnerable witnesses and to obtain their evidence. It was not until the 1970s onwards, that awareness started to grow for vulnerable, and later, intimidated witnesses. What followed, was an inter-departmental working group commissioned by the government to undertake a review to assist with this type of witness. Their report, 'Speaking Up for Justice' (Home Office, 1998) paved the way for Special Measures – these were introduced under the YJCEA (1999) and were implemented to alleviate the fear and distress associated with giving evidence, often exacerbated by vulnerability and intimidation. Subsequently, vulnerable, and intimidated witnesses are eligible for a number of Special Measures to assist them when they provide their evidence during the investigation and at trial.

However, despite one of the most notable developments in the system of law that has been the change in perception towards the vulnerable and intimidated witness and the subsequent implementation of Special Measures (Tekin & Tekin, 2015), there still remains issues with their use. For example, it is a well-established fact that there are inherent difficulties within the identification of witnesses who may benefit from Special Measures under the YJCEA (1999) (Ewin, 2016); many of those are discussed throughout this chapter. Even when a witness is identified as vulnerable or intimidated, there are large numbers of witnesses whereby their needs and wishes are assumed rather than ascertained (Burton et al., 2007). Furthermore, the research base paints a mixed picture in terms of the use of Special Measures; whilst vulnerable and intimidated witnesses frequently express positive views regarding their use, there is a large field of research that suggests that the credibility of the vulnerable or intimidated witness may come under scrutiny depending on the mode of which they give their evidence. This has implications for the CJS and justice outcomes overall. Thus, much more work is needed in ensuring that the needs of this type of witness can be accommodated for to enable best evidence to be achieved, whilst also guaranteeing that this will not affect the outcome of their case. This is also a key issue with vulnerable defendants at trial and will be the focus of the next chapter.

Key Learning Points

- Vulnerable and intimidated witnesses were typically seen as being unreliable witnesses at trial, despite pressure placed on the police to obtain their evidence.
- Concerns started to grow for this type of witness from the 1970s although it was not until the 1990s that the government made a commitment to provide greater support and assistance.
- The 'Speaking Up for Justice' report (Home Office, 1998) made 78 recommendations in order to improve the way that vulnerable or intimidated witnesses were dealt with by the justice system – many of these were included as Special Measures in the Youth Justice and Criminal Evidence Act (1999).
- Special Measures include the way in which the witness will give their evidence, as well as the assistance of an intermediary.
- A number of Administrative Measures were also made to ensure the witness is prepared for trial, for example, a pre-trial familiarisation visit.
- The views of vulnerable or intimidated witnesses are typically positive when Special Measures have been used (Hamlyn et al., 2004) although there remains procedural issues regarding the identification of a vulnerable or intimidated witness and the implementation of Special Measures.
- The psychological research base has painted a mixed picture regarding the credibility of this type of witness should they use the Special Measures available to them.
- This has implications for the justice outcomes for vulnerable and intimidated witnesses.

References

Asquith, N. (2012). Vulnerability and the art of complaint making. In I. Bartkowiak-Théron & N. L. Asquith (Eds.), *Policing vulnerability* (pp. 147–161). Western Sydney University Research Collection.

Baber, M. (1999). *The youth justice and criminal evidence bill.* (No. 99/40). House of Commons Library.

Birch, D. (2000). A better deal for vulnerable witnesses? *Criminal Law Review*, 223–249.
Bunting, L., Hayes, D., & Clifford, G. (2013). *Special measures for vulnerable witnesses in Northern Ireland*. Department of Justice Northern Ireland.
Burton, M., Evans, R., & Sanders, A. (2006). *Are special measures for vulnerable and intimidated witnesses working? Evidence from the criminal justice agencies*. Home Office.
Burton, M., Evans, R., & Sanders, A. (2007). Vulnerable and intimidated witnesses and the adversarial process in England and Wales. *The International Journal of Evidence and Proof*, *11*, 1–23.
Charles, C. (2012). *Special measures for vulnerable and intimidated witnesses: Research exploring the decisions and actions taken by prosecutors in a sample of CPS case files*. Crown Prosecution Service.
Cook, T., & Tattersall, A. (2010). *Blackstone's senior investigating officers' handbook*. Oxford University Press.
Cooper, D., & Roberts, P. (2005). *Special measures for vulnerable and intimidated witnesses: An analysis of crown prosecution service monitoring data*. CPS.
Davies, G., & Noon, E. (1991). *An evaluation of the live link for child witnesses*. Home Office.
Davies, G., & Pezdek, K. (2010). Children as witnesses. In G. Towl & D. Crighton (Eds.), *Forensic psychology* (pp. 178–194). Blackwell.
Davies, G., Wilson, C., Mitchell, R., & Milsom, J. (1995). *Videotaping Children's evidence: An evaluation*. Home Office.
Durston, G. (2011). *Evidence: Text & materials*. Oxford University Press.
Eaton, T., Ball, P., & O'Callaghan, M. (2001). Child witness and defendant credibility: Child evidence presentation mode and judicial instructions. *Journal of Applied Social Psychology*, *31*(9), 1845–1858.
Ellison, L. (2001). *The adversarial process and the adversarial witness*. Oxford University Press.
Ellison, L. (2012). *Special Measures in rape trials: Exploring the impact of screens, live links and video-recorded evidence on mock juror deliberation*. ESRC Briefing Report. https://www.stmaryscentre.org/application/files/6714/7793/1129/Special-Measures-Briefing-Report.pdf
Ewin, R. (2015). The vulnerable and intimidated witness: A socio-legal analysis of special measures. *Journal of Applied Psychology and Social Science*, *1*(2), 31–54.
Ewin, R. (2016). The vulnerable and intimidated witness: A study of the special measure practitioner. *Journal of Applied Psychology and Social Science*, *2*(1), 12–40.
Farrugia, L., & Maras, K. (2023). Achieving best evidence from victims and witnesses. In G. Oxburgh, T. Myklebust, M. Fallon, & M. Hartwig (Eds). *Interviewing and interrogation: A review of research and practice since World War II*. Torkel Opsahl Academic EPublisher.
Flin, R. (1990). Child witnesses in criminal courts. *Children & Society*, *4*(3), 264–283.
Fullwood, C., Judd, A., & Finn, M. (2008). The effect of initial meeting context and video-mediation on jury perceptions of an eyewitness. *The Internet Journal of Criminology*. https://eprints.glos.ac.uk/id/eprint/11793
Goodman, G., Myers, J., Qin, J., Quas, J., Castelli, P., Redlich, A., & Rogers, L. (2006). Hearsay versus children's testimony: Effects of truthful and deceptive statements on jurors' decisions. *Law and Human Behaviour*, *30*(3), 363–401.
Goodman, G., Tobey, A., Batterman-Faunce, J., Orcutt, H., Thomas, S., Shapiro, C., & Sachsenmaier, T. (1998). Face-to-face confrontation: Effects of closed-circuit technology on children's eyewitness testimony and jurors' decisions. *Law and Human Behaviour*, *22*(2), 165–203.
Hamlyn, B., Phelps, A., Turtle, J., & Sattar, G. (2004). *Are special measures working? Evidence from surveys of vulnerable and intimidated witnesses*. Home Office Research Study 283. Home Office.
Home Office (1998). *Speaking up for justice: Report of the interdepartmental working group on the treatment of vulnerable or intimidated witnesses in the criminal justice system*. Home Office.
Home Office. (2004). Are special measures working? Evidence from surveys of vulnerable and intimidated witnesses, Home Office Research, Development and Statistic Directorate. http://library.npia.police.uk/docs/hors/hors283.pdf.
Hoyano, L. (2005). Youth justice and criminal evidence act 1999: Special measures directions—Compliance with article 6. *Journal of Criminal Law*, *69*(6), 488–493.

Kirby, A., Hunter, G., & Jacobson, J. (2013). *APPG vulnerable victims' inquiry – Written evidence from the Institute for Criminal Policy Research*. Institute for Criminal Policy Research.

Landstrom, S., & Granhag, P. (2010). In-court versus out-of-court testimonies: Children's experiences and adults' assessments. *Applied Cognitive Psychology*, *24*(7), 941–955.

Landstrom, S., Granhag, P., & Hartwig, M. (2007). Children's live and videotaped testimonies: How presentation mode affects observers' perception, assessment and memory. *Legal and Criminological Psychology*, *12*(2), 333–347.

Lindsay, R., Ross, D., Lea, J., & Carr, C. (1995). What's fair when a child testifies? *Journal of Applied Social Psychology*, *25*(10), 870–888.

McDermott, Y. (2013). The admissibility and weight of written witness testimony in international criminal law: A socio-legal analysis. *Leiden Journal of International Law*, *26*(4), 971–989.

McLeod, R., Philpin, C., Sweeting, A., Joyce, L., & Evans, R. (2010). *Court experience of adults with mental health conditions, learning disabilities and limited mental capacity. Report 1: Overview and recommendations*. Ministry of Justice.

Ministry of Justice. (2013). Code of practice for victims of crime. *HMMOJ*, *1*(1). https://www.gov.uk/government/publications/the-code-of-practice-for-victims-of-crime

Morris, J. (1999). Disabled children, child protection systems and the children act 1989. *Child Abuse Review*, *8*, 91–108.

Orcutt, H., Goodman, G., Tobey, A., Batterman-Faunce, J., & Thomas, S. (2001). Detecting deception in children's testimony: Factfinders' abilities to reach the truth in open court and closed-circuit trials. *Law and Human Behaviour*, *25*(4), 339–372.

Plotnikoff, J., & Woolfson, R. (2004). *In their own words: The experiences of 50 young witnesses in criminal proceedings*. NSPCC.

Plotnikoff, J., & Woolfson, R. (2007). *Evaluation of young witness support - examining the impact on witnesses and the criminal justice system: Research summary 2*. Ministry of Justice.

Plotnikoff, J., & Woolfson, R. (2009). *Measuring up? Evaluating implementation of government commitments to young witnesses in criminal proceedings*. NSPCC.

Plotnikoff, J., & Woolfson, R. (2015). *Intermediaries in the criminal justice system. Improving communication for vulnerable witnesses and defendants*. University of Bristol: Policy Press.

R v Iqbal (Imran) & anr [2011] EWCA Crim 1348. https://www.casemine.com/judgement/uk/5a8ff70360d03e7f57ea5a0e

Rock, P. (2004). *Constructing victims' rights: The home office, new labour and victims*. Oxford University Press.

Ross, D., Hopkins, S., Hanson, E., Lindsay, R., Hazen, K., & Eslinger, T. (1994). The impact of protective shields and videotape testimony on conviction rates in a simulated trial of child sexual abuse. *Law and Human Behaviour*, *18*(5), 553–566.

Sanders, A., Creaton, J., Bird, S., & Weber, L. (1997). *Victims with learning disabilities*. University of Oxford: Oxford Centre for Criminological Research.

Smith, K., & Tilney, S. (2007). *Vulnerable adult and child witnesses*. Oxford University Press.

Swim, J., Borgida, E., & McCoy, K. (1993). Videotaped versus in court testimony: Does protecting the child witness jeopardize due process? *Journal of Applied Social Psychology*, *23*(8), 603–685.

Taylor, N., & Joudo, J. (2005). *The impact of pre-recorded video and closed circuit television testimony by adult sexual assault complainants on jury decision-making: An experimental study*. Australian Institute of Criminology.

Tekin, S., & Tekin, A. (2015). The issue of adequateness of special measures applied to vulnerable victims and witnessed in the United Kingdom. *Human Rights Review*, *5*(10), 1–24.

Tobey, A., Goodman, G., Batterman, Faunce, J., Orcutt, H., & Sachsenmaier, T. (1995). Balancing the rights of children and defendants: Effects of closed circuit television on children's accuracy and jurors' perceptions. In M. Zaragoza, J. Graham, G. Hall, R. Hirschman, & Y. Ben-Portah (Eds.), *Memory and testimony in the child witness* (pp. 214–239). Sage.

Ward, D., Pehkonen, I., & Murray, M. (2023). *Process evaluation of section 28. Evaluating the use of pre-recorded cross-examination (section 28) for intimidated witnesses*. Ministry of Justice.

Youth Justice and Criminal Evidence Act. (YJCEA). (1999). London: HMSO.

7 Vulnerable Defendants at Trial

Introduction

Increasingly large numbers of vulnerable individuals, namely those with mental health conditions and learning difficulties, are coming into contact with the criminal justice system (CJS) by way of both adult and child defendant (Anderson et al., 2016; Fairclough, 2017; Jacobson & Talbot, 2009). Indeed, it has been estimated that approximately 20% of prisoners have a recent mental health illness (Vogel et al., 2014), and within the youth justice system (YJS), around 70% of youth have at least one mental health condition, with a fifth struggling with a severe mental illness (Skowyra & Cocozza, 2007). Trends have reported an increase in defendants and prisoners with a mental health condition or disorder since the 1980s with scholars now reporting that there are more vulnerable individuals incarcerated than there are in psychiatric hospital (Fuller et al., 2010).

Consequently, those with such vulnerabilities may find it difficult to follow Court proceedings. For example, the terminology used in courtrooms is rarely used outside of the justice system and can be difficult for the average layperson to understand. For those with vulnerabilities, it can become impossible to engage with the judicial system when such language is used (Snow et al., 2012), and thus present a barrier to effective participation in the CJS (Alger, 2021). This can impede on the defendant's right to a fair trial under Article 6 of the European Convention of Human Rights, given that vulnerable defendant cannot be informed of the nature and cause of which they are charged and standing trial, and subsequently prepare an effective defence. For example, under this Article, the defendant must be able to effectively participate, which reflects the presupposition that the defendant can understand broadly the nature of the trial process including the significance of any penalties/sentencing imposed, be able to follow the general gist of what is being said in court including the evidence of the prosecutions witness(es) and his own defence and make appropriate instructions to his counsel regarding which facts to put forward in his defence (Howard, 2022).

That being said, owing to research and practice developments in dealing with vulnerable defendants, there is a slow shift in the CJS in relation to vulnerable defendants at trials (Gerry & Cooper, 2017), especially since the trial of two juvenile defendants in the murder of James Bulger (Gerry, 2012).

Fitness to Plead and to Stand Trial

Being 'fit to plead' and thus subsequently stand trial relates to whether an individual can participate in a criminal trial. In England and Wales, this approach for Crown Courts is set out in Section 4 and 4A Criminal Procedure (Insanity Act) 1964 and requires a Judge to determine if a defendant is fit to plead and to stand trial. Such a question must be determined

DOI: 10.4324/9781003386735-7

as soon as it arises and is usually determined on the balance of probabilities if the defence raise the fitness to plead issue. Should the prosecution raise the issue, then the prosecution must satisfy the court beyond reasonable doubt. This is usually achieved by written or oral evidence from two or more registered medical practitioners, at least one of whom must be approved by the Home Secretary (CPS, 2019). If the defendant is found to be incapable of the following, then he will be deemed not fit to plead:

1 Being able to understand the charges of which he faces;
2 Being able to make an informed decisions regarding their plea, for example, to plead innocent or guilty;
3 Understanding the right to challenge the jurors;
4 Being able to effectively instruct solicitors and counsel;
5 Understanding and generally being able to follow the course of the court proceedings; and
6 Being able to give evidence.

Many scholars argue that the procedure whereby a defendant may be found unfit to plead is very draconian in that it denies a defendant from putting forward any evidence or explanation as to their involvement in the charges against them (Gerry, 2012). For example, case law has reported that finding a defendant unfit to plead deprives him of his rights and should the defendant be guilty of the act, also severely limits the courts powers to sentence the defendant appropriately (see, e.g., R v Walls 2011, p. 2, Cr App R 6).

Should a defendant be found unfit to plead and thus stand trial, the act can or may be proved but the reasons are ignored. What leads from this is a finding of fact (rather than a conviction). Thus, the jury will be instructed to consider whether the defendant did the act, without consideration of the defendant's mens rea (e.g., intent). Depending on the outcome, the defendant may be subjected to a hospital order (with or without a restriction order), a supervision order, or an absolute discharge (CPS, 2019; Gerry, 2012). In a recent case, minimum requirements were set out for a fair trial based on an earlier ruling in SC v UK (2004) EHRR 10. These included the defendant being able to understand what he had done wrong, any defences available to him, and be able to instruct and make appropriate representations if he so wished, and give proper instruction to his legal team, as well as the court being satisfied that the defendant understood the act that was wrong (see R(TP) v West London Youth Court). As such, case law has repeatedly highlighted that it is essential that the vulnerable defendant be dealt with in a manner that takes full account of age, level of maturity, and intellectual and emotional capacities, whilst ensuring that steps are taken to promote understanding and participation at trial. Thus, vulnerable defendants are entitled to a fair trial but may require accommodations to suit their needs (Gerry, 2012); for a vulnerable defendant who is capable of understanding the charges against them, denying them every assistance to engage with the justice system and put their case across is wrong (Gerry, 2012). Many argue, for example, that being able to plead and subsequently stand trial may be dependent on modifications made to the trial processes and the inclusion of Special Measures (CPS, 2019). This is where the chapter now turns.

The Vulnerable Defendant and Special Measures

Many jurisdictions across Europe now have a range of Special Measures available to support vulnerable defendants during trial and to ensure that communication is made more accessible and participation more effective (Turner & Hughes, 2022). Depending on the country and jurisdiction, these may be available for all vulnerable individuals in the justice system, or more specialised in certain courts only available to a certain vulnerable population (e.g., those with a learning disability; see, e.g., Marinos & Whittingham, 2019, or juveniles; see, e.g., Hoyano & Rafferty, 2017). Generally, the aim of the Special Measures is to ensure the courtroom and trial process seems less daunting and formal and can include measures such as the removal of wigs and gown, and a change in language used during cross-examination (Fairclough & Greenwood, 2023; White et al., 2021).

In England and Wales, however, the position is slightly different. Whilst Special Measures for vulnerable and/or intimidated witnesses are automatically available as per the Youth Justice and Criminal Evidence Act (YJCEA, 1999), this is not the case for the vulnerable defendant. Indeed, in their 'Speaking Up for Justice' report, the working group did not consider the use of Special Measures for vulnerable defendants in their recommendations on the basis that pre-trial proceedings are already adapted for vulnerable suspects, defendants (including vulnerable ones) are already privy to fair trial rights and that the use of Special Measures are to protect the witnesses from the defendant and so would not be of any benefit to the defendant themselves (Home Office, 1998). They have been heavily criticised for doing so (Fairclough, 2018). Furthermore, much case law has evidenced how the courts have consistently refused the use of Special Measures, highlighting that defendants should be excluded from the provisions of the YJCEA (Gerry, 2012). Indeed, for vulnerable defendants, the YJCEA only permits the use of the video live link whilst a defendant is giving their evidence (YJCEA, 1999, s.33A). Thus, the requirement as per the Criminal Procedure Rules (2020; see s.3.8(3)(b)) in taking 'every reasonable step to facilitate the participation of any person, including the defendant' is often deemed lacking.

The video live link is defined within the YJCEA (1999) as 'an arrangement by which the accused, whilst absent from the place where the proceedings are being held, is able to see and hear a person there, and to be seen and heard by the judge, justices, jury, co accused, legal representatives and interpreters or any other person appointed by the court to assist the accused' (s.33B). A defendant over the age of 18 years old may give their evidence using this special measure in a Magistrates or Crown Court in England and Wales if they suffer from a mental disorder or has a significant impairment of intelligence or social function and is unable to effectively participate in the trial proceedings by giving oral evidence. Furthermore, if the use of the video live link will enable more effective participation and the court is satisfied that it is in the interests of justice for the defendant to give evidence in this manner, then it is likely to be allowed. Such similar requirements are in place for juvenile defendants giving evidence in the Youth Court, Magistrates Court, and the Crown Court. One of Special Measure of note is the defendant intermediary.

Despite the implementation of this special measure under the YJCEA (1999), research has highlighted that there is a lack of awareness of its existence for vulnerable defendants (Fairclough, 2017). Furthermore, when discussing the use of Special Measures for vulnerable defendants, the use of the video live link was entirely omitted from an article written by a high-profile barrister (see Gerry, 2012).

The Defendant Intermediary

The emergence of the defendant intermediary and their provision within the justice system arose as a result of the YJCEA excluded defendants from the majority of available Special Measures usually available to witnesses. As such, judges have exercised their inherent jurisdiction to appoint defendant intermediaries where deemed necessary for a fair trial (Taggart, 2022). This was recognised in case law – for example, in R (on the application of

AS) v Great Yarmouth Youth Court, it was recognised that a judge may be under a duty to appoint a defendant intermediary to assist the vulnerable defendant in following the proceedings and giving evidence, particularly if a lack of an intermediary resulted in an unfair trial. Thus, it was recognised that defendants with communication difficulties may require the need for assistance in some cases. Following this case, the need for defendant intermediaries gained recognition. Several inquiries into the operation of the courts highlighted the communication difficulties amongst youth offender, for example (Carlile, 2014). More recently, in their report, 'Unfitness to Plead', the Law Commission made recommendations regarding a statutory basis for intermediaries for defendants and a system similar to the Witness Intermediary Scheme that exists for vulnerable witnesses (Law Commission, 2016).

In England and Wales, it is Section 104 of the Coroners and Justice Act (2009) that states that intermediaries may assist with the communication needs of vulnerable defendants, much like they do with vulnerable witnesses (see Chapter 6, although please note the provisions for the two groups differ). However, this legislation is yet to be enacted (Turner & Westwood, 2023). In reality, what occurs is that provision of the defendant intermediary is based on common law. For example, in C v Sevenoaks Youth Court [2009] EWHC 3088 (Admin), it was held that whilst the court have an inherent power to appoint an intermediary to assist with a defendant to prepare for the trial, and during the trial so that they can participate effectively, there is no presumption that the defendant will be assisted. Furthermore, it was held that even where the intermediary would improve the trial process, the appointment of such is not mandatory and that the specific communication problems faced by a defendant should be dealt with by the judge as part of their ordinary control of the judicial process (see also R v Cox [2012] EWCA Crim 549). The case of Sevenoaks is the current authority for appointing a defendant intermediary for a vulnerable defendant in England and Wales (Cooper & Wurtzel, 2013).

C v Sevenoaks Youth Court [2009] EWHC 3088 (Admin)

In October 2008, a 13-year-old male was returning home from a meeting of the Army Cadet Force. Still wearing his uniform, he was approached by 'C' – a 12-year-old male, and 'P', a 15-year-old male, who roughly held the cadet against a wall and demanded his mobile phone. The cadet told both males that he did not have his mobile with him after which they pushed him to the ground and repeatedly punched and kicked him. One of the males ran off with the cadet's torch. 'C' and 'P' were identified nearby and subsequently arrested. 'C' was interviewed the following day under caution with an appropriate adult present but without legal representation. 'C' admitted speaking with the cadet and claimed that he had only asked him what the time was. He denied the assault on the cadet. He was subsequently charged with assault with intent to rob and theft.

On 19 February 2009, 'C' made his first appearance at Court where he was seen by the duty solicitor; his solicitor realised that 'C' had serious mental health issues and set about obtaining medical evidence. A week later at the next Court hearing, 'C' formally entered 'not guilty' pleas to the charges. 'C' was assessed by Dr Marriot, a Chartered Clinical Psychologist – during the meeting, he presented as severely overactive with poor concentration and low tolerance. Of the tests she was able to complete, they suggested a Learning Disability within the range of 'exceptionally low'. She concluded that his comprehension was considerably below his chronological age and confirmed the long-standing diagnosis of Attention Deficit Hyperactivity Disorder which was not being controlled appropriately by the medication 'C' was currently taking. 'C' was also diagnosed with Oppositional Defiance Disorder and Dr Marriot thought that he presented with many symptoms of Asperger's syndrome, for example, 'C' demonstrated an obsessive conduct and became upset at the change to his routines, he was unable to recognise or understand the emotional state of others and had an inability to understand nonverbal communication. Dr Marriot concluded that whilst she thought 'C' understood the nature of his charges and his plea, and would be able to give a coherent and consistent account of the events surrounding the alleged offences, and thus fit to plead and to be tried at trial, she indicated that 'C' would not be able to concentrate during the trial, nor listen to evidence, nor instruct his solicitor, and would find it difficult to cope with cross-examination. Dr Marriot made recommendations pertaining to 'C' having regular breaks and all questions being phrased using simple language. In addition, she identified that 'C' would be more effectively able to participate in his trial if the Court appointed an intermediary who would explain the trial process, assist with his evidence and communication between 'C', his solicitor, and the Court. Her recommendations were supported by a Consultant Forensic Neuropsychiatrist, Dr Staufenberg who also suggested that 'C' give evidence behind screens or by video link.

On 28 April 2009, the trial was adjourned, and the Court made a direction that an intermediary for 'C' be appointed. No consideration was given to whether the Court had the relevant statutory power and who was to pay for the intermediary costs. Subsequently, the justice's clerk questioned whether the Court had the power to make an order appointing an intermediary for a defendant and during a hearing on 15 June 2009, the Court revoked the direction for an intermediary to be appointed during legal arguments. The reasoning related to the fact that the statutory regime for Special Measures for vulnerable and intimidated witnesses under the Youth Justice and Criminal Evidence Act (1999) does not apply to defendants; in fact, defendants are specifically excluded from its provisions in Section 16(1). As such, no order for the provision of an intermediary could be made under the Act.

Following appeals to the decision, the Court of Appeal Criminal Division recognised that the Courts have an inherent duty to appoint an intermediary to help a defendant follow the proceedings and to give evidence, and without such assistance, he would not be able to have a fair trial. The Court identified that whilst there is no statutory power permitting the appointment of an intermediary for a defendant, there is some procedural powers in the Criminal Procedure Rules, particularly under Article 6 of the European Convention on Human Rights. The decision to revoke the appointment of an intermediary was quashed and an intermediary was appointed but not under the Youth Justice and Criminal Evidence Act (1999), rather by the Court's inherent powers.

As is evident, without a statutory entitlement to a defendant intermediary, vulnerable defendants have to rely on ad hoc use of intermediaries dependent on the courts' inherent powers (Taggart, 2022). Scholars have indicated that given the often-conflicting decisions that have followed in recent case law, that the legal position of the use of the defendant intermediary is uncertain, and thus provision is unequal (Fairclough, 2019; Taggart, 2022).

Furthermore, even when a defendant intermediary is appointed, there remains concerns with the duration of their appointment, for example, evidence only or for the duration of trial. Whilst many defendant intermediaries initially were required to assist the vulnerable defendant for the entirety of the trial, this trend has since been reversed and many defendant intermediaries are appointed only when the defendant is giving their evidence (Hoyano & Rafferty, 2017). That said, some scholars highlight merits of the ad-hoc system. For example, some have noted that an approach is needed that acknowledges the individuality of the vulnerable defendant (Hoyano & Rafferty, 2017); indeed, such needs-led assistance can be advocated for by the defendant intermediary themselves with examples including the intermediary recommending that she only attends the pre-trial legal consultation to ensure the defendant understood the nature of the charges. In this regard, it has been suggested that the defendant intermediary should be inherently ad hoc so that the individualised recommendations suggested by the intermediary can be incorporated (Backen, 2017), and that a binary approach whereby a defendant intermediary is granted either for the entire trial or just for evidence only does not reflect the spectrum of communication issues that vulnerable defendants may face (see R v Yahya Rashid [2017] EWCA Crim 2, for example). However, the general consensus appears to be that a failure to allocate a defendant intermediary to a vulnerable defendant is arguably a breach of their human rights, as they are not afforded the opportunity to provide their best evidence at trial and effectively participate in trial (Cooper & Wurtzel, 2013). Furthermore, others have indicated that the extension of the defendant intermediary for the entirety of the trial rather than just for the purpose of evidence, safeguards the fairness of criminal trials (Fairclough, 2017).

In addition to the ad hoc use of the defendant intermediary, concerns have been raised as to who enacts the role. Intermediaries that work with defendants are known as 'non-registered intermediaries' to distinguish between Registered Intermediaries that work with vulnerable witnesses and are accredited by the Ministry of Justice. Defendant intermediaries or non-registered intermediaries receive no formal training from the Ministry of Justice but tend to be employed by an organisation who are responsible for their training (see, e.g., Triangle at www.triangle.org.uk). However, this means that defendant intermediaries are not regulated in the same way that Registered Intermediaries working within the Witness Intermediary Scheme are; for the latter, governance of the Witness Intermediary Scheme is overseen by an 'intermediaries registration board' and a separate 'Quality Assurance Board' that are responsible for the regulation and monitoring of all professional standards of the Registered Intermediary (Ministry of Justice, 2023). The intermediaries that work with vulnerable defendants do not have the same type of governance; there is no formal policy that stipulates what experience of knowledge of the justice system is required to enact this role, there is no accreditation system in existence, no regulated rates of pay, and there is no standard manner of matching an intermediary to a vulnerable defendant in the same way which exists for vulnerable witnesses (Plotnikoff & Woolfson, 2015).

That being said, a high percentage of Registered Intermediaries that work with vulnerable witnesses also complete work as a defendant intermediary and thus are able to bring transferable skills and maintain the same quality standards required (Taggart, 2022). Furthermore, whilst defendant intermediaries are not governed in the same way as those that work with witnesses, the majority of defendant intermediaries are appointed from two leading commercial providers, 'Triangle' and 'Communicourt'; both of which provide training and ongoing continuing professional development. In addition, research has highlighted that defendants accompanied by an intermediary are perceived more positively than those who remain unassisted (Smethurst & Collins, 2019).

Despite the growing recognition that vulnerable defendants need intermediaries to assist them in the same manner than vulnerable witnesses do, the development of similar provisions for the former has been slow. It was not until 2020 that the Ministry of Justice issued a pre-procurement notice for the provision of 'Court Appointed Intermediary Services'. Designed to help meet the obligations of the Ministry of Justice, the scheme aimed to implement minimum standards across the provision of intermediary services that fall outside of the Witness Intermediary Scheme available to intermediaries working with vulnerable witnesses (Taggart, 2022). Furthermore, it ensured that the current ad hoc provision of defendant intermediaries was replaced by a more formal scheme. A few years later, an executive agency of the Ministry of Justice, HMCTS, awarded contracts to a selection of suppliers for the provision of the new intermediary services; Triangle was selected as a managed and approved service provider for the new HMCTS Appointed Intermediary Service framework (HAIS; see www.triangle.org.uk). However, this has been met with some opposition. For example, significant concerns have been raised about the commercialisation and the privatisation of intermediary services with a lack of consultation with relevant bodies cited. In addition, despite this significant development in the provision of intermediaries for vulnerable defendants, it does not formally implement s.104 of the Coroners and Justice Act (2009) and so there remains no legislative or statutory power for the use of the defendant intermediary. The differences between provisions provided for vulnerable witness and vulnerable defendants continue and are explored in further detail next.

Vulnerable Witnesses vs. Vulnerable Defendants at Trial

The recognition of an individual's vulnerability and the necessary adjustments to procedures required to manage cases and enable effective participation has been driven by academic research and case law in recent decades (Gerry & Cooper, 2017). Despite the increasing acceptance regarding the impact of vulnerability on an individual's ability to effectively engage with the justice system, there remains significant differences in the provision afforded to vulnerable witnesses compared to vulnerable defendants. The introduction of legislation in England and Wales that provides a statutory regime of 'Special Measures' for vulnerable witnesses for example, has inevitably led to comparisons regarding the measures available for vulnerable defendants (McEwan, 2013). Many scholars have highlighted that the needs of vulnerable defendants may have been overlooked and that there is an imbalance between the Special Measures afforded to vulnerable witnesses compared to those provided to vulnerable defendants (Turner & Westwood, 2023). For example, the provision of intermediaries and their use in England and Wales has focused predominately on vulnerable witnesses (Fairclough, 2019). The statutory scheme for vulnerable witnesses is supported by the Witness Intermediary Scheme who are responsible for training, funding, and matching appropriately qualified intermediaries to vulnerable witnesses. However, for vulnerable defendants, this is not the case; they are not privy to this scheme which had led to many documented difficulties in finding and funding appropriate defendant intermediaries (Morrison & Taggart, 2023). More recently, the Victim's Commissioner highlighted the inequality in the provision of intermediaries between witnesses and defendants and called for the implementation of s.104 of the Coroners and Justice Act (2009). Thus, whilst the fundamental principle of Special Measures is to enable vulnerable individuals to give the best evidence they can (Gerry & Cooper, 2017), the availability of Special Measures designed to assist the vulnerable remain far more advanced for witnesses than for defendants (Fairclough, 2017), with many highlighting that 'a person's vulnerability should not be ignored when they become a defendant' (Curen, 2005, p. 4).

Under the YJCEA (1999), vulnerable and/or intimidated witnesses are eligible for a wide range of Special Measures. However, as a consequence of the way that the law has developed, the provision remains inferior to that which is available for vulnerable defendants, and is based on case law, statutory provisions, and sources of 'soft law' (Fairclough & Greenwood, 2023). For example, the power to remove wigs and gowns for the duration of trials involving a vulnerable defendant, and allowing the defendant to give evidence in private arose from a high-profile case. In T v United Kingdom, the two 11-year-old defendants were on trial for the murder of a 2-year-old boy. During their appeal to the European Court of Human Rights, it was ruled that whilst their treatment was not inhuman or degrading (as per Article 3 of their human rights), it was deemed that they were unable to participate effectively in their trial given the large amount of publicity and media coverage. In another case, the common law power for vulnerable defendants to use screens was maintained (see R v Waltham Forest Youth Court). Thus, whilst changes are being made for the vulnerable defendant, there remains a disparity in the measures available for vulnerable witnesses when compared to vulnerable defendants.

Defences at Trial and Disposal Options

Should a defendant be found fit to plead and thus stand trial and perhaps receive the necessary Special Measures, they must still demonstrate criminal liability or culpability to be convicted of a crime. For criminal liability or culpability to be demonstrated, there are certain conditions that have to be fulfilled.

Four Requirements for Criminal Liability (Lacey & Zedner, 2012)

Capacity

Individuals must have 'basic cognitive and volitional capacities' to be considered capable of committing a crime (Lacey & Zedner, 2012, p. 170). The most obvious exclusion for criminal liability is the doctrine of doli incapax ('incapable of crime') that is applied to individuals under a certain age. The age of criminal responsibility differs depending on country and jurisdiction; children in England and Wales cannot be held criminally responsible for a crime under the age of 10 years.

Conduct

Individuals can only be held criminally liable for an offence when their behaviour has transgressed a stated legal boundary. Thus, individuals cannot be held criminally liable if they only have thoughts of a transgression or as a result of status or identity.

Responsibility

To be criminally liable, the individual must have had a causal role in the crime; that is, individuals cannot be held accountable for genuine accidents. It is for the prosecution to prove that the action was negligent or reckless, for example. That being said, there are some crimes that automatically fall under strict liability whereby the prosecution need not prove responsibility – for example, driving on the wrong side of the road.

Defences

Even if the other requirements are met, it is still possible for an individual to argue that they are not fully responsible for a crime by forwarding a defence. In doing so, the defendant is submitting evidence concerning some aspect of the circumstances regarding the offence.

Although there are a number of defences available to a defendant at trial, the chapter focuses on those that are perhaps more often linked to mental health, namely loss of control, diminished responsibility, and insanity.

Loss of Control

This type of defence can be used as a partial defence to murder, resulting in the individual being convicted of manslaughter instead. Section 54 of the Coroners and Justice Act (2009) states that an individual can use this defence if they are involved in killing another individual but can raise sufficient evidence of the following:

1 The individual's acts or omissions in killing came from a loss of self-control (not as a result of voluntary intoxication).
2 The self-control has a qualifying trigger defined by Section 55 – fear of serious violence, things said or done which constituted extremely grave circumstances or caused the individual to have a sense of being seriously wrong that was justifiable.
3 An individual of the same sex and age, whom has a 'normal' degree of tolerance and self-restrain may have reacted in a similar manner in the same circumstances of the individual on trial.

The use of this defence is determined by the Judge after they consider each of the criteria in turn, and they are not disproved beyond reasonable doubt by the prosecution (CPS, 2019). How this defence can be interpreted and used is evidence in the following case.

R v Rejmanski [2018] WLR 2721

The defendant, who suffered from post-traumatic stress disorder (PTSD) had been an active member of the Polish Army and had spent time serving in Afghanistan. The circumstances of the case are that the defendant who lived in a shared house got into an argument with his housemates over some food that had gone missing. At the time, he was heavily intoxicated. During the heated exchange, one of the housemates slapped him and made derogatory remarks about the army; he alluded to the fact that people like the defendant only join the army to make money, rape women, and kill children. The defendant lost control and beat the housemate to death.

During his trial for murder, his defence team attempted to use loss of control as a defence. However, the murder conviction was upheld on the basis that the third criteria – evidence that the mental disorder acted to reduce the person's capacity for tolerance and self-restraint was not admissible.

Diminished Responsibility

Diminished responsibility is also known as a partial defence in England and Wales and is used in cases of murder. If successful, the offence of murder is reduced to manslaughter, thus changing the type of sentence the defendant is likely to receive (McGuire & Duff, 2018). Section 2 of the Homicide Act (1967) states that on the balance of probabilities, the following must be proved to use this defence successfully:

1 The individual was suffering from such abnormality of mind that substantially impaired their mental responsibility for the acts and omissions involved in the killing; or,
2 The individual was suffering from an abnormality of mental functioning that (i) has arisen from a recognised medical condition which (ii) substantially impaired the defendant's ability to understand the nature of their conduct, form a rational judgment and/or exercise self-control, and (iii) provides an explanation for their acts or omissions in killing.

This type of defence cannot be used if the defendant was intoxicated at the time of the murder unless it was shown that the intoxication came about due to an abnormality of mental functioning that then substantially impaired the defendant's mental responsibility.

Insanity

The insanity defence came into law following an incident in 1843 during which Daniel M'Naghten shot Edward Drummond, who was the Private Secretary to the Prime Minister, Sir Robert Peel. M'Naghten shot Drummond believing he was the Prime Minister at the time. It was reported that M'Naghten had been suffering from delusions and that these related to the government persecuting him (Mackay, 2010). What followed was the M'Naghten Rules becoming the basis for insanity decision.

To establish this defence, it must be clearly proved that, at the time of committing the act, the defendant was labouring under such a 'defect of reason', from a 'disease of the mind' such that the defendant did not know the nature and quality of the act being done or that the defendant did not know what was being done was wrong contrary to the law (Criminal Procedure (Insanity) Act 1991). By using this type of defence, it does not mean that there is an absence of men rea, for example, a lack of intention, but it does have a significant impact on the type of sentence or disposal option available to the defendant. The types of disposal options that are available to vulnerable defendants will now be visited.

Disposal Options

Should the Court be satisfied that the defendant committed the offence and offered a successful not guilty by reason of insanity defence, the 1991 Act allows the Judge to impose a range of disposal options depending on the defendant and the case, thus the defendant is rarely free to go. The disposal options include hospital orders, restriction orders, mental health treatment, and supervision or guardianship orders.

A hospital order (under Section 37 of the Mental Health Act, 1983) may be imposed for a defendant when the verdict is not guilty by reason of insanity. In doing so, medical evidence must be obtained from at least two registered medical practitioners that the defendant is suffering from a mental health condition or disorder, that makes it appropriate for the defendant to be detained in hospital to receive medical treatment (CPS, 2019). The Court must also be satisfied that it is the most suitable method of disposal for the defendant after taking into consideration the nature of the offence and the character of the offender. Furthermore, a hospital order can only be made if the defendant is able to be admitted to a hospital within 28 days of the order being made. In imposing the hospital order, the defendant is authorised for detention in hospital for medical treatment for an initial period of six months which can be renewed for a further six months if required.

Similarly, an interim hospital order can be made (see Section 38 of the Mental Health Act 1983) following the conviction of an offence usually punishable by imprisonment. The Court must receive medical evidence from two registered medical practitioners that confirm the defendant is suffering from a mental health condition or disorder. However, unlike the hospital order, an interim order can only be made for a period of up to 12 weeks, after which it may be renewed for 28-day periods for a maximum of 12 months.

In addition to the hospital order or an interim hospital order, the defendant can receive a restriction order. Whilst the previous two orders are available at a Magistrates and Crown Court, the restriction order is available only at Crown Court. A restriction order (under Section 41 of the Mental Health Act, 1983) can only be made if a hospital order is in place, and if one of the two medical practitioners who have provided medical evidence has given evidence orally. Considerations are also given to the nature of the offence, the antecedents of the offender and the level of risk relating to the offender committing further offences. By imposing a restriction order, the offender has restrictions placed on them relating to discharge and transfer of leave or absence in order to protect the public from serious harm. The consent required to allow discharge, or a transfer of leave or absence must come from the Secretary of State (CPS, 2019). Given that this order is only available in the Crown Court, a Magistrates Court can make a committal to the Crown Court with a view to a restriction order being imposed; that is, an offender aged 14 years and over who has been convicted of an imprisonable offence can be sent to Crown Court to receive a restriction order.

A Judge may also impose a hospital and limitation directions (as per Section 45A of the Mental Health Act, 1983). This order is only available to the Crown Court and only applies to offenders who are aged 21 years and over who have been convicted of an offence punishable with imprisonment (this does not necessarily mean murder). Offenders who receive this order are detained primarily on the basis of a prison sentence and whilst a limitation direction ends automatically on the day of release (e.g., the day they would have been entitled to be released from custody had they not been detained in hospital), should the offender still be in hospital on their release date, they may remain liable to be detained in hospital from then, much like an offender under an unrestricted hospital order. Furthermore, whilst the limitation direction remains in effect, the Secretary of State can direct that they be removed from hospital to prison to serve the remainder of their sentence, or release them on licence, although this is subject to medical evidence (CPS, 2019).

A mental health treatment requirement can be imposed on those who have been convicted of an imprisonable offence and whose mental health condition requires treatment but not necessarily treatment under a hospital order. By imposing this order (under Section 207 of the Criminal Justice Act, 2003), an offender must accept treatment for a specified period of time under the care of a registered medical practitioner with a view to improve their mental health. The treatment may be delivered to the offender as a resident patient in a care home or a hospital, or as a non-resident patient in such an institution. Treatment may also be received by the offender under the direction of a registered medical practitioner outside of the above requirements and the offender must express a willingness to comply (CPS, 2019).

The other disposal options that can be imposed on an offender relate to a supervision order and a guardianship order (see Section 37 if the Mental Health Act, 1983). A supervision order, available only in the Crown Court, enables treatment to be given to the defendant and is supervised by either a social worker or probation officer. The maximum length of the supervision order is two years. Similarly, a guardianship order is available at both the Magistrates and Crown Courts and medical evidence from two medical practitioners must be provided that evidences that the offender has a mental health condition or disorder which warrants guardianship and that the guardianship is the most appropriate method of assisting the offender. The guardian may be a local authority or an individual related to the offender who is approved by the local authority (CPS, 2019). Throughout all of the disposal options, the focus is on ensuring the vulnerable offender and the public are kept safe, and that the most appropriate form of treatment is provided to the offender.

Summary

There is a general and growing recognition that all defendants, including vulnerable ones, must be able to understand and effectively participate in criminal proceedings (Jacobson & Talbot, 2009). The right to effective participation in trial is a long-established principle in England and Wales and is implicit in the very notion of an adversarial procedure; it is also reflected in the criteria used to determine whether a defendant is fit to plead and thus stand trial (Jacobson & Talbot, 2009). The provision of Special Measures to vulnerable defendants is an important part of upholding this right to effective participation (Fairclough, 2018). However, scholars have frequently highlighted that the current provision of Special Measures do not go far enough in protecting this right nor ensuring effective participation within the justice system, especially when one considers the impact of vulnerability at trial (Owusu-Bempah, 2020), and when one considers the measures available in statute to vulnerable witnesses.

The current inadequacy of the Special Measures provision for vulnerable defendants may risk wrongful conviction of the innocent where, for example, insufficient adjustments were made to help the defendant give their best evidence (Fairclough, 2017). Not only does this impact upon the right to a fair trial but can lead to miscarriages of justice. That said, there are changes being made to the provision of Special Measures for the vulnerable defendant, although a lot of this remains largely reliant on case law and at the Court's inherent discretion. The development and implementation of the HMCTS Appointed Intermediary Service framework demonstrates a positive step forward in recognising the importance of defendant intermediaries to assist the most vulnerable at trial. It must be noted, however, that there are concerns regarding the commercialisation and privatisation of intermediary services, and that despite its development, s.104 of the Coroners and Justice Act (2009) remains unimplemented. This means that there is still no legislative or statutory power for the use of the defendant intermediary.

The chapter has concluded with the consideration of defences that a vulnerable defendant may use at trial and what this can mean for the disposal options that may be imposed upon them. Here the focus remains on the individuals' mental health condition; however, it appears beyond belief that whilst some of these defences have been used for over 100 years, the use of Special Measures during the trial still remains so under-developed. There remains much more work needed to assist vulnerable defendants during the trial stage.

Key Learning Points

- An increasingly large number of vulnerable defendants are coming into contact with the justice system; subsequently, they may find it difficult to follow Court proceedings and effectively participate in the trial process.
- Barriers to effective participation during trial can impede upon the defendant's right to a fair trial under Article 6 of the European Convention of Human Rights.
- Being 'fit to plead' and stand trial related to whether an individual can participate in their criminal trial – this is usually determined by a Judge and is based on how well the defendant can understand the charges of which they face, make informed decisions regarding their plea, understand their rights and follow court proceedings and effectively instruct counsel, and be able to give their evidence.
- There are a range of Special Measures available to vulnerable defendants across many jurisdictions in Europe. The case is different for those in England and Wales.
- Whilst Special Measures are automatically available for vulnerable witnesses as per the YJCEA (1999), these are limited for vulnerable defendants.
- One Special Measure is that of the defendant intermediary; however, this is not enacted in law, rather the provision of such is down to the inherent power of the Judge at trial.
- Despite the development of the HMCTS Appointed Intermediary Service framework, there remains issues with the use of defendant intermediaries and s.104 of the Coroners and Justice Act (2009) remains unimplemented, thus there is still no legislative or statutory power for the use of the defendant intermediary.
- This is in contrast to the defences available to vulnerable defendants when considering their criminal liability. Vulnerable defendants have a range of defences available to them at trial such as loss of control, diminished responsibility, and insanity; this can impact upon the type of disposal option imposed on them should one be used successfully.

References

Alger, K. (2021). More than what meets the ear: Speech transcription as a barrier to justice for African American vernacular English speakers. *Georgetown Journal of Law and Modern Critical Race Perspectives*, *13*, 87.

Anderson, S., Hawes, D., & Sno, P. (2016). Language impairments among youth offenders: A systematic review, *65*, *195*.

Backen, P. (2017). They just don't get it: Communication and the work of an intermediary in the vulnerable people in the justice system. Independently Published.

Carlile [Lord] (2014). *Independent Parliamentarians' inquiry into the operation and effectiveness of the youth court.* Ministry of Justice.

Cooper, P., & Wurtzel, D. (2013). A day late and a dollar short: In search of an intermediary scheme for vulnerable defendants in England and Wales. *Criminal Law Review*, *1*, 4–22.

Coroners and Justice Act. (2009). https://www.legislation.gov.uk/ukpga/2009/25/contents

Criminal Justice Act. (2003). https://www.legislation.gov.uk/ukpga/2003/44/contents

Criminal Procedure (Insanity Act). (1964). https://www.legislation.gov.uk/ukpga/1964/84

Criminal Procedure (Insanity) Act. (1991). https://www.legislation.gov.uk/ukpga/1991/25/contents

Criminal Procedure Rules. (2020). https://www.legislation.gov.uk/uksi/2020/759/contents/made

CPS. (2019). *Mental health conditions and disorders*. https://www.cps.gov.uk/publication/mental-health-conditions-and-disorders-draft-prosecution-guidance

C v Sevenoaks Youth Court [2009] EWHC 3088 (Admin).

Curen, R. (2005). Vulnerable adults and the criminal justice system in England and Wales: Some proposals for reform. *Criminal Lawyer, 155*, 3–5.

European Convention on Human Rights (ECHR).

Fairclough, S. (2017). It doesn't happen ... and I've never thought it was necessary for it to happen: Barriers to vulnerable defendants giving evidence by live link in crown court trials. *International Journal of Evidence and Proof, 21*(3), 209–229.

Fairclough, S. (2018). Speaking up for injustice: Reconsidering the provision of special measures through the lens of equality. *Criminal Law Review, 1*, 4–19.

Fairclough, S. (2019). The consequences of unenthusiastic criminal justice reforms: A special measures case study. *Criminology and Criminal Justice, 21*(2), 151–168.

Fairclough, S., & Greenwood, H. (2023). Vulnerable defendants, special measures and miscarriages of justice in England and Wales. In R. Dehaghani, S. Fairclough, & L. Mergaerts (Eds.), *Vulnerability, the accused, and the criminal justice system* (pp. 162–176). Routledge.

Fuller, T., Kennard, A., Eslinger, D., Lamb, R., & Pavle, J. (2010). *More mentally ill persons are in jails and prisons than hospitals: A survey of the States*. The Treatment Advocacy Centre.

Gerry, F. (2012). *Vulnerable defendants and the courts*. https://www.thejusticegap.com/vulnerable-defendants-and-the-courts/

Gerry, F., & Cooper, P. (2017). Effective participation of vulnerable accused persons: Case management, court adaptation and rethinking criminal responsibility. *Journal of Judicial Administration, 1*, 265–275.

Home Office (1998). *Speaking up for justice: Report of the interdepartmental working group on the treatment of vulnerable or intimidated witnesses in the criminal justice system*. Home Office.

Homicide Act. (1967). https://www.legislation.gov.uk/ukpga/Eliz2/5-6/11/section/2

Howard, H. (2022). Effective participation of mentally vulnerable defendants in the English magistrates' courts: The crucial role of liaison and diversion. *The Howard Journal of Crime and Justice, 61*, 203–220.

Hoyano, L., & Rafferty, A. (2017). Rationing defence intermediaries under the April 2016 criminal practice direction. *Criminal Law Review, 2*, 93–105.

Jacobson, J., & Talbot, J. (2009). *Vulnerable defendants in the criminal courts: A review of provision for adults and children*. Prison Reform Trust.

Lacey, N., & Zedner, L. (2012). Legal constructions of crime. In M. Maguire, R. Morgan, & R. Reiner (Eds.), *The Oxford handbook of criminology* (pp. 159–181). Oxford University Press.

Law Commission (2016). *Unfitness to plead. Volume 1: Report*. Law Commission. No. 364.

Mackay, R. (2010). Mental disability at the time of the offence. In L. Gostin, P. Bartlett, P. Fennell, J. McHale, & R. Mackay (Eds.), *Principles of mental health law and policy* (pp. 721–755). Oxford Unviersity Press.

Marinos, V., & Whittingham, L. (2019). The role of therapeutic jurisprudence to support persons with intellectual and developmental disabilities in the courtroom: Reflections from Ontario, Canada. *International Journal of Law and Psychiatry, 63*, 18–25.

McEwan, J. (2013). Vulnerable defendants and the fairness of trials. *Criminal Law Review, 2*, 100–113.

McGuire, J., & Duff, S. (2018). *Forensic psychology: Routes through the system*. Palgrave.

Mental Health Act. (1983). https://www.legislation.gov.uk/ukpga/1983/20/contents

Ministry of Justice. (2023). Registered Intermediary Procedural Guidance Manual. https://assets.publishing.service.gov.uk/media/64e4858e4002ee000d560cf5/registered-intermediary-procedural-guidance-manual.pdf

Morrison, J., & Taggart, J. (2023). The role of the intermediary in ensuring the effective participation of vulnerable defendants. In R. Dehaghani, S. Fairclough, & L. Mergaerts (Eds.), *Vulnerability, the accused, and the criminal justice system* (pp. 177–191). Routledge.

Owusu-Bempah, A. (2020). Understanding the barriers to defendant participation in criminal proceedings in England and Wales. *Legal Studies*, *40*(4), 609–629.
Plotnikoff, J., & Woolfson, R. (2015). *Intermediaries in the criminal justice system: Improving communication for vulnerable witnesses and defendants*. Policy Press.
R (on the application of AS) v Great Yarmouth Youth Court [2011] EWHC 2059 (Admin).
R v Cox [2012] EWCA Crim 549. https://www.casemine.com/judgement/uk/5a8ff7af60d03e7f57eb1369#:~:text=The%20case%20highlights%20the%20importance,intermediaries%2C%20on%20the%20trial%20process.
R v Rejmanski [2018] WLR 2721. https://www.casemine.com/judgement/uk/5b2897fa2c94e06b9e19e903
R v Walls [2011] 2 Cr App R 6. https://www.casemine.com/judgement/uk/5a8ff70960d03e7f57ea656f
R v Waltham Forest Youth Court [2004] EWHC 715. https://www.casemine.com/judgement/uk/5a8ff73660d03e7f57ea9b4e
R v Yahya Rashid [2017] EWCA Crim 2. https://www.casemine.com/judgement/uk/5a8ff7b760d03e7f57eb1735
R(TP) v West London Youth Court. https://www.casemine.com/judgement/uk/5a8ff74060d03e7f57eaa730
SC v UK (2004) EHRR 10. https://www.yumpu.com/en/document/view/50649659/sc-v-the-united-kingdom-2005-40-ehrr-10#google_vignette
Skowyra, K., & Cocozza, J. (2007). *Blueprint for change: A comprehensive model for the identification and treatment of youth with mental health needs in contact with the juvenile justice system.* The National Centre for Mental Health and Juvenile Justice: Policy Research Associates.
Smethurst, A., & Collins, K. (2019). Mock jury perceptions of vulnerable defendants assisted in court by intermediaries – Are jurors' expectations violated? *Applied Psychology in Criminal Justice*, *15*(1), 23–40.
Snow, P., Powell, M., & Sanger, D. (2012). Oral language competence, young speakers, and the law. *Language Speech and Hearing Services in Schools*, *43*, 496.
Taggart, J. (2022). Vulnerable defendants and the HMCTS court appointed intermediary services. *Criminal Law Review*, *6*, 432–447.
Triangle. www.triangle.org.uk
Turner, K., & Hughes, N. (2022). Supporting young people's cognition and communication in the courtroom: A scoping review of current practice. *Criminal Behaviour and Mental Health*, *32*(3), 175–196.
Turner, K., & Westwood, C. (2023). Speech, language and communication needs and the role of the speech and language therapist. In R. Dehaghani, S. Fairclough, & L. Mergaerts (Eds.), *Vulnerability, the accused, and the criminal justice system* (pp. 147–161). Routledge.
T and V v United Kingdom (1999) 22 EHRR 330. http://hudoc.echr.coe.int/eng#{%22itemid%22:[%22003-68456-68924%22]}
Vogel, M., Stephens, K., & Siebels, D. (2014). Mental illness and the criminal justice system. *Sociology Compass*, *8*, 627–638.
White, R., Bornman, J., Johnson, E., & Msipa, D. (2021). Court accommodations for persons with severe communication disabilities: A legal scoping review. *Psychology, Public Policy, and Law*, *27*(3), 399–420.
Youth Justice and Criminal Evidence Act (YJCEA). (1999). London: HMSO.

8 Future Directions

Vulnerability in the Criminal Justice System: A Historical Overview

Crime has always been and will continue to be a political, social, and contentious issue within society, with scholars frequently reporting that crime was seen as being out of control in the latter part of the 20th century (Rock, 2004), and being a part of 'normal' life for many (Young, 1999). It was not until the early 1990s that a reduction in crime was reported in England and Wales and many countries around the world (Barclay & Tavares, 2002). How vulnerable individuals were treated within the justice system played a big part in this. Historically, juries were required to convict an individual regardless of their mental health condition and whether the act was intentional or not. What could happen is the Court would grant a 'charter of pardon' to any 'insane' individuals found guilty of an offence, thus entitling the convicted individual to a full release (Walker, 1985). However, there were many vulnerable individuals convicted of crime that were confined to bridewells or houses of correction, particularly by the 16th and 17th centuries (Seddon, 2007). Thus, scholars frequently highlighted how prisons were frequently occupied by 'lunatics' who did not receive appropriate treatment or care (Howard, 1784), and thus posed a threat to prison order and prison officers' lives. Whilst many advocated for vulnerable individuals to be moved to a place of seclusion, this was not implemented until the 18th century (Symonds, 1995).

The development of hospitals and workhouses were primarily for those who were 'poor, decrepit and dependent' (Symonds, 1995, p. 96). Indeed, the Lunacy Act (1845) in England and Wales meant that the building of asylums became a reality for such vulnerable individuals, leading to those with mental health conditions in particular, being isolated. Such practices were enforced until the 20th century (Houston, 2019), with asylums, such as Bethlem Hospital in London often 'showing off' the most vulnerable of their patients to the public who would pay to view them (Dvoksin et al., 2020). The implementation of asylums and other similar institutions occurred around the world. However, despite the popular use of such institutions for housing the vulnerable, they were often criticised for being 'overcrowded, inhumane, and ineffective' (Lomax, 1921, p. 10), often resulting in the mistreatment of patients (Scull, 1979). It was not until after World War II that significant changes in psychiatry led to an international consensus that mental health care needed to change (Freeman et al., 1985).

The term 'deinstitutionalisation' was coined as a move away from the traditional mental health hospital to a more community-based approach occurred (Novella, 2010). Thus, asylums were closed and the care and support for vulnerable individuals moved to the community (Fakhoury & Priebe, 2002), with it was believed they should be activity treated and supported (Ballerini, 2002; Schmiedebach et al., 2002). This process occurred at varying

DOI: 10.4324/9781003386735-8

rates around the world with some countries, such as Hong Kong and Japan, still treating those with mental health concerns in asylums or similar institutions (Kuno & Asukai, 2000; Yip, 2000). Thus, mental health reforms remain an ongoing process (Becker & Barquero, 2001). Despite the progress that other countries have made around the world, there remains concerns as to the treatment of vulnerable individuals. For example, some have indicated that community-based settings for individuals with mental health conditions would lead to further alienation and stigmatisation of such vulnerable individuals (McCulloch et al., 2000) and that those who receive treatment in the community face hostility and opposition from other community members (Fakhoury & Priebe, 2002). In addition, those with vulnerabilities are often seen as more dangerous than the average member of the public, leading to the stereotyping and stigmatisation of those with mental health conditions (Daff & Thomas, 2014; Link et al., 1999). In fact the concept of 'dangerousness' has led many individuals to believe that those with a mental health condition are unpredictable and responsible for a disproportionate level of serious and violent crime (Yap et al., 2014). This perception is not limited to England and Wales but has been reported around the world (Reavley & Jorm, 2012). Given that those who have mental health difficulties are at an increased risk of entering the criminal justice system (CJS), (Blaauw et al., 2000) and are over-represented in custody and in prisons (Baldry et al., 2013; Indig et al., 2011), this has implications for their treatment and justice outcomes.

This is also true for vulnerable witnesses; originally termed the 'forgotten actors' in the CJS, (Sanders, 2002), the history of witness' rights has been markedly different to that of suspects or defendants' rights. Historically, their views were not given much interest by the police nor the prosecution, other than the type of evidence they could provide in Court. Thus, witnesses were often left in the dark in terms of the progress of their case. As such, the consideration of witness views and their rights is a relatively new development compared to the vulnerable suspect/defendant. Indeed, it was not until the late 1950s that attention started to develop towards the experiences of witnesses in America (Edwards, 2014), and the 1960s when witnesses started to be considered more in England and Wales. This was largely due to the development of bodies such as the Criminal Injuries Compensation Board (established in 1964). However, the position of the witness was ill-defined and contested with much debate about who was eligible as a witness and what their entitlements should be (Rock, 2004). But, with only a small number of cases successfully moving through the justice system, there developed a focus on coaxing witnesses to report a crime and go to trial. Subsequently, witness' rights have progressed fuelled, perhaps, by the activism of witness groups and organisations, and due to growing attention from politicians. Indeed, witnesses now are kept up-to-date with the progress of their case, are encouraged to give evidence at trial and can make victim personal statements to inform the Court and Parole Board of the impact the crime has had on their lives. Thus, there is now a commitment to witnesses to ensure their voices are heard in the justice system (Kilcommins et al., 2010).

Although progress has been made in recent decades regarding witnesses and their involvement in the justice system, it was not until 2010, in a recent Court of Appeal case in England and Wales, that it was highlighted that, 'until recently, there was no possibility of the Court even considering the evidence of complainants with serious communication difficulties' (R v Watts [2010] EWCA, 1824, para 56). Indeed, even as recently as 1999, a 16-year-old's evidence in rape trial was deemed unacceptable because her 'mental age' was considered less than an eight-year-old, and it was thought that children under the age of eight, could not give evidence under oath at trial due to their communicative and cognitive abilities (McCormack, 1991). In 1998, the Labour Government published a consultation document that underpinned proposed legislation to assist vulnerable witnesses. The 'Speaking Up for Justice' report (Home Office, 2001) was published to propose 'a coherent and integrated scheme to provide appropriate support and assistance' for this vulnerable group (p. 1) and includes an explicit acknowledgment of the difficulties that vulnerable witnesses face when engaging in the justice system. Consequently, recommendations were made to improving identification of vulnerability and/or intimidation in witnesses, greater communication, and the implementation of a range of Special Measures for use at trial. Similar measures were implemented in European countries around a similar time. However, whilst progress has been made in the way that vulnerable individuals are now treated within the CJS, such recommendations can only be put in place if the individual is identified as such.

Defining and Identifying Vulnerability in Witnesses and Suspects

The term 'vulnerability' is frequently used in public, political and academic discourse (Misztal, 2011). Generally, it refers to the neediest of those facing difficulties, risk or exposure and refers to the possibility of being physically or emotionally harmed. Vulnerability has also been described generally as a state or condition whereby an individual is in danger, under threat, or experiencing health challenges and thus requires support or protection (Larkin, 2009). Defining vulnerability within the CJS context is more complex, however, given its widespread implications (Bartkowiak-Theron & Asquith, 2012). Conventional and popularist views of vulnerability tie it to individuals who are witnesses of crime (Dehaghani & Newman, 2017; Enang et al., 2019). Others have alluded to specific characteristics such as youth or old age, physical and mental health, and low socioeconomic status, or the types of circumstances the individual finds themselves in Brown (2015). Some suggest that there are different levels of vulnerability (Smith & O'Mahony, 2018). Consequently, many scholars argue that there is no internationally agreed definition of vulnerability in relation to witnesses and suspects, and that it is largely dependent upon the lens or context in which it is being considered. However, within the justice system, vulnerability is often viewed with reference to procedures such as the police interview because of the impact it may have on obtaining evidence (Smith & O'Mahony, 2018).

One major body of psychological knowledge concerning vulnerability in the CJS, is the work of Gudjonsson. He defines vulnerability as, 'psychological characteristics or mental state which renders an [individual] prone, in certain circumstances, to providing information which is inaccurate, unreliable or misleading' (Gudjonsson, 2006, p. 68). In developing his definition, Gudjonsson draws upon four main types of vulnerability:

1. Mental disorder including mental health conditions such as mood disorders, schizophrenia, and personality disorders.
2. Abnormal mental state that refers to those experiencing anxiety, intoxication, or withdrawal from alcohol/drugs.
3. Intellectual functioning measured by an individual's IQ level.
4. Personality such as how susceptible to suggestibility, compliance, and acquiescence an individual may be.

Whilst his work remains pivotal in our understanding on the degree of risk and characteristics an individual may possess that can impede on the police interview, it also suggests that vulnerable witnesses and suspects may be susceptible to providing unreliable or misleading evidence, and so should not be considered in isolation.

Other scholars highlight that defining vulnerability should not necessarily focus on specific characteristics but be used as a conceptual tool to compel the state to respond appropriately by implementing the necessary safeguards. Fineman (2013) defines vulnerability, therefore, as 'universal and constant...' that must be '...understood as particular, varied, and unique on the individual level' (p. 21). Fineman identifies two forms of vulnerability – the first is physical which includes mental and intellectual states, and the second relates to a socially constructed state. Thus, Fineman posits that all individuals can be vulnerable and prone to dependency, and the state has an obligation to assist with this.

In practice, it can be very difficult to define who is and who is not vulnerable, and using psychological theories alone may not adequately capture vulnerability. In England and Wales, there are two key pieces of legislative guidance that also provides definitions of who may be vulnerable; the Youth Justice and Criminal Evidence Act (YJCEA, 1999) and the Police and Criminal Evidence Act (1984) and the accompanying Codes of Practice. The former identifies vulnerable witnesses as those under the age of 18 years and who have a mental disorder, who are significantly impaired in relation to intelligence and social functioning and who have a physical disability. The YJCEA also identifies 'intimidated' witnesses as those whose quality of evidence is likely to be diminished due to fear or distress in relation to giving evidence. The latter, in particular, Code C identified vulnerable suspects as those under the age of 18 years, and those who as a result of a mental health condition or mental disorder has difficulties in understanding or communicating effectively, does not appear to understand the significance of what they are told, or their replies to questions, and who may be particularly prone to becoming confused, providing unreliable or misleading information, and accepting or acting upon suggestions from others and readily agreeing to suggestions without any protest or questions. Whilst both pieces of legislation have ensured that large numbers of vulnerable individuals are assisted throughout the justice system, they are not without their criticisms, for example, the use of over-inclusive terminology and a preoccupation with definitions and labelling in the YJCEA (Bartkowiak-Theron & Asquith, 2012; Gibbs, 2018; Walklate, 2011), or the complexities of the definition in Code C and thus the interpretation of vulnerability for individuals first entering custody (Dehaghani & Bath, 2019; Farrugia, 2021). As such, there still remains difficulties in defining vulnerability.

Given the difficulties in defining vulnerability, it is not wholly surprising that there are difficulties in identifying vulnerable individuals. When a vulnerable individual enters the justice system, the onus is on the investigating officer to identify if a vulnerability exists based on the legislative guidance provided in the YJCEA (1999) and the Achieving Best Evidence in Criminal Proceedings guidance (ABE; MOJ, 2022), and the PACE (1984; Home Office, 2018) and associated Codes of Practice. However, research has consistently shown this to be problematic for both vulnerable witnesses and vulnerable suspects. For example, research has highlighted that up to half of all vulnerable witnesses are not identified (Ewin, 2010), particularly if the crime is a minor offence (HMIC, 2015; Sherman et al., 2017). In addition, it has been suggested that many assessments to identify vulnerable witnesses rely initially on perception and judgment (Majeed-Ariss et al., 2019). Similarly, vulnerable suspects also face failures in being identified as such. Research has reported that there is ambiguity in the understanding of what vulnerability means and that there are inconsistencies in police force areas in terms of how vulnerability is defined and thus operationalised (Farrugia, 2021). This has been echoed in other countries around the world (see, e.g., Baldry et al., 2013). Furthermore, the screening tools used have been deemed not fit for purpose due to missing many cases of vulnerable individuals entering custody (McKinnon &

Grubin, 2012). However, this is not surprising given that those responsible for identifying vulnerability in the first instance receive little to no formal training in mental health (Vigurs & Quy, 2017). The ability to define and thus identify vulnerable individuals entering the CJS is crucial and has implications for the treatment and outcome of vulnerable witnesses and suspects. If a vulnerable individual is not identified as such, then they will not receive the appropriate support or safeguards to assist them.

Safeguarding Vulnerable Witnesses and Suspects –

It has been reported that mental ill-health, for example, will affect one in four of us at some point in our lives (World Health Organisation, 2001). Vulnerability is a complex area within policing and one that can be very time-consuming (HMICFRS, 2018). Mental health care is becoming increasingly part of the core business of policing and this has been exacerbated by a steep rise in funding cuts leading to many community services being reduced. What this has led to is many police services in England and Wales working beyond their duty when responding to mental health needs. Thus, working collaboratively with the appropriate services in assisting vulnerable individuals is crucial (HMICFRS, 2018); the form of safeguards enshrined in legislation to assist vulnerable witnesses and vulnerable suspects is designed to assist with this. Although there exists many issues and difficulties in identifying vulnerability, when vulnerable individuals are identified as such, they should be afforded safeguards to assist them as they navigate their way through the CJS. Two such safeguards are the role of the Registered Intermediary and the role of the Appropriate Adult.

The Registered Intermediary is one type of Special Measure for vulnerable (and intimidated) witnesses. Their role primarily is to communicate to the witness, any questions put to them and to any persons asking the questions, the answers given by the witness in reply to them, and to assist with any necessary explanations (s. 29(2), YJCEA, 1999). Described as 'new players in the CJS' (Plotnikoff & Woolfson, 2015, p. 3), the Registered Intermediary Scheme was only rolled out nationally in England and Wales in 2008, despite the concept of the intermediary role dating back to the 1950s. Initially, Israel introduced the 'youth examiner' in 1955 which enabled a social worker to question children (Libai, 1969). Similarly, in Africa in 1977, legislation was passed to allow an intermediary to relay questions to children from lawyers (Henderson, 2012). In England and Wales, the use of a 'child examiner' was proposed to relay lawyers' questions to children and allow their evidence to be videotaped before trial (Williams, 1987a, 1987b). Following an advisory group led by Judge Thomas Pigot QC who made recommendations for all children's evidence, including cross-examination, to be captured before trial and lawyers' questions to be relayed to children through an approved person (Home Office, 1989), the Criminal Justice Act in 1991 was implemented. However, the legislation did not allow for a child examiner (Plotnikoff & Woolfson, 2015). In fact, it was not for another seven years that recommendations were made for the Court to hold statutory powers to order intermediary assistances where it would assist vulnerable witnesses to give their best evidence (Sanders et al., 1997). What followed was a number of pilot schemes of the role of the intermediary which was eventually rolled out nationally in 2008.

Accredited by the Ministry of Justice in England and Wales, Registered Intermediaries are trained to facilitate communication between the legal professional and the vulnerable witness so as to obtain the best quality evidence from the vulnerable witness (Plotnikoff & Woolfson, 2015; Taggart, 2021). Upon being matched to the vulnerable witness, an assessment is made of their communication needs and recommendations are made on how best to facilitate obtaining best evidence. The Registered Intermediary is then present throughout the police interview and any subsequent trial where the vulnerable witness is required to give their evidence at Court. Described as 'little short of revolutionary' (Henderson, 2015, p. 155), some suggest that what intermediaries have achieved as a body may have done more than anyone to affect a culture change in the way that the justice system now deals with vulnerable witnesses (Wurtzel & Marchant, 2017). Many international developments of the scheme follow a similar model.

Research has frequently highlighted how vulnerable witnesses, such as children for example, become very stressed when providing their evidence, which can impact upon their overall accuracy and consistency especially at trial (Righarts et al., 2015). Whilst early work found that Registered Intermediaries are helpful in terms of aiding communication and helping vulnerable witnesses cope with the stress of giving evidence (Plotnikoff & Woolfson, 2007), the effectiveness of this Special Measure has not been well examined. Collins et al. (2017) examined the perceptions of jurors and the impact on their decision-making where an intermediary is assisting a vulnerable witness. Their findings indicated that ratings for children's communication and the quality of cross-examination were greater when a Registered Intermediary was present compared to when one was not present, and supports earlier work (Ridley et al., 2015). Other work that has explored the effectiveness of the Registered Intermediary has focused on the views of legal professionals that are required to work alongside the intermediary. Overall, positive responses have been received from Judges and legal professionals (Henderson, 2015; VC, 2018). However, work is limited with vulnerable adult witnesses that have different types of mental health conditions or disorders and learning disabilities.

The Appropriate Adult was introduced in England and Wales as part of the legislative framework of the PACE (1984; Home Office, 2018) and accompanying Codes of Practice designed to regulate police powers and suspects' rights. The Appropriate Adult's role is defined by Code C (Home Office, 2018) as a parent, guardian, social worker, or some other responsible person aged 18 years and above, who does not have any association with the police (para 1.7). The role of the Appropriate Adult is to 'safeguard the rights, entitlements and welfare of juveniles and vulnerable persons' (para 1.7A, p. 7). As such, they are to support and advise, and assist the vulnerable suspect whilst they are in custody. In addition, the Appropriate Adult is required to ensure the police are acting properly and fairly and assist with and facilitate communication whilst ensuring that the vulnerable suspect understand their legal rights. Initially, the role of the Appropriate Adult fell to the vulnerable suspects' parents, particularly if the suspect was a child. This meant that many vulnerable suspects were supported by Appropriate Adults that had little or no training – research frequently indicated that when parents acted within this role, their contributions were more consistent with control or punishment (Brown, 1997; Bucke & Brown, 1997; Leggett et al., 2007), and assisting the police in obtaining a confession (Dixon et al., 1990). Furthermore, research has indicated that parents acting as Appropriate Adults led to little contribution in assisting the vulnerable suspect (Evans, 1993; Howard et al., 2015; Pierpoint, 2001).

Consequently, recommendations were made for the use of professionally trained Appropriate Adults over 30 years ago and have since been encouraged in more recent years (Pierpoint, 2004). This has led to the development of the professional Appropriate Adult; such individuals either volunteer or are employed within dedicated Appropriate Adult schemes which are organised and funded locally. The development of the National Appropriate Adult Network (NAAN) assists with supporting and representing organisations that deliver Appropriate Adult support. Registered as a charity, the NAAN identify as an independent centre of expertise that provide training to around 100 member organisations (NAAN, 2023). Subsequently, there now exists a number of schemes that operate under the NAAN whereby individuals are trained specifically for this role and support vulnerable suspects in custody. However, whilst progress has been made in this area, there remains a disparity in the provision available (Farrugia, 2023). There is still no statutory duty for any agency to provide an Appropriate Adult for a vulnerable suspect (Jessiman & Cameron, 2017) and not all police force areas have access to an Appropriate Adult scheme (Bath et al., 2015). Furthermore, police forces remain consistent in their use of Appropriate Adults (Bath & Dehaghani, 2020; Farrugia, 2021), and there have been concerns raised about the passive nature of the Appropriate Adult during the police interview (Bradley, 2009; Evans, 1993; Farrugia, 2023; Medford et al., 2003; Pierpoint, 2001) – this is not surprising given that the Appropriate Adult can be actively discouraged from completing their duties during the vulnerable suspect's interview (Dehaghani, 2021; Jessiman & Cameron, 2017). Thus, there still remains issues with the Appropriate Adult role and ensuring the vulnerable suspect is adequately protected.

One consideration to support the vulnerable suspect is to introduce the role of the intermediary to them. In England and Wales, the term, 'Registered Intermediary' is restricted to those who are recruited and trained by the Ministry of Justice who then assist vulnerable witnesses as per the requirements of the YJCEA (1999). Currently, vulnerable suspects and defendants are excluded from this Act thereby meaning that they are not eligible for the same Special Measures as vulnerable witnesses. This includes not being able to access the Registered Intermediary (Plotnikoff & Woolfson, 2015). An amendment to the Act added by s.104 of the Coroners and Justice Act (2009) considers examination of a defendant through an intermediary, however, this amendment is yet to come into force. It is only when a Judge exercises their inherent jurisdiction to appoint an intermediary for a defendant, that one can be used. In reality, some Registered Intermediaries take on the role as a defendant intermediary but there are also private sector organisations that recruit and train intermediaries for vulnerable defendants (Plotnikoff & Woolfson, 2015). However, having an intermediary to assist a vulnerable defendant is a contentious issue (McEwan, 2009). They are only likely to be appointed whilst the vulnerable defendant gives their evidence at trial rather than during the earlier police interview stage; this has been and continues to be heavily criticised. Unfortunately, the vulnerable suspect's safeguards are not yet on par with those of the vulnerable witness. This is particularly concerning, especially during the police interview.

Interviewing Vulnerable Witnesses and Suspects

Given the high prevalence rates of vulnerable individuals entering the CJS, the reality is that many police interview conducted with witnesses and suspects involve those that are vulnerable. Their vulnerabilities, whether that be mental or physical health difficulties, or a learning disability, are likely to impede upon their ability to effectively give their evidence, and thus place them at a disadvantage (Farrugia & Maras, 2023; Gudjonsson, 2018). As such, it is vital that their needs are accommodated for. The direction that is provided to police officers when interviewing vulnerable witnesses lies within the ABE guidance (MOJ, 2022). Prior to the development of this guidance, the Memorandum of Good Practice was developed; this was initially published by the Home Office in 1992 to assist with conducting video-recorded interviews with vulnerable witnesses. What followed was a significant amount of psychological research into its implementation. Early work found that less than a quarter of 15,000 videotaped interviews that had been conducted in the first nine months of the guidance had been submitted to the Crown Prosecution Service (CPS), but only 44 of those interviews had been played at trial (Butler, 1993). Davies et al. (1995) reported that interviewers were not always following the guidance provided to them in terms of encouraging a free recall and that questioning techniques were poor. However, they also reported that 75% of cases at trial included an application to use a video-recorded interview. Other research has reported similar mixed findings. As a result, and following further working groups and governmental reports, the ABE guidance was developed and implemented. Largely consistent with the Memorandum of Good Practice, the ABE guidance provided further recommendations to ensure that all vulnerable witnesses are supported prior to the police interview and trial.

Being able to obtain detailed and reliable information from vulnerable witnesses is essential (Gabbert et al., 2018). The ABE guidance emphasises the importance of four phases during the interview, namely:

1 Rapport, pivotal to the interview and advocated for in all major interviewing guidelines in order to achieve best evidence (Fisher & Geiselman, 1992; Gabbert et al., 2021; Lamb et al., 2007).
2 Obtaining a free recall, so that the witness has the opportunity to provide their uninterrupted, free narrative regarding their account of what occurred.
3 Using appropriate questioning techniques such as open questions to elicit as much accurate and reliable information as possible (Myklebust, 2009; Phillips et al., 2011; Snook et al., 2012), and
4 Closure which should occur at the end of the interview to allow for the interviewer to provide a summary of the witness' account and correct any inaccuracies.

The ABE guidance advocated for the use of the Cognitive Interview (Fisher & Geiselman, 1992) which incorporates the above phases. Initially developed over 25 years ago and based upon well-established psychological principles relating to human memory and information retrieval, the Cognitive Interview consists of four techniques in order to support the witness in their recall. Much psychological work has focused on the Cognitive Interview, and it has been enhanced and modified several times (Davis et al., 2005; Holliday, 2003a, 2003b).

Alongside the development of interview techniques for witnesses, those for suspects were also being developed. Prior to the 1980s, police officers received little or no training in interviewing suspects. This led to police officers using coercive and manipulative techniques with the aim to obtain a confession (Walkley, 1987). This ethos was bolstered by influential training manuals at the time which drew on inappropriate interview tactics. Thus, police officers were encouraged to interrogate rather than interview suspects. The Reid Interrogation technique (Inbau et al., 2013) is perhaps one of the most well-known techniques and encourages interviewers to observe non-verbal behaviour as an indicator to deception and then subject suspects to a nine-step interrogation technique. This has been heavily criticised throughout academic and psychological literature for the use of psychological tactics such as the fabrication of evidence, and the confession-seeking ethos. Research has continuously demonstrated the heightened risk of a vulnerable suspect falsely confessing should they be interrogated in this manner and there have been many high-profile miscarriages of justice that have occurred (Gudjonsson, 2018; Meissner et al., 2014).

It was the Fisher Inquiry in 1977 that changed the course of how suspects in England and Wales were interviewed (Price & Caplan, 1977). Following another high-profile miscarriage of justice (the Maxwell Confait case), Sir Henry Fisher conducted an inquiry to explore how suspects were being interviewed and to make recommendations. What followed was the Royal Commission on Criminal Procedure in England and Wales (RCCP; Home Office, 1981) which made recommendations for policy change relating to police powers and the rights of suspects. Despite the introduction of the PACE (1984; Home Office, 2018), police interviewing of suspects remained poor and the same confession-seeking ethos was still in place (Baldwin, 1992). As such, there remained a need to shift from the ineffective use of coercive and manipulative questioning techniques towards a more information-seeking style of interviewing.

The introduction of the PEACE model of interviewing ensured this (Williamson, 2006). A mnemonic for the five stages of the model, the aim is to gather accurate and reliable information through the use of appropriate questioning techniques. The implementation of the model was to ensure that all police officers were provided with the necessary skills and training to conduct effective, information seeking investigative interviews. However, early research into its efficacy produced mixed results. For example, McGurk et al. (1993) found an improvement in interviewer skillset after the training had initially been received, but Clarke and Milne (2001) found that interviews were still interviewer driven, and the use of open questions was limited. A mixed picture within the literature still remains (Soukara et al., 2009; Wright & Powell, 2006).

Although interview methods have improved and been developed for interviewing all types of witnesses and suspects, their use with vulnerable populations casts doubts on their effectiveness. For example, when a Cognitive Interview is used with witnesses that have an Autism Spectrum Condition, research suggests that this type of vulnerable witness actually report more incorrect details (Maras & Bowler, 2010). Other work has highlighted the ineffectiveness of one of the techniques used in the Cognitive Interview when being conducted with a witness with an Autism Spectrum Condition (Maras & Bowler, 2012). Concerns regarding the ineffectiveness of the Cognitive Interview have been reported in research conducted with adults that have an intellectual disability also (Robinson & McGuire, 2005). This is also the case with vulnerable suspects; that is, current interview models may not be the most effective. The work of Farrugia and Gabbert (2020) found that suspects with mental health conditions typically performed worse in terms of amount of and accuracy of information when asked open questions compared to when they were asked more specific questions. Whilst the general consensus is that the use of open questions tend to elicit more detailed and accurate information (Oxburgh et al., 2010), vulnerable suspects in their sample provided more information and more accurate information in response to a modified interview model; one that contained more closed questions. Their findings add to a growing literature base that suggests best practice may not be best practice for vulnerable witnesses and vulnerable suspects. Consequently, work continues to develop better interview techniques for such vulnerable groups (see Maras et al., 2020).

The Trial for Vulnerable Witnesses and Defendants

In the same way that vulnerable witnesses and vulnerable suspects are required to give their best evidence during the police interview, the ability to do so at trial is equally as crucial. Traditionally, vulnerable witnesses were not seen as being reliable, and they were so mistrusted that juries were warned of relying on their evidence at trial (Burton et al., 2006). However, despite being met with untrustworthiness at trial, police officers were being urged to recognise the special needs of vulnerable witnesses in order to obtain their evidence and pursue a prosecution. Support for vulnerable witnesses at trial grew in England and Wales from around the 1970s. For example, Victim Support services were developed to provide support and specialised services to all witnesses, and the Witness Service is now situated in all Magistrates and Crown Courts in England and Wales (Rock, 2004). The implementation and use of Special Measures are provided as per the YJCEA (1999) to alleviate the fear and distress associated with giving evidence, and to enable vulnerable witnesses to give their best evidence using measures to assist them, when they be too frightened to do so in ordinary circumstances (Birch, 2000). The Special Measures available for vulnerable (and intimidated) witnesses include:

- Screening from the defendant (s.23)
- Evidence given by video live link (s.24)
- Evidence given in private (s.25)
- Removal of wigs and gowns (s.26)
- Video recorded evidence-in-chief (s.27)
- Video recorded cross-examination (s.28)
- Examination of witness through intermediary (s.29)
- Aids to communication (s.30)

The application to receive Special Measures must be made by the prosecution counsel to the Court and approved by the Judge (Burton et al., 2006). Many of the Special Measures allow for the vulnerable witness to give their evidence in a more suitable and less daunting environment, thus reducing the impact of the defendant and their presence on the witness giving their evidence (Tekin & Tekin, 2015). For example, the use of screen ensures that the witness can give their evidence in the courtroom but not be seen by the defendant.

There have been a number of key studies that have explored the implementation and use of Special Measures. Hamlyn et al. (2004) found that the use of Special Measures had increased between November 2000 and June 2003, as had satisfaction for their use. Plotnikoff and Woolfson (2004), however, found ongoing difficulties in the implementation of Special Measures and the support available to child witnesses. As a result, they concluded that only a few of the young witnesses in their sample had been able to give their evidence in 'optimum circumstances'. The same authors conducted later research and found that although Special Measures were becoming more frequently used, there still remained problems (Plotnikoff & Woolfson, 2009). The majority of research that has been conducted examining the effectiveness of Special Measures has typically explored one or two Special Measures at a time with child witnesses. There have only been a handful of studies that have explored such measures with vulnerable adult witnesses. In addition, whilst the research work that has been conducted largely paints a positive view in that vulnerable witnesses frequently expressed positive views regarding their use and felt more relaxed (Goodman et al., 1998), there is an increasing amount of research that suggests that the credibility of the vulnerable (or intimidated) witness may come under scrutiny depending on the mode in which they give their evidence (Davies & Pezdek, 2010; Landstrom & Granhag, 2010). Thus, there is much more work needed in ensuring that the needs of vulnerable and intimidated witnesses can be accommodated for to enable their best evidence to be achieved, but also in guaranteeing that this will not affect the outcome of their case. This is also true for vulnerable defendants at trial.

It is estimated that approximately 20% of prisoners have a mental health condition or disorder (Vogel et al., 2014) and 70% within the youth justice system (Skowyra &

Cocozza, 2007). Trends have reported an increase in defendants and prisoners with a mental health condition or disorder since the 1980s; indeed, scholars have reported that there are now more vulnerable individuals incarcerated than there are in psychiatric hospitals (Fuller et al., 2010). As such, vulnerability amongst defendants is likely to be high. Although it cannot be argued that defendants are witnesses, it does not mean that they do not find the trial process daunting. For example, vulnerable defendants may have difficulties in following the Court proceedings (Snow et al., 2012) and thus prevent a barrier to effective participation (Alger, 2021), thus impeding on the defendant's right to a fair trial under Article 6 of the European Convention of Human Rights. That being said, there is a slow shift in the CJS in relation to vulnerable defendants at trial (Gerry & Cooper, 2017), particularly since the trial of two juvenile defendants in the murder of James Bulgar (Gerry, 2012). The justice system is acknowledging that the needs of vulnerable defendants must also be accommodated for.

One of the earliest stages that this can be seen is when considering if the vulnerable defendant is fit to plead and thus fit to stand trial. In England and Wales, this approach for Crown Courts is set out in the Criminal Procedure (Insanity Act) (1964), where a Judge is required to determine if a defendant is fit to plead and to stand trial. Many scholars argue that this procedure is draconian in that it denies a defendant from putting forward any evidence or explanation regarding their involvement in the charges against them (Gerry, 2012). Should a defendant be found unfit to plead and stand trial, the jury are instructed to consider whether the defendant did the act and, depending on the outcome, the defendant may be subject to a hospital order, a supervision order, or an absolute discharge (CPS, 2019). However, some have argued that for a vulnerable defendant who is capable of understanding the charges against them, denying them assistance to engage with the CJS and put their case across is wrong (Gerry, 2012). Thus, being able to plead and subsequently stand trial may be dependent upon the modification made to the trial processes and the inclusion of Special Measures (CPS, 2019).

Whilst many countries in Europe have a range of Special Measures available to support vulnerable defendants during trial (Turner & Hughes, 2022), the position in England and Wales is slightly different and the polar opposite of what is available to a vulnerable witness. Government reports and much case law has evidenced how Courts have consistently refused the use of Special Measure for vulnerable defendants and have been heavily criticised for doing so (Fairclough, 2018). Thus, the requirement as per the Criminal Procedure Rules (2020) in taking 'every reasonable step to facilitate the participation of any person, including the defendant' is often deemed lacking (s.3.8(3)(b)), particularly when one considers the use of the defendant intermediary. There is a growing recognition that vulnerable defendants must be able to understand and effectively participate in criminal proceedings (Jacobson & Talbot, 2009), and the provision of Special Measures is an important part of upholding this right to effective participation (Fairclough, 2018). The use of Special Measures simply do not go far enough for vulnerable defendants (Owusu-Bempah, 2020).

Final Conclusions

Vulnerability in the CJS is not a new phenomenon and some progress has been made when one considers how vulnerable witnesses and suspects were historically treated. This has led to vulnerable witnesses playing an active part in any investigation or criminal proceedings, and vulnerable individuals, as a whole, now being treated in the community rather than in asylums as used to be the case. However, there remains issues with how vulnerable individuals are perceived, particularly around concepts of dangerousness and unpredictability; this has implications for how they may be treated within the CJS.

Defining and identifying vulnerability in witnesses and suspects has developed over recent decades. This is evident in the research work and psychological literature, although many agree there is still no international definition of what constitutes vulnerability. That being said, many turn to the legislative guidance that seeks to define and thus identify vulnerable witnesses and vulnerable suspects. However, this needs much further work, simply because this has an impact on the way that they are treated in the CJS and their subsequent outcomes; research continuously reports the differences in police force areas for example.

This is also true for how vulnerable witnesses and vulnerable suspects are safeguarded. Vulnerable witnesses are able to access a number of Special Measures, including that of the Registered Intermediary – accredited and trained professionals who are able to assess the vulnerable witness and provide recommendations to the police and Courts on how best to elicit best evidence. In comparison, the vulnerable defendant receives the support of the Appropriate Adult. Whilst this is becoming professionalised, there remains disparity in which police forces have access to Appropriate Adult schemes, and who may act as an Appropriate Adult. There is some catching up to do to ensure there are the same safeguards in place for vulnerable suspects as there currently are for vulnerable witnesses. The implementation of a statutory duty to provide the defendant intermediary would go some way to assisting with this.

Interviewing vulnerable witnesses and vulnerable suspects is not an easy task and one that may be exacerbated by the type of vulnerability the individual has. Whilst interview guidance has been developed to ensure a move away from the confession-seeking ethos previously endorsed by police officers in England and Wales, and around the world, there is an emerging research base that suggests that current best practice may not be best practice for all vulnerable witnesses and vulnerable suspects. Much more work needs to focus on this, although it must be acknowledged how difficult it can be for academics to access the necessary interview data.

The ability for vulnerable witnesses to give evidence at trial is relatively new. It was previously thought that those with communication difficulties for example would not be able to give reliable testimony. However, with the implementation of various Special Measures, including the role of the Registered Intermediary, it has become a reality for many vulnerable witnesses to give their evidence, leading to a successful prosecution. But the implementation and use of Special Measures requires some attention. Whilst the vulnerable witness frequently reports their satisfaction in being able to use the Special Measures of which they are entitled to, some research suggests that this may impact upon jury decision-making. This is an area that needs some further inquiry. The vulnerable defendant at trial also needs some attention especially if they are considered fit to plead and thus fit to stand trial. Ensuring they are afforded the same safeguards as a vulnerable witness so that they can effectively participate in criminal proceedings is their human right, but there are many measures yet to be implemented.

The aim of this textbook was to evidence the progress that has been made for vulnerable witnesses and suspects/defendants alike within the justice system. Whilst it is clear that much progress has been made; further work is needed across all stages of the justice system for all types of vulnerable individuals. Vulnerability remains the biggest challenge for the CJS, and we must continue to strive to ensure that the most vulnerable individuals in society are dealt with fairly and consistently, regardless of whether they are a victim, witness, or suspect.

References

Alger, K. (2021). More than what meets the ear: Speech transcription as a barrier to justice for African American vernacular English speakers. *Georgetown Journal of Law and Modern Critical Race Perspectives*, *13*, 87.

Baldry, E., Clarence, M., Dowse, L., & Trollor, J. (2013). Reducing vulnerability to harm in adults with cognitive disabilities in the Australian criminal justice system. *Journal of Policy and Practice in Intellectual Disabilities*, *10*(3), 222–229.

Baldwin, J. (1992). *Video-taping police interviews with suspects – An evaluation*. Home Office.

Ballerini, A. (2002). The Italian paradox: Expansion of community psychiatry and marginalisation of psychopathology. *Archives of Psychiatry*, *65*, 13–26.

Barclay, G., & Tavares, C. (2002). *International comparisons of criminal justice statistics 2000*. Home Office.

Bartkowiak-Theron, I., & Asquith, N. L. (2012). The extraordinary intricacies of policing vulnerability. *Australasian Policing: A Journal of Professional Practice and Research*, *4*(2), 43–49.

Bath, C., Bhardwa, B., Jacobson, J., May, T., & Webster, R. (2015). *There to help: Ensuring provision of appropriate adults for mentally vulnerable adults detained or interviewed by police*. National Appropriate Adult Network.

Bath, C., & Dehaghani, R. (2020). *There to help 3. The identification of vulnerable adult suspects and application of the appropriate adult safeguard in police investigations in 2018/19*. National Appropriate Adult Network.

Becker, I., & Barquero, J. (2001). The European perspective of psychiatric reform. *Acta Psychiatrica Scandinavica*, *410*, 8–14.

Birch, D. (2000). A better deal for vulnerable witnesses? *Criminal Law Review*, 223–249.

Blaauw, E., Roesch, R., & Kerkhof, A. (2000). Mental disorders in European prison systems: Arrangements for mentally disordered prisoners in the prison systems of 13 European countries. *International Journal of Law and Psychiatry*, *23*, 649–663.

Bradley, K. (2009). *The Bradley Report: Lord Bradley's review of people with mental health problems or learning disabilities in the criminal justice system*. Department of Health.

Brown, D. (1997). *PACE ten years on: A review of the research*. HORS 155. Home Office.

Brown, K. (2015). *Vulnerability and young people: Care and social control in policy and practice*. Policy Press.

Bucke, T., & Brown, D. (1997). *In police custody: Police powers and suspects' rights under the revised PACE Codes of Practice. HORS 174*. HMSO.

Burton, M., Evans, R., & Sanders, A. (2006). *An evaluation of the use of special measures for vulnerable and intimidated witnesses*. Home Office, Research, Development, and Statistics Directorate.

Butler, A. (1993). Spare the child. *Police Review*, 14–15

Clarke, C., & Milne, R. (2001). *National evaluation of the PEACE investigative interviewing course*. Police research award scheme, report no. PRAS/149. Institute of Criminal Justice Studies.

Collins, K., Harker, N., & Antonopoulos, G. A. (2017). The impact of the Registered Intermediary on adults' perceptions of child witnesses: evidence from a mock cross examination. *European Journal on Criminal Policy and Research*, *23*, 211–225.

Coroners and Justice Act (2009). https://www.legislation.gov.uk/ukpga/2009/25/contents

CPS (2019). *Mental health conditions and disorders*. https://www.cps.gov.uk/publication/mental-health-conditions-and-disorders-draft-prosecution-guidance

Criminal Justice Act (1991). https://www.legislation.gov.uk/ukpga/1991/53/contents

Criminal Procedure (Insanity Act) (1964). https://www.legislation.gov.uk/ukpga/1964/84

Criminal Procedure Rules (2020). https://www.legislation.gov.uk/uksi/2020/759/contents/made

Daff, E., & Thomas, S. (2014). Bipolar disorder and criminal offending: A data linkage study. *Social Psychiatry and Psychiatric Epidemiology*, *49*, 1985–1991.

Davies, G., & Pezdek, K. (2010). Children as witnesses. In G. Towl & D. Crighton (Eds.), *Forensic psychology* (pp. 178–194). Blackwell.

Davies, G., Wilson, C., Mitchell, R., & Milsom, J. (1995). *Videotaping of Childrens' evidence: An evaluation.* Home Office.

Davis, M. R., McMahon, M., & Greenwood, K. M. (2005). The efficacy of mnemonic components of the cognitive interview: Towards a shortened variant for time-critical investigations. *Applied Cognitive Psychology, 19*, 75–93.

Dehaghani, R. (2021). Interpreting and reframing the appropriate adult safeguard. *Oxford Journal of Legal Studies, 42(1)*, 187–206.

Dehaghani, R., & Bath, C. (2019). Vulnerability and the appropriate adult safeguard: Examining the definitional and threshold changes within PACE code C. *Criminal Law Review, 3*, 213–232.

Dehaghani, R., & Newman, D. (2017). "We're vulnerable too": An (alternative) Analysis of vulnerability within English criminal legal aid And police custody. *Onati Socio-Legal Series, 7*(6), 1199–1228.

Dixon, D., Bottomley, C., Coleman, M., Wall, G., & Wall, D. (1990). Safeguarding the rights of suspects in police custody. *Policing and Society, 1*, 115–140.

Dvoksin, J., Knoll, L., & Silva, M. (2020). A brief history of the criminalisation of mental illness. *CNS Spectrums, 25*, 638–650.

Edwards, C. (2014). Pathologising the victim: Law and the construction of people with disabilities as victims of crime in Ireland. *Disability and Society, 29*(5), 685–698.

Enang, I., Murray, J., Dougall, N., Wooff, A., Heyman, I., & Aston, E. (2019). Defining and assessing vulnerability within law enforcement and public health organisations: A scoping review. *Health and Justice, 7*, 1–13.

Evans, R. (1993). *The conduct of police interviews with young people.* Royal Commission on Criminal Justice Research Study No.8. HMSO.

Ewin, R. (2010). The vulnerable and intimidated witness: A study of the special measure practitioner. *Journal of Applied Psychology and Social Science, 2*(1), 12–40.

Fairclough, S. (2018). Speaking up for injustice: Reconsidering the provision of special measures through the lens of equality. *Criminal Law Review, 1*, 4–19.

Fakhoury, W., & Priebe, S. (2002). The process of deinstitutionalisation: An international overview. *Current Opinion in Psychiatry, 15*, 187–192.

Farrugia, L. (2021). Identifying vulnerability in police custody: Making sense of information provided to custody officers. *Journal of Forensic and Legal Medicine, 80*, 102169.

Farrugia, L. (2023). The appropriate adult: Their perspective working in the criminal justice system. *Criminology and Criminal Justice, 0*(0).

Farrugia, L., & Gabbert, F. (2020). Forensic interviewing of mentally disordered suspects: The impact of interview style on investigation outcomes. *Current Psychology, 41*(5), 3216–3224.

Farrugia, L., & Maras, K. (2023). Achieving best evidence from victims and witnesses. In G. Oxburgh, T. Myklebust, M. Fallon, & M. Hartwig (Eds.), *Interviewing and interrogation: A review of research and practice since* World War *II.* Torkel Opsahl Academic EPublisher.

Fineman, M. (2013). Equality, autonomy, and the vulnerable subject in law and politics. In M. Fineman, & A. Grear (Eds.), *Gender in law, culture, and society: Vulnerability: Reflections on a new ethical foundation for law and politics* (pp. 12–28). Ashgate.

Fisher, R. P., & Geiselman, R. E. (1992). *Memory-enhancing techniques for investigative interviewing: The cognitive interview.* Charles C. Thomas.

Freeman, H., Fryers, T., & Henderson, J. (1985). *Mental health services in Europe: 10 years on.* WHO Regional Office for Europe.

Fuller, T., Kennard, A., Eslinger, D., Lamb, R., & Pavle, J. (2010). *More mentally ill persons are in jails and prisons than hospitals: A survey of the States.* The Treatment Advocacy Centre.

Gabbert, F., Hope, L., & Confrey, M. (2018). Witness testimony. In A. Griffiths, & R. Milne (Eds.), *The psychology of criminal investigation: From theory to practice* (pp. 113–132). Routledge.

Gabbert, F., Hope, L., Luther, K., Wright, G., Ng, M., & Oxburgh, G. (2021). Exploring the use of rapport in professional information-gathering contexts by systematically mapping the evidence base. *Applied Cognitive Psychology, 35*(2), 329–341.

Gerry, F. (2012). *Vulnerable defendants and the courts*. https://www.thejusticegap.com/vulnerable-defendants-and-the-courts/
Gerry, F., & Cooper, P. (2017). Effective participation of vulnerable accused persons: Case management, court adaptation and rethinking criminal responsibility. *Journal of Judicial Administration, 1*, 265–275.
Gibbs, P. (2018). *Love, fear and control – Does the criminal justice system reduce domestic abuse?* Transform Justice.
Goodman, G. S., Tobey, A. E., Batterman-Faunce, J. M., Orcutt, H., Thomas, S., Shapiro, C., & Sachsenmaier, T. (1998). Face-to-face confrontation: Effects of closed-circuit technology on children's eyewitness testimony and jurors' decisions. *Law and Human Behavior, 22*, 165–203.
Gudjonsson, G. H. (2006). Disputed confessions and miscarriages of justice in Britain: Expert psychological and psychiatric evidence in court of appeal. *Manitoba Law Journal, 31*, 489–521.
Gudjonsson, G. H. (2018). *The psychology of false confessions: Forty years of science and practice*. John Wiley & Sons Ltd.
Hamlyn, B., Phelps, A., Turtle, J., & Sattar, G. (2004). *Are special measures working? Evidence from surveys of vulnerable and intimidated witnesses (Home Office Research Study 283)*. Home Office.
Henderson, E. (2012). Alternative routes: Accusatorial jurisdictions on the slow road to best evidence. In J. Spencer, & M. Lamb (Eds.), *Children and cross-examination: Time to change the rules?* Hart.
Henderson, E. (2015). Bigger fish to fry: Should the reform of cross-examination be expanded beyond vulnerable witnesses? *The International Journal of Evidence & Proof, 19*(2), 83–99.
HMIC (2015). *Police effectiveness 2015 (vulnerability) - A national overview. HMIC.*
Holliday, R. (2003a). Reducing misinformation effects in children with cognitive interviews: Dissociating recollection and familiarity. *Child Development, 74*, 728–751.
Holliday, R. (2003b). The effect of a prior cognitive interview on children's acceptance of misinformation. *Applied Cognitive Psychology, 17*, 443–457.
Home Office (1992). *Memorandum of good practice*. His Majesty's Stationary Office.
Home Office (1981). *Royal commission on criminal procedure*. HMSO.
Home Office (1989). Report of the advisory group on video evidence. https://www.scie-socialcareonline.org.uk/report-of-the-advisory-group-on-video-evidence-thomas-pigot-chairman/r/a11G00000017xaaIAA
Home Office (2001). *Speaking up for justice*. Home Office.
Home Office (2018). *Police and Criminal Evidence Act (1984) and codes of practice*. https://www.legislation.gov.uk/uksi/2018/829/pdfs/uksiem_20180829_en.pdf
Houston, R. (2019). Asylums: The historical perspective before, during, and after. *The Lancet Psychiatry, 7*(4), 354–362.
Howard, J. (1784). *The state of the prisons in England and Wales*. William Eyres.
Howard, R., Phipps, E., Clarbour, J., & Rayner, K. (2015). "I'd trust them if they understood learning disabilities" support needs of people with learning disabilities in the criminal justice system. *Journal of Intellectual Disabilities and Offending Behaviour, 6*(1), 4–14.
Inbau, F., Reid, J., Buckley, J., & Jayne, B. (2013). *Criminal interrogation and confessions*. Jones & Bartlett Learning.
Indig, D., Vecchiato, C., Haysom, L., Beilby, R., Carter, J., Champion, U., Gaskin, C., Heller, E., Kumar, S., Mamone, N., Muir, P., van den Dolder, P., & Whitton, G. (2011). *2009 NSW young people in custody health survey: Full report*. Justice Health and Juvenile Justice.
Jacobson, J., & Talbot, J. (2009). *Vulnerable defendants in the criminal courts: A review of provision for adults and children*. Project Report. Prison Reform Trust.
Jessiman, T., & Cameron, A. (2017). The role of the appropriate adult in supporting vulnerable adults in custody: Comparing the perspectives of service users and service providers. *British Journal of Learning Disabilities, 45*, 246–252.
Kilcommins, S., Leane, M., Donson, F., Fennell, C., & Kingston, A. (2010). *The needs and concerns of victims of crime in Ireland, Dublin*. Commission for the Support of Victims of Crime.

Kuno, E., & Asukai, N. (2000). Efforts toward building a community-based mental health system in Japan. *International Journal of Law and Psychiatry*, *23*(3–4), 361–373.
Lamb, M. E., Orbach, Y., Hershkowitz, I., Esplin, P. W., & Horowitz, D. (2007). A structured forensic interview protocol improves the quality and informativeness of investigative interviews with children: A review of research using the NICHD investigative interview protocol. *Child Abuse & Neglect*, *31*(11), 1201–1231.
Landstrom, S., & Granhag, P. A. (2010). In-court versus out-of-court testimonies: Children's experiences and adults' assessments. *Applied Cognitive Psychology*, *24*, 941–955.
Larkin, M. (2009). *Vulnerable groups in health and social care.* Sage Publications.
Leggett, J., Goodman, W., & Dinani, S. (2007). People with learning disabilities' experience of being interviewed by the police. *British Journal of Learning Disabilities*, *35*, 168–173.
Libai, D. (1969). The protection of the child victim of a sexual offence in the criminal justice system. *Wayne Law Review*, *15*, 977–984.
Link, B., Phelan, J., Bresnahan, M., Stueve, A., & Pescosolido, B. (1999). Public conceptions of mental illness: Labels, causes, dangerousness, and social distance. *American Journal of Public Health*, *89*(9), 1328–1333.
Lomax, M. (1921). *The experiences of an asylum doctor: With suggestions for asylum and lunacy law reform.* Allen & Unwin.
Lunacy Act (1845). https://www.cambridge.org/core/books/abs/manual-of-lunacy/lunacy-act-1845-8-and-9-vict-c-100/E94034B6BFB6C398417B6CF17D2A9B5F
Majeed-Ariss, R., Brockway, A., Cook, K., & White, C. (2019). 'Could do better': Report on the use of special measures in sexual offences cases. *Criminology & Criminal Justice.* https://journals.sagepub.com/doi/full/10.1177/1748895819840396
Maras, K., & Bowler, D. (2012). Context reinstatement effects on eyewitness memory in autism spectrum disorder. *British Journal of Psychology*, *103*(3), 330342.
Maras, K. L., & Bowler, D. M. (2010). The cognitive interview for eyewitnesses with autism spectrum disorder. *Journal of Autism and Developmental Disorders*, *40*, 1350–1360.
Maras, K., Dando, C., Stephenson, H., Lambrechts, A., Anns, S., & Gaigg, S. (2020). The witness-aimed first account (WAFA): A new technique for interviewing autistic witnesses and victims. *Autism*, *24*(6), 1449–1467.
McCormack, B. (1991). Sexual abuse and learning disabilities. *British Medical Journal*, *303*, 143–144.
McCulloch, A., Muijen, M., & Harper, H. (2000). New developments in mental health policy in the United Kingdom. *International Journal of Law and Psychiatry*, *23*(3–4), 261–276.
McEwan, J. (2009). The testimony of vulnerable victims and witnesses in criminal proceedings in the European Union. *ERA Forum*, *10*, 369–386.
McGurk, B. J., Carr, M. J., & McGurk, D. (1993). *Investigative interviewing courses for police officers: An evaluation.* (Police Research Series Paper 4). Police Research Group, The Home Office.
McKinnon, I., & Grubin, D. (2012). Health screening of people in police custody – Evaluation of current police screening procedures in London, UK. *European Journal of Public Health*, *23*, 399–405.
Medford, S., Gudjonsson, G., & Pearse, J. (2003). The efficacy of the appropriate adult safeguard during police interviewing. *Legal and Criminological Psychology*, *8*(2), 253–266.
Meissner, C., Kelly, C., & Woestehoff, S. (2014). Improving the effectiveness of suspect interrogations. *Annual Review of Law & Social Science*, *11*(1), 211–233.
Ministry of Justice (2022). *Achieving best evidence in criminal proceedings: Guidance on interviewing victims and witnesses and using special measures.* HMSO.
Misztal, B. (2011). *The challenges of vulnerability: In search of strategies for a less vulnerable social life.* Palgrave Macmillan.
Myklebust, T. (2009). *Analysis of field investigative interviews of children conducted by specially trained police investigators* [Unpublished PhD thesis]. University of Oslo.
National Appropriate Adult Network (2023). https://www.appropriateadult.org.uk/about-us/our-work
Novella, E. (2010). Mental health care in the aftermath of deinstitutionalisation: A retrospective and prospective view. *Health Care Analysis*, *18*, 222–238.

Owusu-Bempah, A. (2020). Understanding the barriers to defendant participation in criminal proceedings in England and Wales. *Legal Studies*, *40*(4), 609–629.
Oxburgh, G., Myklebust, T., & Grant, T. (2010). The question of question types in police interviews: A review of the literature from a psychological and linguistic perspective. *International Journal of Speech, Language and the Law*, *17*, 45–66.
Phillips, E., Oxburgh, G., & Myklebust, T. (2011). Investigative interviews with victims of child sexual abuse: The relationship between question and investigation relevant information. *Journal of Police and Criminal Psychology*, *27*, 45–54.
Pierpoint, H. (2001). The performance of volunteer appropriate adults: A survey of call outs. *Howard Journal of Criminal Justice*, *40*(3), 255–271.
Pierpoint, H. (2004). A survey of volunteer appropriate adult services in England and Wales. *Youth Justice*, *4*(1), 33–45.
Plotnikoff, J., & Woolfson, R. (2004). *In their own words: The experiences of 50 young witnesses in criminal proceedings*. NSPCC.
Plotnikoff, J., & Woolfson, R. (2007). *The 'Go-between': Evaluation of intermediary pathfinder projects. Research summary*. https://www.researchgate.net/publication/344219930_The_%27Go-Between%27_evaluation_of_intermediary_pathfinder_projects
Plotnikoff, J., & Woolfson, R. (2009). *Measuring up? Evaluating implementation of government commitments to young witnesses in criminal proceedings*. NSPCC.
Plotnikoff, J., & Woolfson, R. (2015). *Intermediaries in the criminal justice system. improving communication for vulnerable witnesses and defendants*. Policy Press.
Price, C., & Caplan, J. (1977). *The Confait confessions*. Boyars.
R v Watts [2010] EWCA 1824. Retrieved July 1, 2023, from https://www.casemine.com/judgement/uk/5b46f1fb2c94e0775e7ef591
Reavley, N., & Jorm, A. (2012). Stigmatising attitudes towards people with mental disorders: Changes to Australia over 8 years. *Psychiatry Research*, *197*(3), 302–306.
Ridley, A. M., van Rheede, V., & Wilcock, R. (2015). Interviews, intermediaries and interventions: Mock jurors', police officers' and barristers' perceptions of a child witness interview. *Investigative Interviewing: Research and Practice*, *7*, 21–35.
Righarts, S., Jack, F., Zajac, R., & Hayne, H. (2015). Young children's responses to cross- examination style questioning: The effects of delay and subsequent questioning. *Psychology, Crime & Law*, *21*, 274–296.
Robinson, J., & McGuire, J. (2005). Suggestibility and children with mild learning disabilities: The use of the cognitive interview. *Psychology, Crime & Law*, *12*, 537–556.
Rock, P. (2004). *Constructing victims' rights: The home office, new labour and victims*. Oxford University Press.
Sanders, A. (2002). Victim participation in criminal justice. *The Centre for Crime and Justice Studies*, *49*, 30–31.
Sanders, A., Creaton, J., Bird, S., & Weber, L. (1997). *Victims with learning disabilities: Negotiating the criminal justice system*. University of Oxford.
Schmiedebach, H., Beddies, T., Schulz, J., & Priebe, S. (2002). Housing and work as criteria of the 'social integration' of the mentally ill – Developments in Germany from 1900 to 2000. *Psychiatrische Praxis*, *29*, 285–294.
Scull, A. (1979). *Museums of madness. The social organisation of insanity in nineteenth century England*. Pengrum.
Seddon, T. (2007). *Punishment and madness: Governing prisoners with mental health problems*. Routledge.
Sherman, L., Strang, H., & O'Connor, D. (2017). Introduction - Key facts about domestic abuse: Lessons from eight studies. *Cambridge Journal of Evidence Based Policing*, *1*, 59–63.
Skowyra, K., & Cocozza, J. (2007). *Blueprint for change: A comprehensive model for the identification and treatment of youth with mental health needs in contact with the juvenile justice system*. The National Centre for Mental Health and Juvenile Justice: Policy Research Associates.

Smith, K., & O'Mahony, B. (2018). Vulnerability and criminal investigations. In A. Griffiths & R. Milne (Eds.), *The psychology of criminal investigation; From theory to practice* (pp. 91–112). Routledge.

Snook, B., Luther, K., Quinlan, H., & Milne, R. (2012). Let 'em talk! A field study of police questioning practices of suspects and accused persons. *Criminal Justice and Behaviour*, *39*(10), 1328–1339.

Snow, P., Powell, M., & Sanger, D. (2012). Oral Language competence, young speakers, and the law. *Language Speech and Hearing Services in Schools*, *43*, 496.

Soukara, S., Bull, R., Vrij, A., Turner, M., & Cherryman, J. (2009). What really happens in police interviews of suspects? Tactics and confessions. *Psychology, Crime and Law*, *15*, 493–506.

Symonds, B. (1995). The origins of insane asylums in England during the 19th century: A brief sociological review. *Journal of Advanced Nursing*, *22*, 94–100.

Taggart, J. (2021). 'I am not beholden to anyone...I consider myself to be an officer of the court': A comparison of the intermediary role in England and Wales and Northern Ireland. *The International Journal of Evidence and Proof*, *25*(2), 141–162.

Tekin, S., & Tekin, A. (2015). The issue of adequateness of special measures applied to vulnerable victims and witnessed in the United Kingdom. *Human Rights Review*, *5*(10), 1–24.

Turner, K., & Hughes, N. (2022). Supporting young people's cognition and communication in the courtroom: A scoping review of current practice. *Criminal Behaviour and Mental Health*, *32*(3), 175–196.

Victims Commissioner (2018). A voice for the voiceless: The victims' commissioner's review into the provision of registered intermediaries for children and vulnerable victims and witnesses. https://victimscommissioner.org.uk/document/a-voice-for-the-voiceless-provision-of-registered-intermediaries-for-children-and-vulnerable-victims-and-witnesses/

Vigurs, C., & Quy, K. (2017). *What works: Crime reduction systematic review series. no. 6: Police responses to people with mental health needs: A systematic map of the literature*. University College London.

Vogel, M., Stephens, K., & Siebels, D. (2014). Mental illness and the criminal justice system. *Sociology Compass*, *8*, 627–638.

Walker, N. (1985). The insanity defence between 1800. *The Annals of the American Academy of Political and Social Science*, *477*, 25–30.

Walklate, S. (2011). *Handbook of victims and victimology*. Routledge.

Walkley, J. (1987). *Police interrogation: A handbook for investigators*. Police Review Publication.

Williams, G. (1987a). Videotaping children's evidence. *New Law Journal*, *351*, 108–112.

Williams, G. (1987b). Child witnesses. In P. Smith (Ed.), Criminal Law: Essays in Honour of J.C. Smith. *Cambridge Law Journal*, *46*(3), 539–541.

Williamson, T. (2006). *Investigative interviewing: Rights, research, regulation*. Willan.

World Health Organisation (2001). *Mental health: New understanding, new hope*. https://apps.who.int/iris/handle/10665/42390

Wright, R., & Powell, M. (2006). Investigative interviewers' perceptions of their difficulty to adhere to open-ended questions with child witnesses. *International Journal of Police Science and Management*, *8*, 316–325.

Wurtzel, D., & Marchant, R. (2017). Intermediaries. In P. Cooper & H. Norton (Eds.), *Vulnerable people and the criminal justice system: A guide to law and practice* (pp. 363–389). OUP.

Yap, M., Mackinnon, A., Reavley, N., & Jorm, A. (2014). The measurement properties of stigmatising attitudes towards mental disorders: Results from two community surveys. *International Journal of Methods in Psychiatric Research*, *23*(1), 49–61.

Yip, K. (2000). Have psychiatric services in Hong Kong been impacted by the deinstitutionalisation and community care movements? *Admin and Policy Mental Health*, *27*, 443–449.

Young, J. (1999). *The exclusive society*. Sage.

Youth Justice and Criminal Evidence Act (1999). London: HMSO.

Index

Achieving Best Evidence 21, 30, 54–55, 102, 128
acquiescence 15, 59, 87–89, 127
Appropriate Adult 19–20, 22, 29, 39–44, 46–47, 113, 129–131, 136
asylum 1–2, 4, 8–9, 125–126, 135

Bath 19–20, 38, 40, 42, 128, 131
Behaviour Analysis Interview *see* Reid Interrogation Technique
Bethlem Hospital *see* asylum
Bradley 40, 42, 45, 131

Code C *see* Police and Criminal Evidence Act (1984)
Cognitive Interview 59–62, 64–65, 67–68, 82, 132–133
College of Policing 14, 16, 38–39, 45, 58, 65, 81, 83–84
compliance 15, 18–19, 59, 88–89, 127
context reinstatement *see* Cognitive Interview
Conversation Management Approach 82

dangerousness 2, 4–5, 126, 136
defendant intermediary 43–44, 112–116, 121–122, 131, 135–136
Dehaghani 14, 19–21, 38, 40–43, 127–128, 131
deinstitutionalisation 1–5, 8–9, 14, 23–24, 125
diminished responsibility 79, 118–119, 122
disposal options 40, 117, 119, 121–122

empathy *see* rapport
Enhanced Cognitive Interview *see* Cognitive Interview
Evans 39, 42, 130–131

false confession 18, 74, 76–80, 84, 87–88, 90–91
Farrugia 7, 14, 20–21, 23, 40–43, 45, 53, 57, 59, 63, 66, 74, 83, 85, 89–90, 98, 128, 131, 133
Fineman 15–16, 128
Fisher 55, 59–62, 64, 67, 79–80, 82, 90–91, 132–133
fit to plead 110–111, 114, 117, 121–122, 135–136

Gabbert 14, 42, 55–57, 59, 65, 67–68, 82, 85, 89–90, 132–133
Gudjonsson 7, 15–16, 18–19, 23–24, 38, 43, 53, 59, 63, 66, 75–79, 81, 87–90, 127, 131–132

Inbau *see* Reid Interrogation Technique
insanity defence 119
intermediary *see* defendant intermediary
interrogation *see* Reid Interrogation Technique
investigative interviewing *see* PEACE model

Jessiman 40, 42, 131

Kassin 18, 77–79, 87, 91

learning difficulties *see* Learning Disability
liaison and diversion 44–47
Lunacy Act (1845) 2, 9, 125

Maras 21, 53, 56–57, 59, 62–68, 98, 131, 133
Mattison 34, 61–62, 64, 67–68
McKinnon 22–23, 37–38, 41, 128
Medford 40, 42, 131
Memorandum of Good Practice 53–54, 59, 61, 66–68, 131–132
Mendez 84
miscarriages of justice 43, 55, 74–77, 79–80, 87–88, 90–91, 98, 121, 132
Modified Cognitive Interview *see* Cognitive Interview

National Appropriate Adult Network *see* Appropriate Adult

PEACE model 80–81, 83–84, 90–91, 133
Pierpoint 39–40, 42, 130–131
Pigot 31, 53, 68, 129

Plotnikoff, J. 7, 20, 30–32, 36, 43, 45–46, 99, 101–104, 115, 129–131, 134
Police and Criminal Evidence Act (1984) 17–18, 38, 47, 80, 91, 128

question types 57–59, 61, 63

rapport 54–57, 59–61, 67–68, 82, 84, 132
Registered Intermediary 17, 29–37, 43–47, 115, 129–131, 136
Reid Interrogation Technique 74–76, 90–91, 132
report everything *see* Cognitive Interview
Royal Commission *see* Fisher Inquiry

safeguards *see* Appropriate Adult
Self-Administered Interview 65–66
Shepherd 81–82
sketch reinstatement of context 64
Speaking Up for Justice 8, 54, 98–99, 106–107, 112, 127
Special Measures 8, 17–18, 20–23, 30–31, 34–36, 43–44, 46, 97, 99–100, 103–107, 111–112, 114, 116–117, 121–122, 127, 131, 134–136
suggestibility 15, 18–19, 59, 78, 87–88, 127

Taggart 32, 44, 112, 114–116, 129
temporal order *see* Cognitive Interview

variety of perspectives *see* Cognitive Interview
Victims charter (1990) 6

Williamson *see* PEACE
Witness-Aimed First Account 66

Youth Justice and Criminal Evidence Act (1999) 17, 30, 46, 54, 98–99, 107, 112, 114, 128